Gotta Find a Home 4

More Conversations
on the Streets

Amazon Reviews

5.0 out of 5 stars

`People are strangers only until you meet them. We are all the same, we seek happiness and an end to suffering.'

By Grady Harp

HALL OF FAMETOP 100 REVIEWERVINE VOICE

on July 17, 2014

Canadian author Dennis Cardiff has a heart as big as all outdoors. He seems to be a pretty selfless guy as he doesn't provide much personal resume on which to base a beginning to read his book and he contributes a portion of the proceeds to supporting the homeless. From references within his writing it seems he lives in Toronto and spends his walk to work each day talking to the street folk he has gathered into his circle of friends.

The book is a series of conversations with and about the homeless people he encounters. Cardiff is also a poet and he generously sprinkles some of his poems through out the book that spans eighteen months of experience - growth, laughter, kindness, endless biographical information, and simply people who have no home but the street seeking some sense of dignity and understanding from those who have homes.

Early on in his book he lets us know how this concept originated: `2010 - How It Began - My lungs ached, as frost hung in the bitterly cold December morning air, making breathing difficult. I trudged in the falling snow toward the building where I work, in one of the city's grey, concrete, office tower canyons. I dodged other pedestrians, also trying to get to work on time, I noticed a woman seated cross-legged on the sidewalk with her back against a building wall. A snow-covered Buddha, wrapped in a sleeping bag, shivering in the below freezing temperature. I guessed her to be in her forties. Everything about her seemed round. She had the most angelic face, sparkling blue eyes and a beautiful smile. A cap was upturned in front of her. I thought, There but for the grace of God go I. Her smile and blue eyes haunted me all day. In the past I've been unemployed, my wife and I were unable to pay our mortgage and other bills, we went through bankruptcy, lost our house, my truck. Being in my fifties, my prospects looked dim. It could have been me, on the sidewalk, in her place. I was told not to give money to panhandlers because they'll just spend it on booze. I thought to myself, What should I do, if anything? What would you do? I asked for advice from a friend who has worked with homeless people. She said, `The woman is probably hungry. Why don't you ask her if she'd like a breakfast sandwich and maybe a coffee?' That sounded reasonable, so the next day I asked, "Are you hungry? Would you like some breakfast, perhaps a coffee?""That would be nice," she replied. When I brought her a sandwich and coffee she said to me, "Thank you so much, sir. You're so kind. Bless you." I truly felt blessed. This has become a morning routine for the past four years. The woman (I'll call Joy) and I have become friends. Often I'll sit with her on the sidewalk. We sometimes meet her companions in the park. They have become my closest friends. I think of them as angels. My life has become much richer for the experience.'

As a coda to this street symphony, Cardiff states: `After eighteen months of daily conversations with people living on the streets, in shelters or sharing accommodation, I have made the following observations. A full-fledged member of the street family is one who has been with the group for over ten years. Jacques and Joy are the matriarch and patriarch. Everyone else is a newbie -- on probation. To gain acceptance one must be vouched for and have proven themselves not to be an *******. The group expects honesty and sincerity. That may seem strange when you consider that most of these people have prison records. Many have been involved in scams of one sort or another, but if you're family they expect the truth. How else, they explained, can they help you? They'll share with you what little they have, even the jackets off their back. The same is expected in return. The people who come around only when they're in need of money, cigarettes, booze, drugs or food are soon put on notice. On check day, all debts are paid in full.'

These are the words of a man who cares, and in his caring and sharing we discover an entirely new outlook on the people whose street homes are beneath benches, in cardboard boxes, in doorways - any place that provides shelter. Dennis Cardiff brings them into our hearts. Grady Harp, July 14

5.0 out of 5 stars

A Powerful Must-Read For Everyone With a Soul

By Veritas Vincit on July 17, 2014

I have been very fortunate in my life to have traveled extensively throughout the world, and have also lived in Chicago, a city known for its homeless population and rampant issues of people living below the poverty line. I have seen thousands of street people in my life, but it wasn't until I was considerably older that I began to genuinely consider what their lives might have been like. It is so easy to dismiss homeless people, as though they blend into the background of a city, like breathing architecture. This is a terrible viewpoint that hundreds of millions of people around the world share in some way.

This book was a tremendous achievement and I have to stand up and applaud Cardiff for not only seeing the value in pursuing this subject, but approaching it in such a unique and eye-opening way. This book will absolutely change the way that you live your daily life and will certainly change your perspective on those less fortunate. He exposes the personality of his characters, befriends them, helps them, reveals the depth of their struggle, and acquits some of them of the unjust judgments that they have surely experienced for decades. Although it feels terrible to say, "I loved this book", given how emotionally charged and challenging it was at times, I can't deny it. Cardiff is a bold and passionate author who is choosing to use his gifts for the betterment of the people he has come to know as friends. Hopefully everyone that reads this book will re-draw the lines in the sand when it comes to their beliefs on homelessness - If we want to improve society, we will have to do it ourselves. Reading this book and opening your eyes is the right way to start.

5.0 out of 5 stars

An Excellent & Very Thoughtful Read

By The Notebook Blogairy on November 20, 2014

Gotta Find A Home: Conversations with Street People by Dennis Cardiff is one of those books that you pick up on a lark. I picked it up because the second part of the title intrigued me. Conversations with street people? What the heck?!

So, I added this book to my to-be-read bookshelf and went on my merry way. Why did my mind keep wandering back to the question that Cardiff's title implies? What kind of conversations are we talking about? Real conversations? Fictionalized conversations? More importantly, my brain had this question. What could street people have to say?

I'm not (too) ashamed to say that prior to reading this book I, among the masses, averted my eyes when passing a panhandler on the street. I assumed that they were there because they wanted to be there; they missed/lost opportunities and now had to fight and claw their way to get back to 'normalcy'.

Gotta Find A Home did not disabuse me of these notions. For the most part, those beliefs of mine remain largely intact. The conversations that Cardiff shares with his readers are actual factual retellings of his many conversations with people he met on the streets who identified themselves as "Street People."

According to Cardiff, Street People are people who panhandle for a living and have done it for a long time (like a decade or more). But I digress.

Gotta Find A Home is a book that pulls no punches. It is a straight forward daily account of the day-to-day lives of this close-knit group of panhandlers in Toronto.

There is no plot. There is no structure other than the loose timeline of these conversations. There is no true end. This book is a fly-on-the-wall view of what life is like for various members of this group of people who in one week have more crises than the UN, the Pentagon and the Middle East put together. Members of this group have fatal illnesses, severe health issues, psychological issues, financial woes, and of course, issues with finding stable clean housing.

Add on top of these major issues the normal squabbling among a large group of close-knit friends (which many times devolves into fist fights...) and you have what Cardiff calls a 'soap opera'.

Gotta Find A Home: Conversations with Street People will leave you feeling haunted, questioning and, I believe, sympathetic. While many of the people in this book did not change one iota their stories and back-stories are compellingly sad. It makes one realize that with just a different decision (or two) any one of us could have chosen the path that some of the people in Cardiff's book have chosen.

This is an excellent and very thoughtful read. I give it 5 stars for content.

5.0 out of 5 stars

This book might make you cry, shout, feel completely helpless and think really hard, but it's absolutely worth it!

By Leire on February 2, 2015

Reading this book has made me think a lot about homeless people, pan handlers and anyone that seems an outsider in developed countries. I've always found it difficult to know how to interact with someone in the street that asks for money or help. As a young woman I find some of them scary or aggressive and with those that seem really in pain, ill or in great need, I don't really know how to treat them because I'm afraid of sounding condescending or pitying them. Where I live, there are not many people living in the streets and those that do are never in groups, usually alone with a cat or a dog, or sometimes as a couple, when they're young, which is highly unusual. Then, there are organized groups of beggars from different groups but they have nothing to do with the people in the book like Joy. Reading the book has been a humbling experience and also a scary one. It's unfair and totally unacceptable that in developed countries with a lot of money there are so many people suffering, ill and with no roofs over their heads. It doesn't matter what they've done before or how they got there, it's everybody's business to take care of them, to provide them with basic needs and make their life human. If they don't want the help, let them say so. Today I've bought honey to an old man that produces it and was selling in the street. He looked really old and spoke very well but not much, he just sold me the honey and kept asking people to buy him some of it. I wonder what happened to him, although I'm sure he has his own home, but how come you need to sell in the streets when you've worked your whole life? Questions keep pouring into my head...brace yourself for this read...

5.0 out of 5 stars

Street Level! Real People!

By Desmond1979 on September 11, 2014

Having discovered Dennis' Blog when he liked a post of mine on Wordpress I followed him back. At first I was only casually observing the Blog, but once I bought the book and started going through it it really churned out the milk of human kindness. A rarity in this misanthropic world.

The stories of the panhandlers, all of whom have drink and drugs problems and are mainly Native Canadian/Inuit, underlines just how easily it is to end up on the streets if you lose track in the rat race of life. The Heroine of the book is Joy, who is tough as old boots having lived a life which was a series of wars and is the Alpha Female of the group. She always looks out for the group and keeps everything running like clockwork.

Another issue raised in the book is how much Canada has become a Police State by its Political Class. The fear is that Europe is also becoming 'Americanised' in that department. (Ireland and Britain has had noted incidents of Police Corruption)

The book itself reads just like a series of Blog entries. Which will make this book more readable in this age of short attention spans. Having Asperger's myself, reading for over 5 minutes at a time can be a challenge. However I managed to complete the book with a couple of reading sessions over an hour to read the final two Months of entries. This underlines how to promote reading to a new generation of young adults.

Reading these entries makes me appreciate what I do have, therefore the book is uplifting in that sense. Fully recommended.

5.0 out of 5 stars

An Introspective Journey of a Man's Views of Homelessness

By Imy Santiago (RISC Books, New York) on February 17, 2015

This is the first book I've read from the author, and I'll admit I've never read such an intriguing story about homeless panhandlers in Canada.

The book in itself is a journal recounting multiple encounters with different people whom Dennis socializes with on a daily basis. Gotta Find a Home depicts the heartbreaking stories of those who got left behind or the choices they made turned them to the streets.

The author paints a real scene with real characters who have back stories; some with painful pasts and others who do what they do to survive. I especially connected with Joy and her story truly touched me.

Cardiff displays poignant prose abilities and the writing style is real and gritty. Reading this book has shown me the unknown side of homeless people and sometimes we forget they are human beings like us- seeking a connection without judgment or prejudice. They simply desire understanding and their voices need to be heard.

Next time I see a panhandler, I won't look the other way. Perhaps a sesame bagel, tea and a hug is what needs to be done.

Brava, Cardiff. Five stars from me.

5.0 out of 5 stars

Gotta Find A Home : Inspirational and Heartwarming

By Reggie on February 11, 2015

Dennis Cardiff has written a book that inspires, and I believe would assist others; help the unemployed or anyone going through hard times. The interconnecting stories that author Dennis Cardiff tells shows me that Dennis has a lot of love for the people who he mentions in the narrative of this fascinating book. The story takes place over an eighteen-month period.

I've worked with students who display the types of features mentioned throughout this story, and they are often very hard to keep on the straight and narrow. They would often prefer to be out shooting up than learning a trade that would help them overcome some of the adversities in their lives.

Cardiff made me smile at times. At other times, my emotions were tugged at. I became deeply concerned, as I was when I was a teacher, as I was caught up in the author's efforts to understand the complexities of the troubled characters portrayed.

It takes writing skill to engage a reader intensely as I was drawn into this work. Five stars.

5.0 out of 5 stars

like the homeless

August 8, 2014 by Jackie Paulson © 2014

This book is for anyone at any age group! I have been homeless for three months and three days, so it is a book of interest and that is why I wanted to read it. It really gives you the feel of hope even during trials such as being homeless. This is one of my top ten MUST KEEP AND READ for 2014! The author documents homeless people around the world and their true stories. It is heart breaking and breath taking all at the same time.

Yes, some are yucky, stinky, and weird, but they are Children of God. We all come into the world, and we all will go out of this world. If you are a very emotional person this book will bring you to tears because of the reality in all of the stories. Most people pass by a panhandler at a park or where they are at thinking their own perceived thoughts, but mostly to walk by and gossip about it. Did you ever think that some are homeless because of medical reasons, house foreclosures, job loss or even running away? It's often said that if you walked a day in someone's shoes, like the homeless, that it would give you a life changing perspective, and change your life for the best. It will make you realize that when things are tough someone else out there has it worse than you do. If you liked this book you will love: Homeless Bound: By Jeremy Reynalds "UNDER THE OVERPASS" where just a couple of years ago, Christian college student Mike Yankoski and a friend voluntarily plunged themselves into the unfamiliar world of homelessness.

5.0 out of 5 stars

Eye opening.

By Dan Clarke on December 1, 2014

Gotta Find a Home, is not a quick read or a happy one. It's a journal about the lives of the homeless, and while it isn't all doom and gloom, its anything but light hearted.

Dennis Cardiff has helped street people for years, and it shows in his understanding of their worries, concerns and needs. Rather than throwing money at them, he tries to help them gain more control over their situation. One very refreshing part of reading this book, is that he didn't really push politics or an idea that "You Must" do whatever he says to make things better. It would be so easy to preach his point of view, the fact that he didn't shows his respect for the reader. I appreciated it.

Through the journal like chapters, it shows just how widespread the homeless community is. People are constantly being mentioned and talked about that we never learn much about, but everyone else knows. It gets confusing, but it lets us see that these groups aren't isolated from each other, even if they're ignored by the mainstream. Its kind of eye opening.

I really liked this despite feeling depressed while reading parts of it, because Cardiff shows through his work that small bits of kindness can really help people. So despite wanting to give my daughter a big hug after reading parts of it, I'm happy I got it.

5.0 out of 5 stars

By David Bryant on February 4, 2015

It's a most unusual concept for a book. It takes us into an underworld we often glimpse but shudder from exploring. Personally, I thank the author, Dennis Cardiff, for taking my hand and leading me to a greater understanding of the homeless as human beings. There but for the grace of God go many of us.

Dennis is obviously a driven and magnanimous person. It's enough that he works on behalf of the under-privileged. It's a bonus that he's written their story. And what a tale it is. All life is there: pathos; humour; the full range of emotions, desires, disappointments. These are ordinary people without one ordinary thing – money.

The book's anecdotes are presented through conversation. The central character is Dennis Cardiff himself and we come to learn how his crusade has changed him personally. Dennis also provides some entertaining poetry at various points.

For me, this book made a welcome break from fiction and took me to a different universe much more effectively than any sci-fi could have done.

5.0 out of 5 stars

Heartwarming

By Scott on October 25, 2014

Have you ever wondered what it is like to be homeless, jobless, or simply underemployed? In "Gotta Find a Home: Conversations with Street People," Dennis Cardiff gives us a glimpse into the lives of some kind individuals whose lives have been struck with misfortune. I know I have been told countless times that giving money to a homeless person is unwise as they will just spend it on alcohol and/or drugs, and while that can be true, this story showed a picture of human beings beyond the stereotypes.

In "Gotta Find a Home…" Cardiff shares real life conversations that he has had with friends he has made on the street. My favorite conversations were those that he had with a woman named Joy. While she often had a roof over her head, that roof came with an abusive boyfriend, unsupportive friends, extra hands that demanded of her time and care.

While Joy was my favorite, all of the stories really brought to life the reality that all of these people are real human beings, not just some statistic that we walk past on the street and avert our eyes. I found it all very moving and well worth the read.

5.0 out of 5 stars

A Collection of Conversations with a Huge Heart

By horrorgirldonna on December 2, 2014

Dennis Cardiff, a Canadian author, spends his days writing about and helping the homeless. What he's done with this collection is open up the eyes of people who have a negative view of street people—he gives them a face. The real heroine of the book is Joy, a woman who made the choice of a roof over her head with an abusive boyfriend, or life on the street, but free from the abuse.

It's an often difficult reminder that we're all human. What I thought was especially interesting is the lack of homeless stereotypes. Instead, each one of the people Cardiff mentions is a strong and interesting individuals who has experienced some tough circumstances. Although this journal reads like fiction, it is indeed very real. The writing is not flowery, but instead a no-nonsense daily account of a group of panhandlers in Toronto through conversation. How did these people get there, and are they very different from you or me?

This is an interesting look into a world that is thankfully unfamiliar to most of us. It's a difficult, yet heartwarming read. I would recommend it to anyone who enjoys good nonfiction.

5.0 out of 5 stars

An inspirational look at an important societal issue - Gotta read this book!

By Catherine Grainger on January 27, 2015

Author Dennis Cardiff uses an interesting technique to tell us this story, which is actually comprised of many stories, real stories of the real lives of real people; the street people that most of us look right past every day, or look at with unfounded, negative disdain. Cardiff spent time with some of the street people and panhandlers of Canada, and in this book, he gives us a chance to get to know them a little bit, a chance to try to understand how and why they live this life, that they have hopes, dreams, fears, and regrets, just as everyone else does. I really enjoyed the journal style of the writing, and Cardiff writes with a warm and genuine voice that reaches the reader to impart deeper meaning to the bare bones of the story. You can feel the honest emotion in the way that Cardiff shares these stories, and it makes the telling of the stories that much more important.

5.0 out of 5 stars

By Tsutsuji on February 3, 2015

This book is written is short, easily-accessible vignettes, which makes it a quick but very valuable read. The author treats his subject with compassion, yet doesn't apologize nor make excuses for the people he describes. He presents an honest and engaging portrait of a group of very interesting lives.

The author also has a blog by the same name that is well-worth reading. (http://gottafindahome.com)

I wasn't sure what to expect, but the originality of this wonderful book was stunning. I have spent the past 6 years traveling extensively in dozens of countries, and have made an effort to meet and speak with "street people" as often as possible. I know that there are thousands of stories and hundreds of explanations and issues when it comes to the homeless populations of major cities, but I admire an author that is willing to delve into their lives, not as an observer, but as a participant in certain ways. This was a heartfelt piece of gonzo writing, an honest and uncompromising appraisal of the other side of life. It's this type of writing that can change people's opinions, open their eyes, and generally make the world a more tolerant and accepting place. Cardiff's honest way of writing about these individuals wasn't done in an attempt to garner sympathy, and it wasn't an overly sentimentalized way of tackling this issue. He simply wrote what he saw and explicated the beliefs that he had developed. I was blown away by this book, and it reminded me that I'm not alone in thinking about the lives of those that so many people ignore. This might be one of the best books I've read all year. A must-read for anyone who wants to broaden their view on life as we know it.

5.0 out of 5 stars

a book filled with empathy and humanity for those who need it most
By Didsan on November 8, 2014

So many books depict aliens, vampires, werewolves and chick lit about gorgeous hunks who ravish seductive women or discuss esoteric ideas promulgated by a privileged class. Very few portray the disenfranchised, homeless whose humanity has been brilliantly and sympathetically illustrated by Dennis Cardiff in his eloquent recounting of his day to day experiences with the homeless who usually are bypassed by most of us when we walk by them or altruistically give them a dollar if we stop at a red light as they panhandle in all sorts of clement and inclement weather. His realistic portrait of their plight, their grit and determination to survive their harsh circumstances provided an epiphany to me.

No longer are they stereotypes of ne'er do wells, but through Cardiff's book they emerge as strong individuals who try to cope with difficult situations. Cardiff is a saint for revealing their circumstances to the reading public. His altruistic, non-judgmental description of their lives gives them lives with grace and dignity which might otherwise go unnoticed. A must read for all those who have homes.

5.0 out of 5 stars

Delightful book.

By Robin Perron on October 25, 2014

I have often wondered what it might be like to life on the street. I have also wondered if there was any truth in what people say about people who are homeless. What I found reading "Gotta Find a Home: Conversations with Street People" by Dennis Cardiff is that it doesn't matter what others think of people who are homeless because they are people too.

In "Gotta Find a Home…" I was able to read some very heartwarming stories that Dennis learned directly from the people whom he befriended on the streets where he lived. I enjoyed learning more about his friends' lives. The thing that I gained the most from this book was the understanding and appreciation that while we cannot help everyone we can do something whether it is a bit of breakfast, a coffee, or just a kind smile every little bit of human decency that we exhibit to all those around us is helpful.

If you enjoy reading heartwarming real life stories then you will definitely enjoy this book.

5.0 out of 5 stars

An Inside View

By Clarissa Clemens on January 9, 2015

This book is very refreshing dealing with a topic that most would turn away from. A well put together memoir, Dennis did an excellent job painting scenes of hardship and hope. Reading Gotta Find a Home gave me an inside view of real life for those who find themselves homeless. Mr. Cardiff gave us a gift of compassion with this wonderful book.

5.0 out of 5 stars

This is an great book to read and written for a great cause

ByTara Parkeron September 18, 2014

This book offered a new perspective on the trials and hardships of homeless people. This is an great book to read and written for a great cause. I was interested to learn how the author's life changed as he changed the lives of those around him. An inspiring story about those less fortunate and how service and kindness are the heart of humanity.

5.0 out of 5 stars

Reach Out and Touch Somebody's Hand

By M Le'Mont on September 13, 2014

I will never look at homeless people the same. Yesterday I saw a prostitute walking the streets and gave a homeless man a dollar. What a kind heart I thought. Then I read Gotta Find a Home: Conversations with Street People; now every chance I get I give without judging or asking what happened. The book made me realize that something traumatic happened in their lives, and it could happen to anybody --- a loss job, the death of a loved one, illness, etc. So if you want to know what it's like living on the streets then get this book. There's a good reason, why the book has 20 Five Stars---well make that 21 after this review. It's an easy read, insightful, and touches your heart and soul.

5.0 out of 5 stars

Portion of proceeds help the homeless

By LA Howell on September 7, 2014

Gotta Find a Home: Conversations with Street People Book 1 by Dennis Cardiff is a 317 page book of his personal experiences. He began with his earliest contact with some homeless people in 1968 on his way to work. Cardiff shares his backstory then flash forwards to 2010, giving you a great understanding and introduction as to why he wrote the book. I hope this, and his subsequent books, get the notice they deserve. It is a very touching collection of events that he has recorded.

Cardiff became a volunteer at the Shepherd, a place that offered free meals. He recalls several stories during that time and has compiled them by dates. Cardiff was very candid and compassionate in his story and writing. Something we can all learn from. He is even donating a portion of the books proceeds to help the homeless.

5.0 out of 5 stars

Makes You Think

By Bronsen Earl on August 4, 2014
The Homeless Issue is not only a serious problem, but it is also a highly debated one as well. Highly debated because everyone seems to have their own idea on how to solve it. With answers ranging from "They did it to themselves" to "tax everyone."
    This book was an eye opener for me. I would like to think that I help the homeless as much as I can, but I know I'm
    just as guilty as anyone else when it comes to walking by people like they don't exist. Nevertheless, this book was thought provoking and a great conversation starter. 5/5

5.0 out of 5 stars

Refreshing

By Buster Boyon July 28, 2014

On the subject of homeless people, I haven't put much thought into it. Most of my life has been grinding just to survive. However, when I got a chance to read this book it was a real eye-opener. I was actually surprised how much I liked this book. The author brings a soul to the faceless people that are living on the streets. Some of the conversations are funny and others are gut wrenching. Read this book, I promise you won't view street people in the same light when you are finished.

5.0 out of 5 stars

Eye-Opening

By Sierra Klein on July 25, 2014

Most people will walk right on by a homeless person on the street, completely avoid eye contact and maybe even walk to the other side of the street but not this author. This book will change the way you see the less fortunate human beings who have no idea when their next meal will be or if they will have enough clothes to get them through the winter. The author takes you on an enlightening and heartwarming journey through the world of the people we so often ignore or write off as hopeless cases.

5.0 out of 5 stars

By Diane Glenney on January 7, 2016

This is the best and most honest book on how it is to be homeless. As I read about the people and conversations with the people Dennis knows I truly understood homelessness at a basic level. It is a book of true humanity. Read it from start to finish. Highly suggest it to anyone who has a heart.

5.0 out of 5 stars

Well written and extremely interesting

By Emily on July 7, 2014

I really enjoyed reading this although it did make me feel both sad for the people living on the streets and grateful for everything that I have that I know I sometimes take for granted.

The author has done a great job allowing us a glimpse into these people's lives, and experiences.

5.0 out of 5 stars

It gives you insight in a clear cut fashion on a subject you'd like to forget but should do something about

By Youngatheart on April 25, 2015

Dennis' book should be a must read for everyone. It gives you insight in a clear cut fashion on a subject you'd like to forget but should do something about, no ifs, ands or buts. Thank God for a book that will keep you on a higher moral ground and show you the right thing to do. Forget your preconceptions and help get rid of this blight on humanity.

5.0 out of 5 stars

An Excellent & Very Thoughtful Read

By The Notebook Blogairy on November 20, 2014

Gotta Find A Home: Conversations with Street People by Dennis Cardiff is one of those books that you pick up on a lark. I picked it up because the second part of the title intrigued me. Conversations with street people? What the heck?!

So, I added this book to my to-be-read bookshelf and went on my merry way. Why did my mind keep wandering back to the question that Cardiff's title implies? What kind of conversations are we talking about? Real conversations? Fictionalized conversations? More importantly, my brain had this question. What could street people have to say?

I'm not (too) ashamed to say that prior to reading this book I, among the masses, averted my eyes when passing a panhandler on the street. I assumed that they were there because they wanted to be there; they missed/lost opportunities and now had to fight and claw their way to get back to 'normalcy'.

Gotta Find A Home did not disabuse me of this notions. For the most part, those beliefs of mine remain largely intact. The conversations that Cardiff shares with his readers are actual factual retellings of his many conversations with people he met on the streets who identified themselves as "Street People."

According to Cardiff, Street People are people who panhandle for a living and have done it for a long time (like a decade or more). But I digress.

Gotta Find A Home is a book that pulls no punches. It is a straight forward daily account of the day-to-day lives of this close-knit group of panhandlers in Toronto. There is no plot.

There is no structure other than the loose timeline of these conversations. There is no true end. This book is a fly-on-the-wall view of what life is like for various members of this group of people who in one week have more crises than the UN, the Pentagon and the Middle East put together. Members of this group have fatal illnesses, severe health issues, psychological issues, financial woes, and of course, issues with finding stable clean housing.

Add on top of these major issues the normal squabbling among a large group of close-knit friends (which many times devolves into fist fights…) and you have what Cardiff calls a 'soap opera'. Gotta Find A Home: Conversations with Street People will leave you feeling haunted, questioning and, I believe, sympathetic. While many of the people in this book did not change one iota their stories and back-stories are compellingly sad. It makes one realize that with just a different decision (or two) any one of us could have chosen the path that some of the people in Cardiff's book have chosen.

This is an excellent and very thoughtful read. I give it 5 stars for content.

5.0 out of 5 stars

I highly recommend this book to everyone

By Amazon Customer on July 11, 2014

This book is well written and helpful. The author has put extra efforts in writing such a masterpiece. The quality of material of this book is worth more than its price. Easy to understand content for everyone. From me, I will definitely rate this book and the author's efforts a 5-STAR. I highly recommend this book to everyone.

5.0 out of 5 Stars

This will leave a lasting impression!!!

By J. Summers on September 12, 2014

This story is truly touching! If I could make it mandatory for all to read, I would. It shines light on the homeless, but not in a degrading way. So many people often forget about the homeless situation, ignore those that are homeless, or look down upon them. This book reminds us that regardless of our situation, (ex. being homeless) we are all still people. It will remind you that we all bleed the same, we all have feelings, and we all have a heart. You can never know someone's story until you talk with them.

I really like the concept of this book, how it was written, and the material within! The flow and content is so intriguing and easy to follow, one could zoom through its 200+ pages in a jiffy. Mr. Dennis Cardiff did a fantastic job putting it all together. Through a series of entries, he records different accounts with various street people. People whom he has gotten to know and cherish, and if you read you will too! Through these entries the reader gets to read first-hand, how and why these people are homeless. They get the answers to the questions many want to know. Yet, Mr. Cardiff doesn't bluntly ask his new acquaintances these questions, it is all revealed in casually conversations; similar to ones you would have with a new or old friend. After reading this book, my heart began to widen for these people and their unique situation, and my immediate reaction to a street person has forever been changed. If looking for a book with substance, this is it. It is real, insightful, and will leave a lasting impression!

5.0 out of 5 stars

A must-read diary of not-walking-by

By Sheila Deeth VINE VOICE on July 16, 2014

Dennis Cardiff's Gotta Find a Home doesn't just put a human face on street people; it invites non-street people like me to wear a human face too. Short chapters grouped into months offer a diary of life walking the streets, as the author travels to and from work, helps in a food kitchen, and takes time to chat. Sometimes a gentle poem will lighten the mood — "I want to see your smile each day/A memory – it just won't do." Sometimes he offers the background story of one of the people he's met. And sometimes readers are simply asked to listen to voices of strangers not so different from the rest of us; people who live in apartments, struggle with rent, read books, sometimes drink too much, may have suffered abuse in the home or in jail, may have children, grandchildren even, and might like a bagel with cream cheese for breakfast today.

Joy isn't always joyful, but the author's writing shares his delight when she is. The dog might bite. The law's long arm might threaten. Tempers can flare. And yes, this friend might drink too much, that one take drugs, another make foolish financial r social choices. But these people are friends with loyalties and an oddly different sort of hope. Cold in winter, it angers them if someone freezes to death. It should anger us too.

"I've been sober for two days now." Sounds good. "I'm on the second floor of the Salvation Army." But even shelter life isn't easy, and fear of crowds might keep a friend away. Meanwhile the author doesn't judge; he just joins in, like an outsider gaining entry to the family. He finds a willing ear to listen to his worries, as he listens to theirs. Then worlds that might seem far apart grow closer than we think. And I read his blog to learn who's still alive and who is gone.

Gotta Find a Home is a must-read memoir of real people, real needs, real streets, and a real world we too easily ignore. So go read it!

Disclosure: I was hooked on the blog, signed up for a giveaway, and was given a copy of this book. Thank you Dennis, and I offer my honest review.

The beggar, engraving by Alphonse Legros (1837-1911)

Gotta Find a Home 4

More Conversations
on the Streets

Dennis Cardiff

Published by Dennis Cardiff

Gotta Find a Home 4: Conversations on the Streets
Book 4

by Dennis Cardiff

The author has tried to recreate events, locales and conversations from his memories of them. In order to maintain anonymity names of individuals and places have been changed.
Cover Illustration Copyright © 2014 by Dennis Cardiff
Cover Font is called DJ Gross and the *license can be found at:* *http://www.fontsquirrel.com/license/DJ-Gross*

ISBN-13: 978-0993979965 (978-0-9939799-6-5)

ISBN-10: 0993979963

Dedication

To my wife Daisy, for her love, patience and understanding; allowing me to spend hours at my computer, when she would have preferred that I spend them with her. To my sons Rik and Roger, from whom I continue to learn. To my street friends, aliases: Joy, Shakes, Alphonse, Serge, Rocky, Silver, Anne, Shark, Irene, Debbie, Wolf, Weasel and his dog Bear, who have passed away much to early. Wolf's dog Shaggy is retired and has been given a safe home with Gaston and his partner Yves. Still active on the streets are, Little Jake, Mariah, Bearded Bruce, Jacques, Magdalene, Trudy, Chili, Loretta, Craig, Timmy, and both Chesters.

How It Began

From Book 1

My lungs ached as frost hung in the bitterly cold December morning air, making breathing difficult. I trudged in the falling snow toward the building where I work, in one of the city's grey, concrete, office tower canyons. I dodged other pedestrians, also trying to get to work on time, I noticed a woman seated cross-legged on the sidewalk with her back against a building wall. A snow-covered Buddha, wrapped in a sleeping bag, shivering in the below freezing temperature. I guessed her to be in her forties. Everything about her seemed round. She had the most angelic face, sparkling blue eyes and a beautiful smile. A cap was upturned in front of her. I thought, There but for the grace of God go I. Her smile and blue eyes haunted me all day.

In the past I've been unemployed, my wife and I were unable to pay our mortgage and other bills, we went through bankruptcy, lost our house, my truck. Being in my fifties, my prospects looked dim. It could have been me, on the sidewalk, in her place.

I was told not to give money to panhandlers because they'll just spend it on booze. I thought to myself, What should I do, if anything? What would you do? I asked for advice from a friend who has worked with homeless people. She said, 'The woman is probably hungry. Why don't you ask her if she'd like a breakfast sandwich and maybe a coffee?'

That sounded reasonable, so the next day I asked, "Are you hungry? Would you like some breakfast, perhaps a coffee?"

"That would be nice," she replied.

When I brought her a sandwich and coffee she said to me, "Thank you so much, sir. You're so kind. Bless you." I truly felt blessed.

This has become a morning routine for the past four years. The woman (I'll call Joy) and I have become friends. Often I'll sit with her on the sidewalk. We sometimes meet her companions in the park. They have become my closest friends. I think of them as angels. My life has become much richer for the experience.

Contents

The Usual Suspects

(Alphabetical listing of Dennis' street friends)
People come and go on a daily basis on the street, so this list only includes 'the regulars' – the ones that Dennis refers to as 'the usual suspects'. This list will refresh your memory on their approximate ages and who their 'partners' are:

André
Angela – Joy's probation officer
Anne – with Chester and Nick
Bearded Bruce
Bettie – daughter of Shakes
Big Jake – Joy's boyfriend
Bowser – Shakes' stuffed dog
Buck – sells native cigarettes
Chantal – the 'religious lady' who stops by to chat
Chester – with Anne. Joy's 3rd roommate.
Chili – age 21, had hip surgery
Chuck (Toothless) – Joy's 2nd roommate
Daimon – with Lucy in the Sky
Deaf Donald – age 35
Dillinger – Buck's dog
Debbie -- with Outcast
Fran – daughter of Shakes
Gaston – with Yves
Hippo
Ian – with Marlena
Irene – with Shark
Jacques – age 42, has HIV/AIDS
Little Jake – age 41
Joy – age 47

Luther – plays guitar
Lucy in the Sky – with Daimon
Maggie (Magdalene) – age 22, with Alphonse
Marlena – with Ian
Metro – sells newspapers
Nick – with Anne. Pans to make money to help out his street friends by making them sandwiches and coffee.
Outcast - with Debbie
Raven
Roy – Joy's first roommate
Rocky
Stella
Shakes – age 50
Trudy

Introduction

Throughout the past seven years I have met many people, now friends, who for various reasons are, or were, homeless.

- Antonio slept on a park bench and was beaten; he had his teeth kicked out for no other reason than his choice to sleep outdoors. He is a small, gentle man who has a phobia about enclosed spaces.

- Craig slept on the sidewalk in the freezing cold. I saw him every morning and was never sure if, when I lifted the corner of his sleeping bag, I would find him dead or alive. Sometimes, he confided, he would have preferred never to awake.

- Joy fell on hard times. She slept behind a dumpster in back of the coffee shop. I saw her with blackened eyes, bruised legs, cracked ribs, cut and swollen lips. I usually see her sitting on the sidewalk panning for change.

I can't do much for these people except to show them love, compassion, an ear to listen, perhaps a breakfast sandwich and a coffee. I want to do more. To know them is to love them. What is seen cannot be unseen.

When I'm with the homeless, I don't judge. I ask a minimum of questions, only enough to keep the conversation moving. I don't interrogate or ask about their past. Mostly, I listen and try to understand. I am often asked why I am there. Although the reasons are deeper, I usually answer by saying, "The conversations here are more interesting than where I work." I visit these people on the streets, on the way to my place of employment, and at noon hours.

What I have learned over the past seven years has changed my life. These people, who I consider to be my friends, are alcoholics, drug and other substance users. Some work as prostitutes, some have AIDS, most or all have served time in prison for various offenses. All of them I would trust with my life. They have welcomed me into their street family. I am honored to be considered a member.

I have heard sickening stories of abuse as children and babies born with drug dependencies. Most have mental and physical illnesses, suffer beatings, broken bones, stabbings, and have a fear of abusive partners and the police.

Authority in any form is seen negatively, as a means to control their lives. The homeless shelters are noisy, infested with bedbugs, the scene of fights and a place where personal items are stolen. Many homeless people prefer to sleep inside common areas such as bank foyers, outside under bridges, or behind dumpsters.

I have recalled conversations from memory and recorded them on these pages. I've attempted to be as accurate and truthful as possible. I haven't used any recording devices, so recollections may be faulty. I leave out details that I think may incriminate, but I don't interpret, explain or edit.

What they say is what you read. I have changed names and locations for purposes of privacy. My friends don't choose to be addicts. It's a disease and should be treated as such. They need help. They can't do it on their own, but they want it on their own terms.

Books

I folded my jacket, as a cushion, then sat with the crew at the park.

"Dennis," said Wolf, "just the man I wanted to see. Look at what my ladies — I'm not supposed to call them ladies -- look what my women — that doesn't sound right either. Anyway, there was a book sale at the school where this woman's daughter attends. People bring books, other people buy them, money goes to the school. She knows what kind of books I read so she picked out seven that she thought I'd like. There are two Robert Ludlum -- I may or may not have read them. Anyway, I'll put them at the end of my shelf where I've got his other books. There's an English detective novel — I'll have to be in the right frame of mind to read that. They're sometimes kind of slow. They develop the character – I get a bit impatient if there's no action. Have a look in this bag. Tell me what you think. You're welcome to borrow one, but I get first pick. I have to go for a piss." Wolf is a voracious reader. I've given him books from my collection and enjoy our discussions when he's read them. His preference is for what he calls 'shoot-em-up, crime novels'.

"Hi Mariah," I said, "how have you been since I saw you last?"

"Well, so so. I got a few things done. My air conditioner is in now. Frank is working on my laptop. It has ten gigs now, he wants to replace that with sixty. He cleaned up my hard drive, installed Office and a few other programs. When I get it back it should be just like new."

Joy said, "I was talking to Butcher this morning. He's out to get Jake for what he did to me. I tried to talk him out of it, but this time he's got his mind set. He's stubborn. All the time Jake spent in prison was for times he beat me.

I told Jake, 'When you get your hip operation, don't expect me to be there... 'Well, I said I'd be there, so I guess I will. I said, 'Don't get too used to that wheel chair, or we're over. Have your operation, get on your feet then we'll see what happens.' I don't let him pee standing up, but even when he sits down he manages to leave a puddle on the floor."

Mariah said, "When he's at my place, I have to clean up after him."

Joy said, "He's such a slob. He really gets me going when I find a pile of his laundry at the end of the couch. I told him this morning. 'I bring you clean clothes, the least you could do is put your dirty ones in the hamper.' It pisses me off, and starts my day off wrong."

Wolf returned, "Dennis, I was just showing Jacques an article in the paper. There was this kid who shot someone, then he takes the gun apart and leaves it in a mall parking lot. How stupid do you have to be to do something like that? Of course they caught the guy, he may as well have drawn the police a diagram. What is it with these kids now, they got their video games, they're texting each other all the time. The cops even stop them for texting while they're driving. Can you imagine that.

"There was a driver convicted of striking and injuring five cyclists and leaving the scene of the crash. Hitting one cyclist, I can understand, sometimes they're hard to see, but five?

"Another thing, those bicycles that are low to the ground, you've seen them, the pedals are higher than the seat. What's with that? Are they trying to make themselves invisible, so they'll get run over? Anyway, that's all I got to say about that."

"Hippo, " I said, "how is everything going at your place. Are you still having trouble?"

"It's okay, I just ignore them. They still run up and down the stairs."

Joy said, "Look at Shaggy, isn't she sweet, with her nose sticking out between the spokes of the cart? I don't know what it is. That dog has never liked me. With Bear it was different. Even before I started to have symptoms of my kidney failure, she'd hang around me, put her head on my knee. I was still peeing, but she seemed to sense that something was wrong. A week later I was laying on the floor dialing 911."

The Shep

28 May 2014

I shook hands all around. "Dennis," said Shakes, "you didn't shake with Shaggy, hahaha."

"She knows I love her,"

"Here's a cushion for you," said Jacques.

Shakes said, "You know, I'm staying at the Shep now. They served a big breakfast today, eggs, sausages and home fries. They had the big sausages," making a circle with his thumb and forefinger, "like that. I put one in my pocket for Shaggy. First I asked Wolf if it would be alright. He said, 'Okay,' then I gave her a piece. She's been looking at my pocket ever since."

Jacques asked, "Shakes, have you talked to your worker about getting a new place?"

Shakes nodded his head (yes).

"What did she say?" asked Jacques.

"I find out on Friday. That's when she's going to tell me. I hope I can get a place soon."

Jacques said, "You know it's almost a year since I've been in my castle. It's not really a castle, it's a bachelor, but to me it's my castle. June first, that's the day I moved in last year. I love it there."

I said, "It's nice that you have a balcony."

"Yes, I love my balcony."

"Do you have room to make your rice and raisin wine there?"

"I have the room, but my doctor says I'm not to drink so much. So, I drink until I run out of money, then I go the rest of the month without. He said to me, 'If you drank more expensive liquor, you'd drink even less.' I said, 'Yes, but I like it my way.'

Wolf asked Shakes, "Are you going for a pack of smokes?"

Shakes nodded (yes). "Can you do a count for me?" He hauled a handful of change out of the inside pocket of his leather jacket and put it in a pile on the sidewalk. "How much do I have there?"

Wolf counted, he said, "You got five eighty-five. How much do you need? What's your price?"

"Seven seventy-five."

Wolf said, "Here's a two, you got ten cents more than you need. Now, are you going for smokes?"

Shakes said, "I'm going. I just need a cigarette first." To a man walking past he asked, "'Excuse me, can I buy a cigarette from you? Ma'am, can I buy a cigarette?"

Wolf said, "I don't want to rush you, but fuck off already. I'm waiting for a smoke."

"Hey soldier, can I buy a cigarette?"

Wolf said, "I guess since you're the one going, I shouldn't be trying to hurry you. I'm just, what is it they say? -- busting your balls?"

Two men from the Innercity Mission stopped by. One was driving a refrigerated vehicle, powered by a bicycle. "Would anyone like a sandwich, a bottle of water? How about you, Shakes. Is there anything you'd like?"

"A sandwich please, but not egg. I like scrambled eggs, but not hard boiled or sunny-side-up. I can't eat those. I don't know why."

I said, "Maybe it's the mayo you don't like."

"No, give me a can of ham and some mayo -- Jake'll tell you -- I'll go through that like nothing flat."

"Wolf," the man asked, "anything for you?"

"Water, please, and one for Shaggy."

Shakes said, "I'll take one for Shaggy too. Do you have socks? We'll all take a pair of socks. Shaggy needs two pair."

Jacques said, "When I had my dog, Star, women would get mad at me if I called her a bitch. They'd say, 'That's no way to talk to your dog.' I'd say, 'But, she is a bitch, that's what female dogs are called. I didn't make it up.' "

Wolf said, "Women get mad at me when I call the Queen a bitch."

Jacques said, "That's something we agree with. So, we don't have to go to war now, France against Germany."

Wolf noticed that the man in the red vest was wearing a Montreal hat. "That was some game last night, man? We stayed alive over the Rangers in game five. It was too much stress. We had them four to one, then Nash, Stepan and Kreider all struck within four minutes to even the score. I was tearing my hair out. I put back six beers before the end of the second period. I was throwing empty cans all over the place. I calmed down a bit after Bourke put in two. Then Desharnais scored on an empty net to end the game seven to four. So, now we wait for them to meet in game six on Thursday in New York.

"Thanks for the water and the socks."

After they left Jacques said, "I don't like those guys."

I asked, "Why is that, Jacques?"

"Sometimes they come by and ask everyone but me if they want something."

I said, "They asked you today."

"Yeah, but I still don't like them."

Jacques asked Wolf, "How much do you pay for your smokes?"

"If I buy Du Maurier, or Export A, it's twelve bucks, but I only get them on check day. I bring them here and share with everybody. Other days, I buy natives for seven bucks."

"So, it costs me less for my one gram of pot a day, than it does you for your cigarettes."

Wolf said, "I never thought about it that way, but you're right."

Jacques pulled out his pot pipe. "Once, when the cops came by, I was holding this in my fist, but they noticed the end sticking out. The cop asked to see it. He asked, 'Do you have anything to put in this?' I said, 'No, I have to go downtown to buy some.' Maybe I should have asked him if he had any. You know, it's not illegal to have a pipe, as long as there's nothing in it. I scraped the bowl with a screwdriver. I got nearly half a gram. That makes a good smoke, that stuff that gets caked around the edge, but I don't like the resin. I tried those water pipes. I don't like them... and when they put wine or cognac in them, ugh, it makes me sick.

"I think I'm going to make this pipe flatter on top." He rubbed it back and forth on the sidewalk. "See, when it's shaped it's white, but when it's handled, the fat from people's hands turns it dark green.

"Shakes, do you still have that big pipe I gave you?"

"Yeah, I still got it at home."

"Dennis," asked Shakes, "would you please help me up.

"Thanks."

Bleeding on the Counter

29 May 2014

"Hi, Dennis," said Little Chester, " it's an honor to see you. Do you have any of those Tim Horton cards? How about bus tickets, do you have any of those?"

"Sorry Chester, I'm all out."

"Here's a cushion, Dennis," said Jacques.

"Thanks, how are you today?"

"Okay, my check should be in the mail today. Last night the fire engines came to our building at about four in the morning. I sniffed the air in my apartment. Stuck my head out the door to the hallway. I could smell something, but not much, so I put my earphones back in and went to sleep. The apartments are all concrete. If a guy came home drunk, started cooking something on the stove, then fell asleep, it might cause a fire, but it would all be contained in the one apartment.

"Look what I found yesterday. It's a case to carry my pot pipe and my lighter."

Mariah said, "It looks like the case for one of those electric shavers, or clippers. It's a good, solid case."

Jacques pulled a tall can of Old Milwaukee out of his canvas bag.

Chester said, "Jacques, I see you've got a beer."

Jacques said to me, "See the cut I got on my thumb. I did something really stupid yesterday. I was cutting the side handles off my bag, because I only use the shoulder strap and the others get in the way. The knife slipped. It cut really deep. I put Polysporin and a band aid on it last night. When I woke up this morning it was bleeding. I put another band aid over top. I took my cans back to the beer store and it started bleeding again, I thought, *Oh, no, they're not going to serve me, I got blood on one of the cans.* That's what happened to me at the liquor store one day. I had a cut that started bleeding on the counter and the guy jumped back. He said, 'This cash is closed. We need to disinfect.' I guess he thought that maybe I have HIV. He didn't know."

Chester asked, "Jacques, can I have a beer?" Jacques poured his beer into a red drinking bottle. Took the can, twisted it, crushed it between the palms of his hands, then put it in his bag."

Chester said, "I got a watch. I found it on the day of the marathon. That reminds me, the government owes me some money. I should go see them about it."

Mariah said, "Maybe you should wait until sometime when you're sober, before you try to do that. It might go better for you," She passed Jacques an empty vodka bottle. He put it in his bag.

Jacques said, "What do you mean when he gets sober. Don't you mean if he gets sober?"

Gnome stopped by and said, "This is Wolf's court date. Does anybody know how it went for him?"

Jacques said, "I hope that he remembered to go."

Chili said, "I got some good news. My hip operation is going to be scheduled for November at the latest."

Mariah said, "That's good, sometimes they'll have a cancellation and will be able to take you early."

"I hope so. I'm really having trouble walking. I can't sit down properly either. I have to keep my leg straight.

"I'm going to meet someone downtown so I'll see you guys."

I said, "Bye Chili. I'll I have to leave also. Will everybody be back tomorrow?"

Jacques said, "I don't know. It being my check day and all. I'm going to read the flyers and make my grocery list. I got a flyer from Target. What's Target, what do they sell?"

Mariah said, "It's just like Wal-Mart, but not as good."

Chili said, "I go to my Independent Grocer on Mondays and pick up their flyers for the week. For clothes I like to go to Winners, or Value Village."

I said, "I buy nearly all my clothes from Value Village. Everything I'm wearing is from there."

Mariah said, "That's a nice shirt."

"I think I paid five bucks for it, a couple of years ago. For the pants, I may have paid seven. As you can see, they're due to be replaced."

Pandemonium

30 May 2014

Pandemonium reigned at the park today. While I greeted Joy, Chester interrupted by asking, "Dennis, do you have any bus tickets?"

Ghyslain said, "I'd get up to shake your hand, but I'm on roller blades."

I came back to Joy who said, "Big Jake has gone for the weekend."

I asked, "Where has he gone?"

Chester asked, "Dennis do you have any bus tickets?"

Joy said, "He's gone to his parent's cottage in the Muskokas. We've been together for eight years now and he hasn't introduced me to his parents. What do you think of that? I'm so pissed off."

Chester asked, "Dennis, do you have any bus tickets?"

"Here, Chester," I said as I handed him the tickets.

Jacques offered me a cushion and I sat between him and Shakes. Ghyslain was on the sidewalk in front of me. He asked, "Dennis, did you see the game last night?"

"No," I said, "I didn't see it."

"You don't follow hockey? It was a real disappointment. Montreal was beat out by New York. It's been twenty-two years since a Canadian team has won the Stanley Cup. It wasn't Tokarski's fault, he was standing on his head to make some of those saves, he allowed only one goal, but that was all it took for the Rangers to win. Now it will be the winner between Chicago and Los Angeles who plays New York for the finals."

Little Jake came over to talk to Shakes, **"You got paid yesterday. It's time to pay your debts."**

"What debts?"

"To me, asshole. Who do you think has been feeding you?"

Jake stormed off with a scowl on his face. Shakes said to me,

"He's on new meds. That's why he's so cranky. He's had a go at everybody today." He pulled a bottle of Jack Daniels from his inside jacket pocket and passed it around.

Debbie stood up to try to soothe Jake. "Come on Jake, sit down and relax."

"You, get away from me. Don't you dare put a finger on me."

"Or what, Jake? What are you going to do to me? Are you going to hit me? Don't you dare touch me again."

As this was going on Joy was yelling at Raven, "You piece of shit. You stole money from Chester. I know he gave you his bank number and you cleaned out his account. You did the same thing when I was living there." Mariah was holding Joy back as Raven walked away. Chester was rocking back and forth on the plastic crate he was sitting on.

Jacques said to me, "Chester isn't supposed to drink hard liquor. It could kill him. His legs go when he drinks that stuff."

I asked, "What's wrong with his legs?"

"He's got a bad knee, but the real problem is when he drinks, he can't stand. Me, I just have a couple of beer and leave it at that. I know I can't drink hard liquor or wine."

Joy said, "I have to get Chester back to his place. We're going to have to get a cab. Can somebody help me get him up." Mariah, Jake and Debbie tried to help get him vertical.

A woman stopped and asked, "Do you want me to call an ambulance?"

Mariah, the voice of reason, said, "He'll be fine, we're going to phone a cab.

"Okay, we got him up, now what do we do? He won't walk. It would probably be better if we took him over to the lawn where he could sleep it off for a while." He was a dead weight and ended up lying on the sidewalk. "The police will be here if we don't move him soon."

Jake said, **"He's not garbage, you're not going to just dump him on the lawn."**

Mariah said, "Nobody's dumping him, Jake. There's nothing else we can do. After he sleeps it off for a while we can get him in a cab."

We all lifted, dragged and pushed Chester to a secluded part of the lawn. He lay down and fell asleep.

Jacques picked up his radio, drinking bottle and cushion and said, "I'm getting away from all this bullshit. I don't need this drama in my life. I'm going home where it's quiet."

Seated on the curb, Debbie had her arm around Joy who was visibly shaking. "She's having one of her epileptic seizures. It's okay girl, you'll be alright."

I asked, "Was it all the stress with Chester that brought this on?"

"Stress, booze, malnutrition, anything can bring one on."

After about five minutes joy awoke. She sobbed, "I hate when this happens. Do I have snot all over my face?"

"No," said Debbie, "you look just fine. If you want you can blow your nose on my sleeve. It's clean."

"I can't do that."

"Sure you can. I do it when I don't have Kleenex. What else am I supposed to do."

Joy said, "Thanks, Dennis. I'm sorry about all this. I'm really hammered."

I said, "Just take care of yourself. There's nothing to be sorry about. I'll see you Monday. Have a good weekend."

June 2014

El Mocambo

"Dennis," said Mariah, "this is my friend, Beast."

"Hi, Beast."

"I'll stand up to shake your hand, just showing respect. Have you lived around here long? The reason I'm asking is I've been out west in Calgary and Medicine Hat, but I lived here in the seventies. I played in a rock band. We use to be at Larry's Hideaway, the Horseshoe, El Mocambo — we called it El Mo. Remember The famous neon palm tree sign hanging out over the sidewalk on Spadina Avenue? "

"Yeah," I said, "I know those places. I lived two blocks from the Victory Burlesque Theater on Spadina. The Stones played the El Mocambo around that time, 1977, maybe."

"It's funny you should mention that. I was working the door that night. Margaret Trudeau, the Prime Minister's wife showed up. There were a lot of big shots there. I was riding my motorcycle home — it was raining — my wheel got caught in the streetcar tracks and threw me in the path of a BMW. I broke both my legs, my arms, my hands are still messed up. I still play guitar, but I can't play like I used to. I play in the market area sometimes. A friend lends me his guitar. I've had a lot of guitars, they all seemed to end up in pawn shops.

"Our drummer's girlfriend was a stripper, hooker. Everyone thought that he was living off her money. Actually, she was living off him, her money was all stashed away. She was murdered. Her name was Jennifer."

"Remember some of the local groups from that time: Foot in Coldwater, Triumph, Lighthouse, Dee and The Yeomen — I knew all those guys."

"Yeah, I saw Lighthouse and McKenna Mendelson Mainline live at an outdoor concert at Humber College. I saw the Yeomen in Yorkville."

"That's great , man. It's good to talk to somebody from the old days. It was a lot different then. I remember some of the dope we got into — hash oil, Moroccan Gold, hash laced with opium. What was that place? … that college downtown?"

I said, "I think you mean Rochdale College on Bloor Street. They used to call it Roach-dale, there was so much marijuana being sold. I had friends there, went to a lot of parties. Motorcycles would be ridden up and down the stairs. I think they closed it in 1975."

"Yeah, those were good times. Lately, I've felt depressed, like I'm not going anywhere.

"Do you hear what's playing on the radio? It's Knockin' on Heaven's Door; except it's not Bob Dylan, or Eric Clapton. It's the Guns and Roses version — weird.

Wolf said, "Dennis, do you recognize my dog? I took her to the spa, Saturday. It cost ninety bucks, ten more than last year. They trimmed her nails, sheared her coat. It'll be a lot cooler for her in the heat. The vet also prescribed some arthritis medication for her. You should see her now, jumping, running. It's like she was five years younger."

I asked, "Did they have any problems with her biting?"

"No, they put a muzzle on her. I didn't stay, but I said to them, 'She's old and in pain, so be very gentle.' They know what they're doing. She's really good about taking her pills. I call her over and say, 'Okay Shaggy, it's time to take your pill'. She comes over and opens her mouth, 'Okay.' She knows I'd never give her anything that would hurt her.

"I'm thinking of getting a Blue Jays cap. What do you think? I wouldn't buy a new one, but I'd acquire it — nothing

illegal. Maybe I could get one from a friend. I'm not a real
baseball fan, not like I am about hockey. When I flip channels I
see Toronto Blue Jays — there's not much else to watch, so I've
started getting into it. I'm probably not making much sense. It
was pay weekend. I did a lot of drinking. I wasn't here
Monday. Tuesday we had rain. I guess I haven't seen you
since last Wednesday. I'm still reading that hardcover book I
told you about. The one with the big print. The others are still
lined up on my shelf -- the ones I haven't read.

"Dennis," said Mariah, "you should have seen all the
activity around our place on the weekend. There was a
stabbing across the street. I knew both guys involved. One
lived in our building. He was taken away, there's a restraining
order against him, so he'll have to move out. The other guy
had to get seven stitches. I saw him yesterday, he had a big
blood spot on his shirt. I pointed it out to him. He said, 'I
guess it's started up again.'

"Big Jake came back after the weekend. Joy is still at home,
her legs are really swollen. She may have to go into hospital
again."

Wolf said, "Would you look at this guy. Is he trying to
blind us with that flourescent pink shirt? It's Little Jake, he's
gone Hollywood on us, with the shades and everything. Jake,
have you seen Shakes?"

"Yeah, he's broke, so he came over to my place. Where else
would he go? He never shows up when he's got money for
food, only when he's broke. He pisses me off.

"Dennis, can you spare me a card? It's been a bad day."

"Sure, Jake. I have to be leaving. Maybe, I'll see all of you
tomorrow."

Crack Doctor

11 June 2014

More uncertain weather. When I approached Metro, the vendor of free newspapers, he said, "Joy's up there."

"Thanks Metro, Have a good day. Stay out of the rain." He waved and nodded his head.

"Hi Sunshine," said, Joy.

"Hi," I said, "Mariah told me that you've been having trouble with your legs and may have to go to hospital again."

"Yeah, my ankles are still swollen, but they're better than yesterday. Big Jake's coming down later. He's having more trouble with his wheelchair. He's thinking it's maybe the crazy guy upstairs. He's had two flat tires in two weeks. That's not right. I told him to chain his chair in front of the window, so he can keep an eye on it."

I asked, "Do you mean at the Sally, or at your place?"

"My place. He's out drinking with the boys now –as long as he keeps away from me, I don't care.

"Did you hear that Willard is coming after Jake? I don't know what that's about. Willard is Raven's boyfriend. Do you know him? Anyway, I thought everything was cool. Last week I grabbed Raven by the throat and told her to get out of my fuckin' sight, for stealing money from Chester. That's what she does, she gets guys drunk — doing whatever it is that she does — then goes for their wallets. Willard does the same thing behind the Mission. He'll sit with a guy, bum a few beers. When the guy runs out he beats the shit out of him for the change he has in his pockets.

"Raven said, 'Willard wants to meet with Frank.' I said, "We know where he hangs out. We'll be there. I may just punch out Willard myself. He's a wife beater, but he hasn't come up against a someone like me before. I don't punch like a woman."

Rodeo Ride

18 June 2014

"Good morning, Joy," I said, " how are your legs?"

"They're aching. It seems to help if I rock back and forth. I have arthritis as well. My knees and hips are sore."

I asked, "Have you tried Aleve? On television they say that it's good for arthritis."

"That's bullshit, they say that it's clinically proven to relieve the pain of arthritis for 12 hours with just one pill.' Shit, I took four of them and they didn't do a thing. I'm going to buy one of Jake's Tylenol 3. They usually help."

I said, "If you can get an appointment with your doctor, he may recommend Celebrex. It's an anti-inflammatory drug used to treat pain or inflammation, especially arthritis.

"So how was your weekend?"

"It was quiet, we had a few barbecues. I think my upstairs neighbor is pissed off with the number of barbecues we've had."

I asked, "Is the smoke going up to his apartment?"

"Probably, he hasn't mentioned it, but if he did I'd tell him to close his window. We don't have any kind of patio, we're just set up at the end of the driveway. He's been stomping up and down the stairs, so I don't care what he likes or doesn't like.

"I've got a problem with my stove. I was baking some potatoes and Jake asked, "What the fuck's with the oven. I see flames in there. I patted the flame out with an oven glove. The potatoes were ready anyway. I waited around all day yesterday for a repairman to come, but he didn't show. I'll have to get on to the landlady about that."

I asked, "Is it an electric or gas stove?"

"It's electric. Have you ever heard of a fire starting like that in an electric stove? It's bizarre.

"Did I tell you the joke about the Rodeo Ride? That's when a guy mounts a woman doggy style, whispers into her ear, 'You're the worst fuck in the world!' then tries to hold on for nine seconds."

...

At noon I walked to the park and the first to greet me was Outcast, "Dennis, I haven't seen you for about a year. Come here, give me a hug. It's good to see you, man."

"It's good to see you, Outcast."

I asked Mariah, "How has your stomach been?"

"So so, I just have to watch what I eat and how I cook it. Occasionally, if I can find them on sale, I'll get some of those filet mignon. A four-pack costs fifteen ninety-nine, so for four bucks, on check day, I'll treat myself. Usually, I eat mostly vegetables. I just love raw vegetables."

Two female outreach workers, dressed in black, came by with bottled water. "Shakes, would you like some water?"

"Yes, please."

She asked Mariah, "Would you like some ma'am?"

"Yeah, okay, thanks."

"What is your name ma'am?"

"What do you need that for?"

"Oh, don't worry, we don't use it for anything. It's just for our own records, to show how much we've handed out."

"My name's Mariah."

The women went around the circle, then walked away in the direction they'd come.

Outcast yelled to me, "Dennis, do you have any plans for Sunday night?"

"Yeah, I'll be out of town."

"Too bad, Steve Martin and the Steep Canyon Rangers are coming to town. They're really good. We can't afford tickets, but it's an outdoor concert, so we'll be listening from across the street.

"Joy," said Mariah," we'll have to get some clothes. I got a thirty-five dollar voucher from Value Village."

Joy said, "Where did you get the voucher?"

"From my worker. She gives me one a year."

"I'll have to check with my worker about that. She's never offered anything like that.

"Remember those red jeans that Loretta got me last year. There's no way I'll be able to fit into them now. I've cut back to one meal a day. Jake says I should eat more, but I'm getting huge. We waste a lot of food. Sometimes I just don't have an appetite. You can only keep stuff so long in the fridge.

"I wouldn't mind going to that church place that sells clothes, except they won't leave you alone. They're always asking, 'Would you like a cookie? Would you like a nice cup of tea?' I just want to get some clothes and get out of there.

"Your son, Paul, came over to my place the other day. He was looking for you. I said, 'When the weather's good, she's most likely at the park.' "

I asked, "How old is your son?"

"He's twenty-eight. He just lost his job. For the past eight years he's been working at one of those fast food places. The manager really liked him. He'd send him to some of the other stores to fill in if someone was sick. Then they changed managers. The new guy was checking them all, before they left, for any food they might have taken. Paul got sick of that bullshit and quit.

"The problem is he's not eligible for unemployment insurance and he's running out of money. He has to walk nearly everywhere. I can't help him much. I said if you want to crash on my floor for a few days, that's okay, but there's no way you're moving in permanently, and don't even think of trying to get an apartment in this building.

"We just had Charlie's brother over for a few days. He's a big guy. He used to spar with Mike Tyson. He's had a few too many shots to the head, so sometimes he just drifts off someplace, or he'll mumble a bunch of stuff that doesn't make sense. We just leave him alone. Eventually, he'll come back.

I asked, "Does he still have both his ears?"

"Yes. People can't believe that he and Charlie are brothers. They're as different as can be."

Joy said, "I was talking to Irene the other day. She's freaking out because there are so many crack heads coming around. They've had their door kicked in twice while they were out; people looking for drugs. You know how tiny she is, and Shark's not much bigger, they wouldn't be able to defend themselves. It was the same way last time she lived with Shark. The landlord is getting pissed off too. He's probably going to evict them."

I asked, "Is Shark selling his medicinal marijuana and morphine pills?"

"Yeah, I think he's dealing crack too.

Spinner

19 June 2014

Joy was marching towards me as I approached her spot. She said, "Can you watch my stuff. The pizza place wont let me use their washroom."

"Sure," I said. I took her place on the plastic box, now with two plastic cushions acquired yesterday. I sat, feeling somewhat conspicuous, ignored by people I work with. I had forgotten my watch at home, so I was watching the wrists of people walking by hoping to get a glimpse of the time. A man's analog wristwatch can be read from at least four feet away.

Joy returned, looking very pissed off, "These damn new people. I'm going to have to deal with this," she said as she marched off in the opposite direction. I could see her gesturing to a man seated on a marble platform, bordering the steps to a public building.

She came back, just as frustrated. "He knows Big Jake," she said to me as Jake rolled up in his wheelchair.

"Hi Jake, " I said. He waved.

"Joy," said Jake, "you don't want to go messing with that guy. He's a spinner. I've seen guys six foot six back down from him. You never know what he's going to do. He's nuts."

"Great," said Joy. "I asked him politely, I didn't hassle him, but he wouldn't talk to me. I said to him, 'I know you can talk, because I've heard you asking people for money. What I'm asking is that you wait until until nine o'clock when I'm finished, or move down the block.' He still wouldn't talk."

"Just leave it, Joy," said Jake.

A small Asian man, wearing a black suit stopped to talk to Joy, "Hi," he said. "I haven't seen you for a long time."

Joy said, "Yeah, how have you been doing. You're looking great."

"Thanks," he said, "I have to go now, but it was great seeing you."

After the man left Joy whispered to me, "That guy used to be a woman. People gave him a really hard time when he was transitioning. Some people are just born that way. A man born into a woman's body, or in his case a woman born into a man's body."

I said, "Why would people give him a hard time? It's not as if it's his choice, but a person has to choose to be an asshole."

Joy said, "I can figure out how a man could be changed to a woman, but how do they change a woman to a man? Do you know?"

"Yeah, I read about it on the internet. There are these pills you can buy. A guy can grow four inches overnight. I guess, if he wants to be bigger than that, he just takes more pills."

Brown Shoes

19 June 2014

"Dennis," said Shakes, "see if you can pull me up." He reached out his hand and I pulled.

I said, "You're not moving. Let me brace my foot against yours. Now, hang on and I'll pull."

Shakes said, "Do you know why you can't pull me up? It's because I don't want to get up, hahaha."

Joy said, "Shakes, don't do that. Act your age."

"Dennis," shouted Wolf, "come over here. I got something to show you. This is from the lady that gives me all the books. I hope it's not as weird as the last one. Have a look. Tell me what you think." Wolf handed me a hardcover book entitled

The Third Rail by Michael Harvey. I read inside the jacket cover:

A woman is shot as she waits for her train to work. An hour later, a second woman is gunned down as she rides an elevated train through the Loop. Two hours after that, a church becomes the target of a chemical weapons attack. The city of Chicago is under siege, and Michael Kelly, cynical cop turned private investigator, just happens to be on the scene when all hell breaks loose.

I said, "I haven't read any of this guy's stuff, but they say here that he writes about Chicago the way Raymond Chandler wrote about Los Angeles and the way Dashiell Hammett wrote about San Francisco. Those are two of my favorite authors. I'm sure that you're going to enjoy this. It's just the type of *shoot-em-up story* you like."

"That's good. That's my reading taken care of for the weekend. So, how are you? Isn't this weather great, not too hot, not too cool, a nice breeze blowing."

Joy said, "I'm getting too hot in the sun here. I think I'll move to the shade."

Big Jake pulled up in his wheel chair, "Joy, do you have any smokes?"

"No, I'll give Shark a call. *Hi, it's me. Are you coming to the park today?* He says he's not coming."

Jake said, "That's okay I'll go to his place."

Joy said, "Jacques is pissed off with me because I bought native cigarettes from Shark instead of from him. The thing is, Shark charged me four bucks for a pack of twenty-five. Jacques charges four bucks for a pack of twenty. He hangs around the Mission selling cigarettes there. He doesn't smoke himself, so he makes a good profit.

"Irene is still afraid to come out of the house. They have two big bodyguards, because there are a lot of thugs hanging around.

Shakes said, "Hey, Wolf, guess how long Joy and I have known each other."

"I know it's a long time, but I don't know how many years."

Joy said, "I met Shakes when I was thirteen. How many years is that, Shakes? How old are you?"

"I was born in the early sixties."

"So, what year — 1960, 61, 62, 63, 64?" Shakes didn't answer.

Joy said, "Thirty-six years, make that thirty-five. I use to buy stuff from Shakes."

Wolf said, "I knew you two were tight, but I didn't know it went that far back. What's the deal between you and Shark?"

"Shark said he'd back me until his nose bled, but he doesn't respect me. I said, 'I don't give a shit about that as long as I know you've got my back.' Irene and I used to do some deals together. We're still close."

A man in a suit was bending down in the flower garden. He seemed to be examining the soil. Joy whispered, "That dude looks cool. I wonder what he's doing."

Wolf said, "Dennis, did you notice something wrong? Joy thinks that guy is a sharp dresser. He's wearing a white shirt, a gray tie, gray jacket and pants, but look at the color of shoes he's wearing — brown. That's just not right. He should be wearing black shoes. Do you agree, or disagree?"

"I agree, Wolf. I was always taught to wear black shoes with grey or navy; brown shoes with brown or green."

Wolf started singing, "Blue and green, should never be seen, except when they're in, the washing machine. That's what my mother taught me. Do you agree?"

"Yes, Wolf, I agree."

Shakes was lying on the sidewalk next to Shaggy. "Wolf, Shaggy picked up her bowl. She's thirsty."

Wolf emptied her bowl, pulled out a water bottle from her caboose, splashed some water in the bowl and said, "Okay, Princess, there you go."

Joy said, "Princess, you bet! That dog gets treated better than people do. No doggy backwash for her, just pure bottled water."

Wolf said, "You know, Shaggy has bitten lots of people, but she's only drawn blood three times. Twice, it was from Joy."

"Yeah," said Joy," and I was being nice to her. Here we were, me, Wolf and Shaggy under the bridge. I had a paper cup full of chili. I was feeding Shaggy with my fingers. She couldn't get to the bottom of the cup, so I picked it up and was going to tear the sides down. That's when she bit me, right in the Achilles tendon. I nearly had to crawl home it was so painful."

You Can't Sleep Here!

20 June 2014

"Hi Dennis, " said a mournful Little Jake, "I fucked up last night. I lost everything: my backpack, my jacket, my sunglasses. I don't know what happened. Shakes and I ended up at a construction site near the cop shop. Some time around three thirty, I felt somebody kicking my foot. I said, **'Fuck off, that's my bad leg!'** It was two cops, one said, 'Hi Jake, what are you doing here? ' I don't know what happened after that. I woke up downtown. I was freezing... No Shakes, no smokes, no pot, nothing to drink. I still don't know where Shakes is. I hope he's got my bag."

Wolf said, "This is a great day. We got the music playing from the Jazz Festival, a light breeze and I don't have to go back to work until Monday. Maybe I'll take Monday off, we'll see."

Ambling up the sidewalk came Shakes. He took a seat on the curb.

"Shakes," asked Jake, "do you have my bag?"

"No, I don't have your bag. The last I remember a cop was kicking my foot. He said, 'Shakes, is that you?' I said, 'Of course It's me. Who else would I be?' He said, 'You can't sleep here, Shakes.' 'Well,' I said, 'not with you kicking my feet, I can't.'

"I saw my mom this morning. She was at the hairdressers. I saw her through the window. She said to the hairdresser, 'That's my son out there. Can you give him five bucks for me?' I hadn't seen her for about four years.

"I was at Rib Fest last night. I made about sixteen or seventeen dollars and people gave me lots of ribs. This guy asked me if I wanted to buy a forty pounder. I said, 'I don't know if I got enough money. Here you count it.' He said, 'No, Shakes you don't have enough.' When I counted my money later, I was short two bucks. He'd stolen it from me. I got two bottles now though."

Outcast walked up, "Have any of you seen Shark?"

Wolf said, "Yeah, he was here a while ago with Irene."

Outcast said, "I got to find him. I'm going to his place."

Wolf said, "He may not be there, why don't you phone him."

"I got no phone."

"I'll give you fifty cents to use the pay phone."

Shakes asked, "Do you want to buy a joint or some cigarettes?"

Outcast said, "I got no money, but I got a credit with Shark. That's why I gotta see him." With that he walked off.

Wolf said, "He seems to be having a hissy fit, same with Jacques. Ever since Joy bought that pack of cigarettes from Shark instead of him, he's been avoiding us."

Paul rode up on his bicycle with a guitar strapped to his back. He said, "This city sure has odd rules for busking. I got a licence to play in the market, but this afternoon I was playing downtown. A cop comes up to me and says, 'You can't play here.' I said, 'Yes, I can.' He asked, 'do you have a licence?' I said 'Yes.' and I showed him my licence. He said, 'This licence is for the market. That's where you have to play.' I said, 'Just because I have a licence for the market, doesn't mean I have to play there. I'll play wherever I want.' The place I used to play is gone, with the new subway construction. It's just gone."

"Dennis," said Shakes, "do you have any bus tickets?

"Here are some tickets, Shakes."

"Can you go on a liquor run for me if I give you the money?"

"I would have earlier, Shakes, but now I have to get back to work."

Rain, Rain Go Away

24 June 2014

Rain was falling lightly. I opened my umbrella. I wasn't expecting to see any of my friends, but from across the street I saw Joy, huddled in her coat. I jaywalked in front of traffic to talk to her. I held my umbrella over both of us.

"Don't worry about me," said Joy, "I'm soaked already, a few more drops won't make any difference."

"How have you been feeling?" I asked. "Big Jake left a message with Wolf that you had sun stroke."

"Yeah, I was feeling pretty sick. Now, my legs really hurt because of the dampness. I saw Chuck earlier. I don't know where he is now. Oh, there he is, talking to that native guy on the corner. I guess he's been cutting Chuck's grass. The guy's coming this way now.

"Did that grumpy guy chase you out of your spot?

"No," he said, "it's just too wet."

After he left Joy said, "I don't know where these guys are coming from. They're not twinkies, coming from the suburbs for the summer. He must be from out of town. Here comes Chuck."

"Hi Chuck," I said. "Was that guy giving you any trouble?"

"No, I just asked him to move along. He did."

Joy said to him, "I'm leaving shortly, so you can set up down there."

I asked Joy, "How was the rest of your week?"

"I'm pissed off with Jake. He phoned me at three o'clock yesterday. He said, 'I saw you down at the park at eleven.' I said, 'You saw me at eleven and you wait until three to call me. Whats with that?'

"He's been hanging around with some junkie friend of his. Jake sells him his morphine pills. I don't know what he gets from this friend. He was over yesterday hardwired on something, talking a mile a minute. That's not Jake. Usually I have to pry words out of him. He stayed for supper, then just left — no explanation, nothing. I'm not his personal cook. It pisses me off. I hope he doesn't come down here this morning.

I'm heading out now. I'm looking forward to some peace and quiet at home. Maybe, depending on the weather, I'll see you tomorrow."

Giant Woodpecker

25 June 2014

A noon I sat with Wolf and Scruffy. Chris rode up on his bicycle, "Hey, Dennis, I haven't seen you for a while."

I said, "I don't think I've seen you since last summer. Your hair and beard are a lot longer now."

Wolf said, "I was talking to Stella this morning. Did you know that Shark and Irene's place was broken into. They were away at the time. They had deadbolts on the door, but someone just smashed it down. That's one of the risks of selling dope. He's been at it for about twenty years.

"Chris, you used to be in that business, didn't you?"

"Not since 1991."

I said, "I heard that Irene is really terrified. I think they've hired some bodyguards. Neither Shark or Irene weigh more than a hundred pounds."

Wolf said, "It's a young man's business. They'll rob you for your stash of drugs, or the money they think you've hidden. They'll even beat you up if you have no drugs or money. It's a rough neighborhood — time to move. Irene is going to take a place by herself — she can't take the stress. Shark will get a room somewhere.

"A couple of days ago somebody came into my place. I was out, but I'd lost my keys, so I left the door unlocked. They stole my margarine, ketchup, mustard, six eggs and a few hot dogs. It really makes me mad that someone in my building, probably someone I say hello to everyday, would do something like that. After a hard day I came home and was looking forward to cooking some supper, but they cleaned me out. I left a note inside the fridge saying, 'Fuck off you piece of shit, stay out of my apartment.'

I asked, "Have you had your keys replaced?"

"No, I'm saving that until check day."

"How much does a new key cost?"

"Thirteen bucks. I've probably got that much on me, but not in the bank. I owe Jake eight dollars. He'll let it slide, just like I would with him. He knows that I'm good for it. With some people I know, like Outcast, I wouldn't feel comfortable lending money. He's too shifty. Jacques is still pissed off with him, so is Shark.

"Now, Jacques is avoiding us because of a buck and a half for cigarettes. Go figure."

Jake said, "Dennis, I saw this giant woodpecker. It was at least a foot high."

Wolf said, "Monday you said it was four feet high."

"Yeah, that was after three bottles of wine, still it was big."

Wolf noticed an earthworm crawling in the grass. "Here's some fishing bait for somebody. Did you know that André is living right across the hall from me? He's been sober for months now and goes fishing every day. I don't think it's good to eat as much fish as he does — all that mercury, raw sewage and whatever else is in that river."

Chester said, "I talked to Joy on the phone today. She yelled, **'What do you want?'** I said, 'I'm just phoning to ask about your health. When I saw you last, you mentioned that your legs were sore.' She said, 'My legs are fine, now my arms are sore.' She's just as grumpy as ever."

Party

25 June 2014

I was on the bus, coming home from the gym, engrossed in a book when I felt a tap on my shoulder. There stood a smiling

Little Jake. "Hi, Dennis, we've been at Shark's partying all afternoon."

There was a vacant seat for two nearby, so I suggested we move there. "Hi, Jake, it's good to see you. So, who was at the party?"

"All the guys from this afternoon and, of course, Shark and Irene. I'd been talking to my mother on Shark's phone, eighteen minutes -- he timed me. Anyway, she said she'd send me sixty bucks."

I said, "That's great to have a mother that loves you and cares about you."

"Well, actually, I suggested that I come home for a visit. She said, 'How be I send you sixty dollars instead. I'll have your uncle Dave bring it to you.' Uncle Dave spent ten dollars, on the way, so that left me with fifty. So, in fact, my mother was paying me not to come home. It doesn't matter, I had fifty bucks. I could have been a hoarder, but that's not me, so the party was on me, or, I should say, my mother. Thanks, mom.

"We just kept passing the bottle. Shark offered me some fried chicken, but I'm a true drunk, I don't eat until I've finished drinking. I finally had to call it quits or I never would have made it home. He packed it for me and I'll have it when I get home.

I said, "I heard that Shark and Irene are thinking of moving. Do you know any more about that?"

"Yeah, I heard the same thing. Shark didn't talk about it, but I guess it's true. Shark doesn't lie. I don't either — I can't."

We passed a building with an *Apartment for Rent* sign. Jake said, "I'm going to check that out."

I asked, "Are you planning to move?"

"Yeah, I have to be closer to downtown. Where I live is just too far out — you know that, we're on the same bus, and you get off after I do."

I said, "It is a long way."

Jake said, "I got my check today. I always get it a few days before everybody else. When I get home I have to write down the names of all the people who I've borrowed money from."

I said, "You mentioned at noon that you owed Wolf eight bucks."

"That's been taken care of. This has been a really great day. It keeps me from thinking of the really gory stuff. October 14, I hate that day. Be warned, if I'm acting crazy that day, there's a reason for it. Now, don't go putting this into your blog. The only other person I've told is Wolf.

"Why am I telling you this stuff?"

"It's okay, Jake, you can tell me whatever you want, or don't tell me whatever you want. It's your choice. I'm not going to ask you any questions about it."

"Well, for some reason I feel comfortable talking to you, and I have to talk to somebody.

"This is my stop. I gotta go. I'll see you tomorrow."

"I'll see you tomorrow, Jake."

July 2014

Shakes, R.I.P.

The sky was overcast, thunder showers were predicted. The crew at the park was somber. I started to pat Shaggy, but she started growling. Wolf handed me some treats to give her to improve her mood, then he handed me a newspaper to sit on.

Jacques said, "I guess you wouldn't have heard the sad news, but Shakes... he died on Sunday at Little Jake's place. He had a heart attack. Jake phoned the police and the ambulance. They tried to shock him with those paddles, but he didn't revive. That's too bad, we all knew him for a long time. Who will be next, I wonder?"

I said, "Little Jake must be taking it hard. He was really upset when Weasel died."

Wolf said, "Yeah, we both found him sprawled on the bed. Another one's gone. Big Chester, the fat, toothless fuck, was worried about the jean jacket that he left at Jake's place. Who gives a fuck about a jacket, the size of a tent, when somebody's died. Everyone's upset. What can you do?"

Little Chester made a comment. Wolf said to him, "Can't you see I'm having a conversation here. Shut the fuck up, so I can keep my train of thought going. The chipmunks are going around in my head, but I have to listen to keep things straight.

"It's not that we didn't all see it coming. Nobody can drink five bottles of sherry a day without it doing real damage to their system. He knew he was sick. We just didn't expect it so soon.

"I'd been drinking for seven days straight, but as soon as I heard the news I stopped drinking. I went two days without a drink, in respect for Shakes. I know, it sounds crazy, most people get drunk when they hear of a death in the family. I did just the opposite. I had to be sober today for Jake. He's a very caring, emotional person — you know that. I didn't know if he'd be able to hold it together, what with Shakes dying at his place."

Little Jake came by. Wolf took him aside to express his condolences. We all shook Jake's hand. Nobody said anything.

Jake said, "Let's get this party started. That's what Shakes would have wanted us to do. Has anybody got a drink? Jacques handed him a Plastic drinking bottle a quarter full of sherry. Jake asked, "Is that all you got? I don't want to take anybody's last swallow."

Jacques said, "Don't worry, I got another bottle."

Wolf said to Jake, "I was supposed to tell you that Mary's daughter — what's her name? Anne? That's right, Anne, brought a bottle of J.D., Shakes' favorite, so we could give him a farewell toast. There were only three of us, Jacques, me and Anne. We thought you'd be here, but you weren't so we split it three ways instead of four. I just wanted you to know that she was thinking about you."

Jake said, "That was thoughtful of her. I didn't sleep well last night so I got up late, otherwise I would have been here. We're going to party on the bridge. I hope the cops don't come by."

Jacques said, "We haven't seen them for a long time."

Two outreach workers came by to pay their respects. They were trying to contact Shakes' daughters Betty and Fran. They asked, "Does anybody know their phone numbers?"

Wolf said, "Phone numbers, we didn't even know his last name. Who would have thought it was Jake Baker? All these decades we only knew him as Shakes."

Jacques said, "I have some of his numbers on my phone, Shakes One, Shakes Two, and Shakes Three. I don't know who they are for. One is probably for a phone that Shakes lost a while ago. Can you read these?"

The worker took down the numbers and asked Jake, "How about the rest of his belongings? His wallet, his hat?"

Jake said, "The police took all the papers out of his wallet. I have his hat to give to Betty."

The worker said, "We'll try to contact her and Fran. Did he have any other family in town? Betty can give us all that information. We're very sorry for your loss. Shakes was very well liked by a lot of people." They then walked away.

Jacques said, "I want to show you the new, handy thing I got. He pulled out a key strap with an electronic fob on the end. This is to get into my apartment. If I lose it they said I have to pay thirty-five dollars for the next one."

Wolf said, "They gave me one of those. I only have to pay twenty-five for a replacement."

"Twenty-five, thirty-five, I don't know.

"I fell asleep at one thirty and didn't wake up until nine or ten when the fireworks started. I couldn't see them, but I heard everything."

Wolf said, "Shaggy nearly went crazy because of all the noise. Some of our neighbors had the street blocked off, so they could light their own firecrackers. I guess they figured that, since it was Canada Day, it was their patriotic duty to make lots of noise. Shaggy wasn't just upset, she went nuts. The only place she could get any peace was in the bathroom with the light turned off.

"Anyway, Dennis, I want to show you the book that one of my ladies gave me. Tell me what you think." He handed me a book. It was the story of two brothers. The wife of one is murdered and the other brother disappears at the same time. Most of the story takes place ten years later when the second brother reappears.

"This looks interesting, Wolf. It has all the things you like: a murder, police investigation, the works. It's on the New York Times best seller list. You're going to enjoy it."`

Little Jake in Mourning

2 July 2014

I had a window seat on the bus home and was, as usual, engrossed in a book to entertain me for the forty-five minute ride. A man sat next to me, invading my comfort zone. He began to lean on me. I looked at him and recognized Little Jake.

He said, "I wondered how long it would take for you to notice who I was."

"Hi Jake," I said. "it's good to see you." He was drinking a dark liquid from a clear plastic bottle. I didn't recognize the smell, but it was strong, maybe brandy, or his favorite sherry mixed with beer. He calls that a Jakinator.

He said, "I'm going back to my place, but I really don't want to go in. Maybe, I'll just sit outside on the steps for a while. The paramedics left all kinds of medical shit behind. They worked on Shakes for about twenty minutes. They got a slight pulse, so they loaded him on the stretcher, but he died on the way to the hospital. I was a mess. I was shaking so bad I needed help to dial 911. I felt so helpless. I'm sorry to vent to you like this."

I said, "I can't imagine how you must have felt. I've lost a father, mother, brother, sister and nephew, but I wasn't there when they died. I know that helpless feeling you're talking about. It never really goes away. After my mother died, my father, brother and I stayed drunk for three days.

"Have you heard anything yet about funeral arrangements?"

"Betty and Fran are looking after that. They phoned around to a bunch of places. I think there's something arranged for Monday, but I don't know the details. I hate the guys those girls are with, Shakes did too. I had to get out of there before I hit one of them.

"Another person who was really upset was Blaine. He really fell to pieces, so did Chris."

"Joy will take it hard. She's known him since she was thirteen years old. We all lived in the same general area, but didn't know each other then. Joy and I were in Cabbagetown, Shakes was nearby in Regent Park.

I said, "Last time we talked, you mentioned moving to a new place."

"Yeah, now I'll have to. I can't stay in a place where my friend died. It was the same when Wolf and I found Weasel, sprawled on his back with his tongue sticking out. It really freaked us out, man. I have to go to my place to pick up the rest of his stuff to give to Betty, otherwise I'd crash somewhere else. I spent one night last week in the park."

I said, "We didn't know where Shakes was for about four days last week. When did he go to your place?"

"I was thrown in the booze can Thursday. After the cops let me out I didn't get home until about three thirty in the morning. When I arrived, Shakes was asleep in front of my door. He was with me ever since. On Sunday we were having a drink together when, all of a sudden, his eyes rolled back and he passed out. I couldn't handle it, so I banged on the apartment next door. A woman came out and dialed 911 for me. My hands were shaking so bad, I couldn't do anything."

I asked, "How old was he? I think he must have been around fifty, but any time we asked, he wouldn't give us a direct answer. He admitted that he was born in the early sixties, so that would make him fifty something."

"He never wanted to tell his age. I'm forty-two and I figure he had about eight years on me. He and Uncle Wolf were about the same age. I wonder who will be the next to go. I hope it's me.

"Now you got all these numbers going around in my head. I'm not real good at doing adding and subtracting — mental gymnastics -- I used to be, when I worked as a waiter, but not any more.

"Is this my stop coming up? I better get going."

I watched Jake stagger across four lanes of traffic. I think he made it safely to the other side. I didn't hear the screeching of brakes or tires sliding on the pavement.

Funeral

4 July 2014

As I approached the group, sitting in a circle at the park, Shaggy was barking. I patted her on the head, then she settled down.

Wolf said, "Shaggy, will you pick a place then lie down."

Mariah handed me a folded newspaper to sit on.

Jacques said, "Before you sit down could you hand me the Food Basics flyer. I'm going shopping this afternoon. They have my favorite paper towels on sale. A pack of four is usually five dollars, but they have it for a dollar off. That's a good price."

Mariah asked, "Could you hand me the Metro flyer. That's where I shop. It's the closest to my place."

I asked, "Anybody else? I've got Rexall Pharmacy here. Nobody interested? how about Loblaw's Superstore? Going once, going twice. No takers?"

Mariah said, "I guess not. Everybody else has their shopping in order.

"I got a new futon this morning. Not new from a store, but one of my neighbors bought it for her daughter when she was planning to visit, but she never came. It's still in the original packaging, just a bit dirty from dragging it along the sidewalk. It's the first new bed I've had. Charlie's brother broke my cot. I've been sleeping on an air mattress. This is going to be so nice. I can't wait to try it out.

"Another neighbor said, 'If you don't want it, I'll give my son a call. He can probably sell it for about two hundred and fifty.' I said, 'No, I really want it. I just have to figure out how to get it up the stairs to my place.' Between my Charlie, the neighbor and me we managed to get it up the stairs and into my apartment."

I asked, "How is Joy? I haven't seen her since last week?"

"She's not doing so well. She's got some kind of rash on her back. She's afraid that it's chicken pox. I gave her some calamine lotion. She's going to try that before going to a doctor.

I asked, "How's everything going, Wolf?"

"It's okay. I've had a few beer. My entire life revolves around my panning spot in the morning, then coming here to have a beer with my friends, then going home again. I traveled the country when I was younger, but now, this is it. Shaggy is a hundred years old in dog years, and I've got no socks. I've had to hide my groceries and any valuables in different places around my apartment, because I have to leave the door unlocked."

I asked, "Didn't you just get a new electronic device to open and lock your door?"

"I don't even want to go there. Yes, I had an electronic key for two days, then I lost it. That's how stupid I am."

Mariah asked, "When was Shaggy born?"

Wolf replied, "I don't know when her actual birthday is. She's between thirteen and fourteen years old. I took her to the river this morning, that's why she has her ball with her. It floats. She just walked into the water a few feet, then plopped down. I'd throw her ball a short distance and she'd bring it back. When she was younger I'd throw it half way across and she'd tear after it." Shaggy lay with the ball near her mouth. Jacques teased her by reaching for the ball. She'd growl, bark then grab the ball in her mouth.

I asked Wolf, "How is Germany doing in the World Cup?"

"Haven't you been listening? The game is on right now, it started at a quarter to twelve, between Germany and France. Jacques and I are at war."

Danny, who was Shakes' former roommate, came walking up the grass. He's been away for the past three months. I stood up and shook his hand, "Hi, Danny. I'm so sorry to hear about Shakes."

"I was only supposed to be away for a few days, but our Chief asked me to stay to help settle some tribal business. Then I stayed with my daughter for a while.

"I had a small smudging ceremony at Shakes' panning spot this morning and I'll have another after the funeral. He told me, before I left, that he didn't have much longer to live. He told me what he wanted done at his funeral, but I guess he didn't tell his daughters. Fran has made arrangements to have some kind of tribute for him at the Shepherd, sometime Monday. I want to have a talk with her because Shakes had hundreds of friends in the downtown area, people who have seen him everyday for the past fifteen years, even government people. It would have been better to have a ceremony at one of the funeral homes nearby. I know that they've done that for other homeless people. I even told her that the tribal council would cover costs. Just because a member doesn't live on the reserve, doesn't mean that he's been abandoned by the tribe."

I said, "I have to go now, Danny, but I'll see you at the funeral on Monday."

Smudging Ceremony

8 July 2014

Our Native elders have taught us that before a person can be healed or heal another, one must be cleansed of any bad feelings, negative thoughts, bad spirits or negative energy – cleansed both physically and spiritually. This helps the healing to come through in a clear way, without being distorted or sidetracked by negative "stuff" in either the healer or the client. The elders say that all ceremonies, tribal or private, must be entered into with a good heart so that we can pray, sing, and walk in a sacred manner, and be helped by the spirits to enter the sacred realm.

Native people throughout the world use herbs to accomplish this. One common ceremony is to burn certain herbs, take the smoke in one's hands and rub or brush it over the body. Today this is commonly called "smudging." In Western North America the three plants most frequently used in smudging are sage, cedar, and sweet grass. (By Adrienne Borden and Steve Coyote: http://www.asunam.com/smudge_ceremony.html)

At noon, as I was passing the entrance to the park, I heard my name being called. I turned and saw Danny sitting at the gate on his rolled sleeping bag. I asked, "Do you know when the memorial service is being held for Shakes?"

It was yesterday at St. Paul's church."

"I'm sorry, I didn't know about it. I would have attended, had I known."

"A lot of people hadn't heard about it. I'm holding my own Smudging Ceremony here. I've been here since midnight and will be staying until midnight tonight. I mix sweetgrass and sage, light it, then waft the smoke with an eagle feather.

"When we were staying together Shakes told me his last wishes. I blame myself for not being there for him. I even showed him my ticket indicating that I would be back in a few days, but our tribal chief, of the Fort William First Nation, asked me to stay to submit a proposal to the government. It kept being delayed, then on the day it was to be presented, the federal Minister of Aboriginal Affairs and Northern Development wasn't in attendance, so they just submitted my notes.

The Fort William Reserve, on the western end of Lake Superior near Thunder Bay, was set aside under the provisions of the Robinson-Superior Treaty of 1850, also known as the Crown Treaty Number 60. The agreements arrived at have never been met. We now have the support of the Supreme Court of Canada and the United Nations.

"I came back to Toronto and on my way to Osgoode Hall, where the Law Society of Upper Canada meets, I met a lawyer friend of mine. He said he would accompany me. Near the end of their session, the judge asked if there was anybody who had anything to add. I asked my friend to open and close the door when he said that. Then I went in and said that I wished to address the Society concerning our proposal. The judge said that they had our proposal on file, but I told him that was only in point form, that I would like to elaborate. He gave me the floor.

"As soon as I heard about the death of Shakes, I came straight home. Unfortunately, when he was evicted from our apartment, he had no way of storing my belongings and art supplies. He tried for three days to contact his worker, but when she didn't return his calls he just said, 'To hell with it.' You know how Shakes is. Someone was able to save my talking stick. I'm very grateful for that. As for the other things, they can be replaced.

"Dennis, would you do me a favor and go to the native store up the street and get me some sage?"

"I'd be pleased to, Danny." I went to the store, but unfortunately, they were out of sage. It was suggested that I try another store about six blocks away. I gave Sammy the news, then I had to return to work.

Before I left I wanted to pay my respects to Shakes. Sammy instructed me to take some tobacco in my left hand, sprinkle a bit in the smoking bowl, say a prayer, then put the rest in a container off to the side. This would be taken to Sacred Mountain, where there would be an Ojibwa tribal ceremony held in his honor. I said my prayer and said goodbye to a great friend.

Little Jake said, "I'm sorry, Dennis, I'm too drunk to talk today. I tried panning, but that didn't seem to work either." He patted Shaggy, rubbed her belly and her ears. Shaggy licked his face.

Wolf said, "I'd be careful getting your face that close to Shaggy's mouth. I can show you lots of scars where she's drawn blood. She's an old bitch and she can get cranky, Just ask Outcast. That was a stupid thing he did, trying to break up a fight between two dogs. He should have known better. The dogs weren't injured, he was the only one dripping blood. My stupid neighbor let her dog near Shaggy's bowl. Of course she's going to be protective. It's her space. It only lasted a few seconds. The other dog was on a leash. The owner pulled it back, fight over."

Jacques said, "It's time for me to go. I've finished my last beer."

Wolf said, "I've got mine timed just right. I'm on my last one now."

Jacques said, "Well, I'm going home to get hydrated, to have another beer. Maybe on my way home I'll buy some groceries. I'm in the mood for a couple of chicken breasts. I'll get some white potatoes, that I don't have to peel, and a can of gravy, that usually lasts me two meals.

"Wolf, don't forget to bring your two dollars on Monday."

I Am The Eagle!!

9 July 2014

I asked Wolf, "Did you attend Shakes' funeral on Monday?"

"No, I didn't. I worked that morning, three hours in the pouring rain. Shaggy jumped out of her caboose and I banged my shin on one of the crossbars. Look, it's still swollen. Imagine how it looked two days ago. I miss Shakes, but I don't do well at funerals. I'm an emotional person, even though I can act like a real prick sometimes. Were you around for Digger's funeral? Maybe that was before your time. I went; when I saw him laying in the casket I broke down crying in front of millions of people. I like to think that Shakes is looking down on us now. I sure hope there is beer in heaven. There must be. Why else would anybody go there."

I said, "Jake is really taking it hard. I spoke to him on the bus the other night. We were wondering who would be the next to die, he said, 'I hope it's me.' "

"Yeah, Jake's an emotional guy. I know from the number of times he's crashed at my place. I wish these guys would get the message. That sherry that they drink, that's got to be hard on their systems. Whenever I drink sherry I get a massive hangover. That's why I have this bruise on my shin. That was a sherry day. I drink a dozen beer a day. I wake up refreshed. Maybe that's not good for me either. Who knows?

"I've talked to Jake. H.I.V. isn't terminal, like it used to be. I told him that he should go to a dentist, have those few teeth pulled and get a set of dentures. If I've walked half way down here and remember that I haven't put my dentures in, I'll go back for them. I lost my bottom set. I tried to get a new plate when I had my jaw broken. I couldn't get them to pay for it. I'm glad I didn't have them in at the time. They coulda done a lot of damage to the inside of my mouth. I shoulda had them replaced, but at least I can smile. What's that they say about shoulda, coulda and woulda?"

I said, *"If the dog hadn't stopped to shit, he woulda caught the rabbit.* I guess that's only woulda."

"Don't say that too loud in front of Shaggy, not that she can catch anything any more. I just don't want her feelings to be hurt."

Danny stopped by with some posters he had printed in memory of of Shakes. His image was in the center, above it a soaring eagle. The caption read, flying above the cloud "I AM THE EAGLE!!" Thoughts and Prayers are on the Wings of many Eagles, for you Shakes… Long May you Soar.

He said, "A friend of mine printed these. I'm selling them for ten bucks each, the cost of reproduction. I thought that friends of Shakes would appreciate a picture of him.

Wolf said, "Here's a picture of Shakes that Stella brought me today. He's lying down, with his bottle of Dr. Pepper, just like we remember him. I thought that was a nice gesture.

Dog Fight

10 July 2014

At noon I sat with Chris, Wolf and Jacques, who was passing around his pot pipe. Chris took a toke and started coughing. He had a hard time catching his breath. He explained, "I've had problems with my lungs ever since I was a kid. It's because of bronchitis. Sometimes, I cough so hard that I pass out (the medical term is cough syncope). When I was at Shark's place it started happening, I got the shakes and my arms started twitching, then I was able to catch my breath and I was fine. Once, I pissed and shit myself, the coughing was so bad. Sometimes, I nearly puke. I guess it's been about three years since I've gone down.

"Twice I've drunk myself blind with gin and vodka. It was at my sister's wedding. Can you imagine, having a wedding the same day as the Super Bowl? All the guys were watching the game, except me. I'm not a football fan, so I was drinking with the ladies. It was a free bar. I started drinking vodka with orange juice. Then it got to be a full glass of vodka with a splash of orange juice. The women kept hauling me up to dance. Maybe, they were trying to get me sober. I don't know. I'd get up, shuffle a bit, wave my arms around. Anyway, it was like I was looking through a thick fog. I remember one time during the night, my mother said to me, 'If you're looking for the bar, it's thirteen steps to your right.' The next morning I had a massive hangover. My head was like a drum

— ba ba ba BOOM, ba ba ba BOOM, ba ba ba BOOM. I was sleeping in the same room as my nephew. I woke up early and was trying to roll a joint. My nephew asked, 'What are you doing?' I said, 'Shut up and go back to sleep.'

Wolf said, "I remember being asked a question at one of the many rehab programs I've been in. Anyway, the question was, 'What gets into your system faster, injecting, smashing coke into your arm or smoking it as crack. I answered, injecting. I was wrong. You get a faster high with smoke. Who'd of guessed?"

He was excited about Germany beating Brazil in the FIFA World Cup. "Can you imagine, seven to one for Germany. I wouldn't want to be a Brazilian soccer player now, they're ready to run the team out of the country. I'm not a big soccer fan, usually I just watch the last half of each game, but I want to see Europe defeat South America. See, I've got my German flag attached to Shaggy's caboose.

He continued, "When I was nineteen, and you were nineteen, all we wanted was to get laid. When my father was nineteen he was carrying a gun for the German army. We lost the war. Our black, red and white flag was dragged through the shit; now it's black red and yellow. They made us change it.

"I nearly got beat up by Outcast last night. We were sitting outside. Shaggy was off her leash, because it was at her place. There were two other dogs on leashes, a Schnauzer and a Dachshund — a wiener dog. Anyway, the owner of the Schnauzer walked into Shaggy's space and she went after the other dog. It was a stupid thing for the owner to do. The dogs were rolling about, like dogs do, then Outcast tried to separate them. His hand got bitten and he was dripping a lot of blood. He blamed me and was ready to fight. I was glad that Hippo was there. He brought out his hatchet. Outcast settled down after that. I don't know if it was Shaggy or the Schnauzer that bit him — or maybe both did. The wiener dog didn't do anything."

Shaggy, the Heroine

11 July 2014

Shaggy gave one half-hearted bark as I approached the group. Wolf handed me a blanket and said, "Dennis, she's just saying hello. Make sure you pat her so she doesn't feel ignored. Did I tell you that she took on a pit bull the other day? A neighbor brought over her little dog with big ears. I don't know what you call them. Anyway, there was also a pit bull. The pit bull attacked big ears, Shaggy intervened and the pit bull backed down. What do you think of that? My girl is a hero, or heroine, for saving Big Ears.

"I've got something to show you. One of my ladies lent it to me. I'm to give her, what's the word? — an appraisal? I don't think that's it, but she wants me to tell her what I think, so she can tell her husband. Here, have a look." The novel was Vengeance by Benjamin Black. I read from the back cover:

A bizarre suicide leads to a scandal and then still more blood, as one of our most brilliant crime novelists reveals a world where money and sex trump everything.

This looks good Wolf, all the things you like."

"I've got my whole weekend planned out. Reading, then on Sunday, Germany plays Argentina. I also may watch the game on Saturday, Brazil versus the Netherlands. I always cheer for Europe."

Jacques said, "I have two dollars bet on Argentina for Sunday. I hope they win. I just bet on them because the German bet against them."

Little Jake said, "Hi, Dennis, how you doin'. I'm still feeling sick. I can't keep anything down. I was over at Bruce's last night, he fed me some Mr. Noodles. I was able to keep that down, but apart from that I haven't eaten all week."

Jacques said, "See, I told you, eat soup. That's the best thing for you now. When you can keep that down, then you can try other things."

Wolf said, "You gotta eat, Jake. If you don't eat, you don't shit. If you don't shit, you die — simple as that."

Gnome wandered over, "Hi, guys."

Wolf said, "Hi Gnome, where are you staying now?"

"At my brother, Gordon's place. It's a condition of my probation. Gordon says I have to be in the house by eight and in bed by eight thirty. I said to him, 'I'm a fifty year old man. I'm not going to bed at eight thirty.' Also, I'm not supposed to drink." He then pulled out a can of Strongbow Apple Cider and opened it.

Jake said, "I'm sorry, Dennis, I'm too drunk to talk today. I tried panning, but that didn't seem to work either." He patted Shaggy, rubbed her belly and her ears. Shaggy licked his face.

Wolf said, "I'd be careful getting your face that close to Shaggy's mouth. I can show you lots of scars where she's drawn blood. She's an old bitch and she can get cranky, Just ask Outcast. That was a stupid thing he did, trying to break up a fight between two dogs. He should have known better. The dogs weren't injured, he was the only one dripping blood. My stupid neighbor let her dog near Shaggy's bowl. Of course she's going to be protective. It's her space. It only lasted a few seconds. The other dog was on a leash. The owner pulled it back, fight over."

Jacques said, "It's time for me to go. I've finished my last beer."

Wolf said, "I've got mine timed just right. I'm on my last one now."

Jacques said, "Well, I'm going home to get hydrated, to have another beer. Maybe on my way home I'll buy some groceries. I'm in the mood for a couple of chicken breasts. I'll get some white potatoes, that I don't have to peel, and a can of gravy, that usually lasts me two meals.

"Wolf, don't forget to bring your two dollars on Monday."

Chickenpox

16 July 2014

I was walking along the sidewalk towards Chuck's spot when I heard somebody call from across the street, "Hey, Dennis, what are you doing over there?" I turned my head and saw it was Joy. I crossed the street.

"Hi, Joy, I haven't seen you for ages."

"No, I've had chickenpox. I'm not contagious now, but I'm still scratching. It bugs the hell out of me and freaks people out, 'cause they think I have fleas.

"Whoa, did you see the look that woman gave me?"

I asked, "Are you sure she was looking at you and not me?"

"She was looking at both of us."

"Perhaps, it was someone I work with."

"She was pissed off with somebody. I feel like going after her, to see what her problem is."

A garbage truck stopped at the curb in front of us. The driver waved, got out of the truck and came over.

"Hi Lemar, I said."

Joy said, "Is that your name? I never remember." He opened his safety vest to show his name tag.

"I've known people with that name, but they were black."

Lemar said, "My dad was black."

I said, "My daughter-in-law is black. My granddaughter is...

"Creamy coffee-colored." said Joy.

"That's right," I said, "she's a beautiful little princess."

Joy said to Lemar, "Are you going to let your partner empty all the bins?"

"Yeah, " he said, "he empties, I drive. I guess I better get back to it. Nice to see you, Joy, Dennis."

"Nice to see you, Lemar."

I asked Joy, "Did you attend Shakes' funeral?"

"I was there, but I didn't go into the church. I don't do funerals. Little Jake went in. He said there were only about twenty people there. Danny was telling everybody that he was having a smudging ceremony and that everyone should be sober. That's a pack of bullshit. All Shakes' friends are alcoholic. When did you ever see Shakes when he was sober? I remember one time, when he was on antibiotics, but that was only for a couple of days. Danny was also selling pictures of Shakes. I didn't like that at all."

I said, "I bought one. He said he was selling them for the price it cost him to have them printed."

"How much was that?"

"Ten bucks."

Joy said, "I've got my own pictures of Shakes. I don't need any more.

I said, "I attended the smudging ceremony that Danny arranged. He was there from 6pm Monday to 6pm Tuesday. I was there Tuesday at noon.

"How's Big Jake?"

"A pain in the ass. He doesn't get up until about one o'clock, then he comes over to my place. I feed him. At nine I kick him out. I have to be up at five thrity. If he had his way he'd stay until one in the morning.

"I can't believe how much he smokes. We bought two cartons of cigarettes from Shark a week ago and already they're gone. I told him that two cartons would last me a month. I'm always butting them out, then relighting them. Now, my place smells like an ashtray. I'm always washing the walls to get rid of the cigarette stains."

I said, "I've been talking to Wolf, Jacques, Little Frank, Mariah and Debbie. Wolf said that Outcast got a nasty bite when he tried to break up a fight between Shaggy and another dog. His hand was dripping blood. Wolf told him, 'That was a stupid thing to do!' Outcast said, "You should have better control of your dog."

Joy said, "Outcast is always whining. This weekend he's helping his ex move into subsidized housing. He said, 'Because of their rules, I won't be able to live there.' I said, 'Outcast, how old are you — fifty? Don't you think it's about time you got a place of your own instead of always living off somebody else.' He's been at Shark's place three months now. He was only supposed to be there a week. He's another person that smokes too much. He has emphysema."

I said, "He also has lung cancer from working with asbestos."

I checked my watch. Joy said, "I see you replaced your watch strap. It's about time."

"This was a present from my sons. I couldn't visit them with a broken watch strap."

Joy pondered, "I have to decide whether or not I want to see Jake today. He'll probably be phoning around one. Will you be at the park at noon?"

"Yeah, it's been a while since I've seen everybody."

August 2014

Medical Marijuana

At the park I asked the group if there had been any further news about the death of Alphonse. Outcast said, "It's official, he was found hanged. Whether or not he took his own life nobody knows. I do know that he's tried it before when he stayed with me. I had to haul him back off the balcony."

I asked, "Do the police suspect that foul play was involved?"

Mariah said, "This is Montreal we're talking about. It's a rough city. If he said the wrong thing to the wrong people, that's all it would take. Personally, I think he was fucked."

Outcast said, "I agree, he was fucked."

Jacques said, "That's another of us gone. I wonder who will be next."

Little Jake put up his hand.

Mariah said, "Me."

I asked her, "How have you been feeling lately? Is your back still giving you problems?"

"Well, my back always gives me problems. Some days are worse than others. Some days I can't get out of bed. I've also got osteoarthritis and rheumatoid arthritis. Either one of those is always acting up, but today isn't too bad."

"How has Joy been feeling?" I asked. "Is she getting out at all?"

"Yeah, she's able to manage the stairs to come up to my place every once in a while. Big Jake was drunk yesterday. She's still trying to get rid of him."

I said, "I heard that she's stopped panhandling because he takes any extra money she gets."

Little Jake said, "Dennis, I'm sorry that I'm drunk."

Jacques said, "You're always drunk. You shouldn't apologize for being drunk. You should apologize if you're ever sober."

"Yeah, " he said, "that's true."

Outcast introduced me to Debbie. He said to me, "You mentioned, the other day, something about a TV interview. I've been giving it some thought and Debbie and I may be interested."

"That's great," I said, "I'll let my brother-in-law know. He has all the contacts."

Debbie said, to me, "Just today I lost my job. I've been bullied lately and had a letter I was going to hand in concerning the situation, when I heard about losing my job. I have some mental illness. I get very depressed sometimes."

I said, "I also have mental illness: bipolar, paranoid personality and obsessive compulsive disorders. I've taken medication for them for the past twenty-five years."

Debbie said, "I have borderline personality disorder. I also take medication, and I have a prescription for medical marijuana. I still have to pay five dollars per gram. I won't be able to afford that, now that I don't have a job."

Outcast said, "We should all move to Smith Falls, they've turned the old Hershey plant into a medical marijuana operation. Maybe they'd give out free samples."

Heat Wave

"Dennis,' said Wolf, "When did I see you last? Was it Friday? I know I haven't seen you this week. Anyway, I got three new books, hard covers, that's nice. Two are by authors we know, one's by an author we don't know; at least I don't know her. I can't remember their names. The book I started is looking good, the stuff we like, spies, espionage. She's a famous author from Sweden, sold millions of copies. There are a lot of people in Sweden, aren't there? I think those countries are all crowded over there. That's what I had to tell you.

"I'll show you my elbow, the swelling's gone down. The doctor said there would always be a bump. That's the way at our age, getting bumps and bo bo's.

"Shaggy's beat. See, she's lying in her water bowl. It's a bit small for her, but at least part of her is cool."

André said, "It's been quite a while since I've seen you. Do you notice a difference?"

"Yeah," I said, "for one thing you've lost weight, and you're wearing glasses."

"I also got all my teeth pulled. That's why I was sick before, they were all infected. That poison was going through my whole system. I got my life under control now. I still drink, because I have to. If I stop I get sick. So, I stick to a couple in the morning when I get up. Then I do some work. I'm fixing bicycles now. People are always bringing their bikes over to my place. They're amazed that I can fix these things.

"I've also got into engraving glass. I get these picture frames at the Dollar Store. They've already got glass in them and a picture. I engrave the picture on the outside of the glass. What started out costing a couple of bucks, I sell for ten. I'm doing a big Harley Davidson now. It's about three feet wide."

I asked, "Where are you selling them?"

"I don't have a regular place to sell them. People buy them as soon as I make them. I was at the hardware store asking for diamond and carbon fiber bits. The salesman asked what I was using them for, so I told him. He asked, 'Are you any good?' I said, 'The people who have bought my work think so.' He said, 'Bring one around, maybe I'll buy it.' So, that's what's happening. I go to buy bits, I end up making a sale."

Mariah said, "I'm waiting for my son to come by. He went to the welfare office this morning. He's hoping to get first and last month's rent, so he can get his own place. Lately he's been sleeping on my kitchen floor. That's kind of awkward. Charlie's pissed with him because he moved some of his stuff. Charlie has this thing that his belongings have to be in a certain place, or he blows up. That's what happened. He said, 'There's the door. Use it and don't come back.'

"My son has always had a mean streak. He gets it from me. When he was a teenager he started to rebel. I told him, 'When you're in my place there are certain boundaries. I'm not your roommate, I'm not one of your friends that you can give shit to. You follow my rules or go live at the Sally.'

"He's not working now. The fast food place, where he had a job, closed down, even their second location closed. So, he's looking for work."

Jacques asked me, "Dennis, you want a lock? It's still in the package. It would be good to lock a suitcase or a backpack. No?"

Mariah said, "Before I got my place I had to lock everything. I know what that's like."

I said to Mariah, "I heard that you visited Joy yesterday. How is she doing?"

"Ehhhhh… so, so. She's able to get out of bed on her own. She can shuffle along with her walker. I call it the Joy shuffle. It's funny to see her. They still haven't figured out what's wrong with her. They've ruled out MS. I knew it wasn't that.

I've been around a lot of people with MS. They didn't have the same problems as she has. They think it's something hereditary."

Outcast came by and said to me, "Hippo's too shy to ask you, but he's not feeling so good. Could you spare him a bus ticket so he can get home? It's not for me, I've got a bus pass."

"Sure," I said, "I've got extra."

Wolf said, "I'm not looking forward to that walk home. It takes me about an hour and a half, but I'll break it up. I'll take Shaggy to the river. After that I'll pick a shady street and take my time. I'll sit down along the way. The last thing I want is to come down with heat stroke."

Check Day

27 August 2014

"Dennis," said Manisee, "This is my friend August. He's from Nain, on the northern coast of Labrador. That's where I'm from as well.

"August, Dennis is a friend of ours. He helps us when he can. He's been where we've been, but now he's sober.

"Did I tell you that I'm going to be a grandfather again. I already have one granddaughter, now my daughter is three weeks pregnant. I'm so happy. When I get my life straightened out I'm going to invite her to come live with me. I can't now because I'm living on the street.

Mariah said, "My son went to the welfare office. He filled out all the forms. Now, he's waiting for approval. He's going to be living with a friend. He thinks that he'll be able to find work at one of the fast food places near where he'll be living. He has a lot of experience."

Manisee said, "Mariah, if your son is looking for work, tell him to come see me. I know a lot of people."

"Do you know of any jobs available?"

"No, but I know a lot of people."

"Thanks, Manisee," said Mariah, "I'll keep that in mind."

André came by carrying an etched glass picture of a Harley Davidson motorcycle. It was very detailed, even including the brand names on the tires."

I said, "That's great, André. Are you going to sell that?"

"Yeah, I'd like to. I was thinking of asking forty bucks."

Everyone said, "You could get much more than that."

"Yeah," said André," but people don't carry much cash with them. I only deal in cash, on the spot. I can go home and in five hours I can make another of these. It's noisy, but I've talked to my neighbors. They said, 'As long as you do it indoors we've got no problem.' My walls are concrete and ten inches thick. I usually do my engraving in my bedroom. I don't have neighbors on that side.

"Have I told you about my new apartment? I've really come a long way since I was living on the streets. I'm sharing a big two bedroom — and I mean big. I've got eleven bicycles on my balcony that I'm repairing. I sold one to Shark this morning for fifty bucks. He wanted it for his brother."

Wolf yelled, "Keep that ball away from here. Shaggy's just gone to sleep. I don't want her riled up again."

Outcast was kicking a small inflated ball around and Buck's dog was chasing it. "Wolf, keep your mouth shut. I'll kick this ball wherever I want." Dillinger seemed to be really enjoying the exercise. Buck looked on, indifferently.

Mary said to me, "My mom, here, is inebriated. She's passed out."

Chester vomited. "Christ, Chester, you could have done that somewhere else. Now we've got two we have to babysit."

Jacques said, "It's because he was drinking that sherry. He was okay before that." He was drinking out of a mason jar with a sock wrapped around it. He explained to me, "If the cops come around, and don't see any open liquor, they'll just ride past."

I asked, "Don't you think they'll be suspicious, seeing you drinking out of a sock?"

Mary said to me, "Did I show you the necklace that Jacques gave me. It's a locket. I'm going to put my niece's picture in it. I'll show you the one he gave my mom." She reached around Mary's neck and showed me the silver charm."

Debbie said, "Jacques gave me this shirt. I really like it. In fact it's my favorite."

I said, "It's really nice. It suits you."

"Yeah, that's what I thought."

I was about to shake hands with Little Jake. He said, "I better not shake hands. I'm coming down with something and I don't want to spread it. I don't feel so good."

Wolf said to me, "Dennis, we didn't get a chance to talk, maybe later this week."

Dog Shit

28 August 2014

André said to me, "Dennis, haven't a cushion for you to sit on, but use my bike, you can sit on the frame. It may not be comfortable, but it's better than sitting on the wet grass."

"Thanks André, is this one of the bikes you fixed?"

"Yeah, that's what's been keeping me in spending money. My check should be in today, but I'm not even going to bother cashing it. I've still got five hundred bucks at home. I'm taken care of.

"See this stereo radio I got. I found it in a dumpster. I was rooting around looking for an empty plastic bag to put something in. I could feel that this one bag had something in it. I was careful, it could have been dog shit for all I knew, but it turned out to be this radio. With some new batteries, it works fine.

"I was off drinking for eleven months. Now I know I can quit if I want. Sometimes, I like to come here and have a drink with my friends. I never said I'd never have a drink again. It's just like getting out of prison. I'd be in for nine years, get out for a month, be back in for two years. When I was leaving I'd always say to the guys, "I'm going to change my life around. I'm never coming back inside again. Of course, I'd get drunk, do something stupid and be back inside. The last time I got out, I didn't say anything. I didn't want to jinx it, and so far it's worked.

"It's the same with drinking. I know I'm an alcoholic, but I also know that I can control it. I stick to a couple of beers at a time and I feel great. I don't have the shakes. I don't have the dry heaves. I'm better off than I've ever been, so I don't want to jinx it."

Shawn had been talking on the phone. I knew he'd been to the welfare office, so I asked how the meeting went.

"I'm screwed, man. The welfare office said I need something to prove that I've found a place to live. I went to my worker and she said all I need is a 'statement of intent to rent'. She helped me out with that. I want back and they said I need some kind of proof that I live there, like a hydro bill, or something. I don't know how I can do that, because the friend I want to stay with is out of their jurisdiction. I'm fucked. I can't stay at my mother's place because her boyfriend came over for the weekend. I don't know what I'm going to do.

"Do you have some bus tickets? That would really help."

"Sure," I said, "How many do you need?"

"Two will do." I handed him the tickets.

"Thanks, this will help a lot."

I said to Jacques, "I see you're still drinking out of your sock," referring to the sock wrapped around a mason jar he was drinking from.

"Yes, it works fine. It maybe insulates, as well. I don't know."

I asked Wolf, "How are you doing?"

"I'm tired," he said. "It's been a long week for me. You may laugh, but it's tough panning five days straight. I'm looking forward to a few days of doing nothing. I told you I have my three new books, beer in the fridge. I'm all set for the long weekend.

"I guess you're going to your cottage, are you?" I nodded in agreement. "I really envy you that. I'd just like to be somewhere quiet for a change. I know there are crickets and bullfrogs, but not the constant sound of traffic."

Debbie said, "I love going to the woods. It's part of my heritage. It's where I feel at peace and at home."

I asked Donald, "Have you any plans for the long weekend?"

"No, not really. My friend and I are living in a cabin on an island, so we have to get there by boat. It keeps the rain off. Sometimes, I come into town to stay with my mother, or to get groceries. I have to come in for my methadone treatments."

I said, "Tell me about your cabin."

"We built it ourselves. It's not a castle, but it keeps the rain off. It didn't cost us anything. The wood was already there, we just nailed it together. It's nice, because nobody can see us when we're there. Like Wolf said, it's 'somewhere quiet for a change.'

Jacques said, "I've got a splitting headache."

André said, "I've got some oxycodone if you'd like some. I just bought it last night."

Robert asked, "Can I see that bottle? This says percocet!"

Wolf asked, "Well, is it oxycontin or percocet? They're two different things."

Robert said, "The print is awfully small, but it has both oxycodone and percocet."

Jacques said, "Never mind. I've got some Motrin in my bag. I'll take a couple of those. Maybe, I just need to drink more."

Little Jake walked up. He asked, "Wolf can I borrow that sweater? It's cold here in the shade."

Wolf said, "It's clean. I don't mind if you wear it, but don't use it to sit on the ground. You can even smell how clean it is."

Jake said, "Yeah, you're right."

It was time for me to leave. I said, to Jake, "I have to go now, but let me smell that sweater first."

Wolf and the crew said, "We'll see you next week, Dennis. Have a good long weekend."

Repay Day

30 September 2014

I approached Chester, sitting precariously on a box. "Dennis, have you got a card?" His blue eyes looked distant. I wasn't sure if he could see me. Later he asked, "Dennis, can you help me up?"

I asked, "Chester, are you sure that's a good idea?"

Debbie said, "Can some more people help here?" Chester was standing, but he was ready to fall on his side. We led him to the curb and helped him sit down. He immediately toppled over. Since the breeze was cool Wolf draped Shaggy's blanket over him.

André rode up on a bicycle. He announced, "I'm too drunk to walk, so I decided to ride. I'm not doing so good. All morning people have been coming to my place bringing booze."

Little Jake said, "Babysitting, first Chester, now André. I hate babysitting. Mind you, I'm drunk too. I've been feeling good lately, that's why I decided to splurge, but my money is dwindling low.

"I've been drinking a lot of milk lately. I went through one of those big bags in no time."

I asked, "Don't you usually drink milk?"

"Not usually, but I had a couple of boxes of cereal to finish. I couldn't very well eat it dry."

André asked Jake, "Have you got ten bucks?"

"What for?"

"I owe you thirty, but I only got two twenties. Give me ten back."

"Yeah, okay. See Dennis, it's good being drunk. I've forgotten all the people who owe me money. It's a nice surprise when someone pays me back."

Wolf asked, "So, Dennis, are you following the hockey draft? Do you have any interest in hockey? I missed you last Friday. I was looking forward to some donuts. I got so wasted, I'm still ashamed of what happened. It's past now. I don't want to talk about it."

"What book are you reading?" I asked Wolf.

"You know, I've been drunk for so long, I haven't been able to read much. I started a book, The Assassins (The President and the Assassin by Scott Miller). I haven't read much, just the first few pages and the back cover. It's really fascinating, the author says that there was a group responsible for all the assassinations of US presidents, from Lincoln through to JFK. There are a lot of details to keep in mind. I wasn't up to that.

"You know me, I'll get myself straight. For a while, I won't leave my apartment, I'll tidy the place. All I'll do is read. I just have to figure out when to do that."

Chili was on her cell phone. "We should get someone to take Chester home. How do I phone the Salvation Army?"

Outcast said, "Just phone three-one-one and ask for Outreach."

"They said, all the workers and the van are out."

Outcast said to Manisee, "Help me get him up near the bridge. They'll pick him up in an ambulance. If we leave him here the cops will come and we've all got open booze. I'm surprised that they haven't been here already, it's been nearly a week since they've visited."

Manisee said, "They know we've been paid, so they'll be checking all the usual places."

Debbie asked Jake for a cigarette. He pulled out a plastic margarine container. Took off the lid and passed her a cigarette.

He whispered to me, "See how she touches my hand when she takes the smoke. She always does that."

Jacques was going through the Metro flyer planning his grocery shopping. "They've got cod for six ninety nine a pound and salmon for three ninety nine each. What I'd really like is a big chunk of Emmental cheese."

Wolf said, "I'm really not into fish, but I like their frozen meals, two for five bucks."

Jake said, "There used to be a place not far from here that made the best fish and chips. They served them in newspaper and had a big hunk of cod on top. The chips were hand cut and cooked to a nice golden color. Each batch was made fresh.

"Dennis, you see how we're always talking about food when you come. I guess it's because it's lunch time.

That's Life

17 October 2014

As I was walking towards the park I met Mariah and the two Chesters. I asked, "Mariah, are you leaving?"

"Yes, I'm not feeling so good. Cramps, I've just started my period. Big Chester is going to walk me home."

The usuals were there, in their usual places.

Marcel said, "Hi Dennis, I haven't seen you for a long time. I'm not drinking now. I haven't necessarily quit, but I'm a binge drinker. I'll get drunk for a few days then I'll stay off it for three months. I still have my weed. I won't give that up. In fact I have a court appearance coming up for that, but the judge knows me. You see, I'm supposed to be getting workmen's comp. for a back injury and the judge knows that. He knows that I'm self-medicating. Last time I told him, 'Your honor, I could go to my doctor and get opiates for the pain in my back, but if I did I'd eventually become addicted, then I'd have another problem. Or, I could sell them on the street, to pay for my marijuana, but if I was caught I'd be in more serious trouble. He didn't like where I was going with this.

"I changed social workers, and every time that happens they cut me off my meds. I have to go in, explain everything to them, get a letter from my doctor, then I'm reinstated. I waited three months and hadn't received a letter from my worker. She had been sending my mail to the wrong address. My old landlord hates me. He was probably throwing my mail in the garbage. Anyway, I told this to the judge. I said, 'Your honor, I

had no pain medication for three months. What was I to do?'
It was only a probation breach, so he had it dropped."

I asked, "What is the charge for marijuana possession?"

"It all depends on the judge. If you're caught with a gram,
they may give you thirty days in jail. If you're caught with an
ounce, that's a different story. They can charge you with
trafficking. You could get sixty days to two years, whatever
the judge decides."

"How did you injure your back?" I asked.

"I was working at the airport. Every so often the 737's
suffer from what is called metal fatigue. The only thing to do is
to take them completely apart, then put them back together
again. It's a big job and takes about two years. At the end I had
a really easy job. I was doing the final inspection. I had a
checklist that was color coded, from red that meant life
threatening, yellow was hazardous, but not life threatening,
and all the way down. So I didn't have to do much, just make
sure that everyone else had done their job. Near the ceiling of
the hangar is where all the gasses collect, from the generators,
the welding equipment, exhaust fumes. One day I passed out
and fell about twenty feet to the cement floor. I had multiple
spinal compression fractures in my lumbar region and neck.

"Why was there a delay in getting workmen's
compensation?"

"It was a grey area. First of all, I lived in Quebec but
worked in Ontario. They couldn't decide which province
should cover my injuries. Second, it was an international
airport, so the federal government was involved. Third, for
safety reasons we were only supposed to work eight-hour
shifts. The union, without permission from the government,
changed it to four twelve-hour shifts, with three days in
between. According to the government, I shouldn't have been
working when I was. I raised a lot of shit. I became a whistle-
blower and pointed out twenty-one safety violations that were
taking place. Things like guys going out for a smoke and

propping the door open with a brick. The inspectors were aware of these things, they just chose to ignore them. That didn't make me very popular with the union. Heads rolled, but I've been waiting fourteen years for my compensation. They say that I'm going to get my money, but I tell them, 'It's been fourteen years. My kids may get my money, but I'll be dead by the time this is resolved.'

"I really ruffled some feathers higher up. One night cops came to my door with a search warrant. They took every piece of paper in the house, photographs, even my kid's drawings on the fridge. Now, why would they take a kid's drawings? They also magnetized my house. Do you know what that means? They took a powerful magnet to every piece of electronic equipment I had, computers, cameras, erased everything. They were gone within an hour, but they were thorough.

"There's something else I did that upset a lot of people. I set up a union for panhandlers. It's still active. We have a list of lawyers we can call, to appear for us in court, at no charge. They're good lawyers."

I asked, "Is there any way that you can go back to the kind of work you were doing at the airport?"

"No, my doctor says that I've developed a sensitivity to certain gasses. Even a whiff could trigger my brain into falling asleep. It's the body trying to protect itself. If you're asleep, then your breathing is shallower. I get ODSP (Ontario Disability Support Program), but because I was in a high paying job, I'd get a lot more from the Compensation Board, but, that's life."

Remembrance Day

11 November 2014

I was on the bus coming home from work when a man sat next to me. I didn't look up, but smelled sherry and beer. It was Little Jake. I asked, "Did you come downtown for the Remembrance Day service?"

"I tried to get down in time, but I missed the bus by this much (indicating with his fingers about an inch). "Damn it, I was so pissed off. I'd wanted to see the planes fly overhead at eleven o'clock. I was walking down Main Street and I heard them fly over. I couldn't see them. I was looking all around, I nearly stepped into traffic. "Jacques was down there. I got pissed off with him too. We're standing there, out in the open, parents and kids standing all around, and he pulls out his pot pipe. I was ready to smack him upside the head, the way a father would do to his son, but that would have only brought more attention. I think it was disrespectful. He could have waited an hour before toking up."

I asked, "Have you seen Joy lately?"

"It's the weirdest thing," said Jake. "She invited Hippo and me over for supper. We knocked on the door and she said, 'What the fuck are you guys doing here?' Hippo looked at me and we both thought, *woo woo. What's up with her?* Hippo saw that she was cooking steaks and asked if he could come in for supper. I didn't think that was right, so I went up to Mariah's place. Later, Hippo said that Joy wasn't looking good. She's lost weight and her face was pale. That's Hippo, anything for something to eat."

"Yes," I said, "that's Hippo."

Jake said, "I hope that Stella comes down tomorrow. I want her to give me a photo of Shakes. She said she'd bring one down.

"Here's my stop. I'll see you soon."

Fiasco

13 November 2014

"Hi, Joy," I said, "it's good to see you. How are you feeling?"

"I'm okay, my legs get stiff, especially in this cold. I'm going to be getting a three-wheeled scooter. That'll make getting around a lot easier.

"Big Jake's going to see his p.o. (parole officer) today, so he'll be coming over early. I'm not too pleased with that. I usually have to shoo him out when it's time for me to go to bed. I get up at five a.m. He phones me around two p.m., which usually means he's been up for about an hour. I've been feeling sick for the past week or so. Jake's been coughing and he doesn't cover his mouth. He stays at the mission, where most people cough without covering their mouths. Who knows what kind of airborne cooties are flying around?

"Have you been up to the park to see the guys?"

"Yeah," I said, I've seen Jacques, Little Chester, Mariah. On Remembrance Day I sat on the bus with Little Jake. He'd been downtown for the services. He was pissed off with Jacques for pulling out his pot pipe in public.

"Little Jake told me that Hippo came over to your place for supper."

"Yeah, what a fiasco that was. He and Little Jake came over at about eleven in the morning. I said, 'What the fuck are you guys doing here. Get lost!' Later, Hippo came over by himself and asked, 'Are you in a better mood now? Did you forget that you invited us over for a meal?' I felt about this tall (indicating with her fingers approximately an inch.) So, he came in and I made lunch. Outcast dropped over later. I had to kick him out after three beer, because he gets to be such a dickhead."

I said, "You mentioned that Big Jake was helping towards the expenses. How is that working out?"

"He's been helping, but he smokes and eats so damn much I'd be better off on my own. We bought a bag of native cigarettes. He filled his container three times before I finished my first. I asked him, 'Why do you smoke so much? You've just put one out, you don't need another so soon.'

I asked, "What do you think of my book?"

"I haven't finished it. I'll reserve judgement until the end."

I said, "I can change anything you disagree with. I'll give a copy to everyone, after it has your approval."

Joy said, "Outcast said something about it, but he's such a bullshitter, I never know what to believe.

"I was debating whether or not to come down here. It means two bus tickets, but I guess it was worth it. I'm not staying long. I'm looking forward to getting a big chicken sandwich, when I leave."

"I'll be here tomorrow. I need the money. It's the end of the week."

Cutting My Grass

14 November 2014

"You look cold, Joy," I said.

"I'm, fuckin' freezing. I can't stay here much longer. My legs are so stiff I can hardly bend them."

I said, "I noticed Ghyslain standing on the corner."

"Yeah, usually he goes over to Silver's old spot. I don't know why he's being such an asshole today. He's cutting my grass."

"Chuck said that he doesn't drink. Is that right?"

"Yeah, he's a crackhead among other things."

"You mentioned that you're getting a three-wheeled scooter. How is that coming along?"

"It belongs to a friend of Buck's mom. She can't get out any more, so they were going to toss it. He asked me before if I'd be interested. I thought it would be too much trouble, since I can't get it downstairs to my apartment, but I'm having so much trouble with my legs that I've changed my mind."

I said, "It would be great for you to drive to the store. You wouldn't have so much trouble carrying heavy grocery bags."

Joy kicked her plastic storage box to the wall and wrapped a scarf around her face. "I'm heading off now. Maybe, I'll see you next week, maybe not."

December 2014

Sore Legs

17 December 2014

"Hi Joy, how are your legs today?"

"They're sore. Yesterday I could hardly walk. I think I may have water on my knee, it's swollen."

"Are you going to see a doctor?"

"Not if I can help it. I have a doctor, but he creeps me out. He's one of those guys under a turban. I just don't feel comfortable around him and it's hard to understand what he's saying.

"I hate that Ghyslain is panning on the corner. He's cutting my grass. I think he's on crack. One day he was bragging about how much he'd collected, the next day he said he was broke. If I'd made that much it would have lasted me a week. Not only that, he's only here when the weather's good, then he fucks off to Rimouski. We don't see him again for six months."

I asked, "Have you read any more of my book lately?"

"Not much. I'm a slow reader. I can only wear my glasses for so long, before I get a headache. I like the parts about Big Jake, though. He want's to read it after I'm finished.

"He's been coming by early lately. The Mission kicks him out at seven thirty each morning. If he doesn't leave then he's stuck there the whole day. I'm going to have to kick him out for a while. I'll be seeing enough of him at Christmas."

I said, "He's got lots of friends, There are plenty of places he could go.

"Is there any word about the scooter you were going to get?"

"I'm waiting for Buck to bring it to me."

"Is André out of hospital now?"

"Yeah he's out. Now he thinks he can drop over to my place anytime he wants. He came over at nine thirty in the morning. I told him, 'Phone first, or I won't let you in.' He tried it a couple of times. I saw him at the window and said, **'Not today, now get lost!'**

"He's pissed with Hippo because of the bike he sold him. It didn't come with a lock, but Hippo took one when he left. I said, 'You know where he lives. Go straighten him out.'

I said, "Big Jake could visit André. They both seem to be looking for friends."

Joy said, "That won't happen, because of the beating André laid on me."

"How has Jake been treating you?"

"He's okay. He knows what'll happen if he raises his hand to me."

Chili Charged

6 January 2015

While engrossed in a novel, as I sat on the bus on my way to work a voice called out, "Hey, Dennis!" I turned my head and saw Chilli. She said, "I haven't seen you for ages." An empty seat opened beside me, so we sat together for the rest of the trip.

"So, how've you been?" she asked.

"I've been fine. I haven't seen many of our friends lately. It's been too cold. I saw Joy about three weeks ago. She's doing fine, but her legs are still giving her trouble.

"How about you?" I asked.

"I had my hip surgery — it went really well. I'm still using a cane, but I can get around a lot better. I don't have much pain. Oh, I broke up with my boyfriend. It happened at a bar. I guess I drank too much. When they handed me the bar bill it was over a hundred dollars. My boyfriend and I had an argument, he took off, leaving me with the bill. I didn't bring any money, because I thought that he'd be paying. Anyway, they called the cops. I guess I flipped out. I got into a fight. I'm on my way to court now. I have six charges, including assaulting a police officer. I even got pepper sprayed, twice. When I went to the hairdresser to have my hair cut I could still smell the spices from the spray. It nearly made me sick. So, I'll have to see how that goes. Hey, I'm still in school."

"That's great Chili, I'm really proud of you. I hope it goes well for you in court." Our stop was approaching so we stood up to exit the bus. She walks faster than I do and we separated somewhere in the crowd.

Homebound Bus

20 March 2014

I was on the bus, on my way home from the gym. It was packed and noisy. Getting closer to the end of the route I took an open seat near the front. Sitting on one of the side seats nearest the driver was Little Jake.

"Dennis, how the fuck are you? I haven't seen you for ages. What are you doing on this bus? Oh, I forgot, you live up this way. Shakes and me met you one other time on this bus.

"I was talking to Bearded Bruce earlier. We were going to cook a big meal. He asked me to get the split peas. You know, the hard ones in the bag. Anyway, I get to his place and he's not there. I don't know what happened. I stopped by to see Snake and Irene, but their place was all locked up. I went to Jacques' place. He was cooking supper. I asked, 'Do you mind if I stop by for a while?' He said, 'Can't you see I'm getting ready to eat? Fuck off!' He hadn't cooked enough for two, so I just pulled up a chair, opened my bottle and had a few joints.

"I got two bottles of wine with me, three grams and some chicken breasts. I'm ready to party and I can't find anybody. It's like everybody's dissin' me; but not really, 'cause they're not home. I got my check today, two days before everybody else. I don't know how that works. It has somethin' to do with the fact that I don't have direct deposit. For some reason, my Trillium check and my G.S.T check come two days later than everybody else. I can't figure that out. It works out for me though. I lend people money when I first get my check. When I'm running low, before my next check, they pay me back. I only lend to people I trust.

"I'm going to stop on my way home to see if Shakes is in. He's just a couple of buildings down. What time is it? — eight thirty? It's near his bed time, he should be home. Am I near my stop yet? Oh no! I'm out of rolling papers. I'm going to have to walk a block down and get some.

"I left my bike near the Market. It's locked, but I've only got a small, cheap lock. I've also got quick release wheels. There's nothing stopping someone from taking my wheel, but I can always steal another one.

"You'll never guess who I saw today, Mariah. She was nearly in tears when she saw me. Well, not really in tears, but her voice sort of choked up. There was Bruce, Jacques, me,

Buck and Mariah. It's the first time the crew has been together in months.

"Jacques has lost a lot of weight, probably about twenty pounds. He still has a pot belly, but he doesn't look like Santa Claus any more. He's cut back to just two beer a day and he stays off the wine. He's eating well too."

I said, "His doctor probably told him to lose a few pounds because of his heart. He's had three heart attacks already, hasn't he? I'm glad to hear that he's taking care of himself. How is Shakes?"

"He staggers around like he always does. He hasn't been panning much because of the cold weather. He's doing more bumming off people. Apart from that, he's the same old Shakes. He knows everybody. If he passed out downtown, when he woke up he'd know somebody nearby who'd put him up for the night. He's collected a few cracked up friends that I don't much care for. You don't want to be bumming off the wrong people, if you know what I mean. It's just not healthy. This is my stop coming up. I'll see you man."

I won't charge you

12 March 2014

The coldest winter in twenty years, that's what the weather forecasters say. None of my homeless friends have been out lately. I don't blame them. I boarded the bus heading east and threw my gym bag on an empty seat. As I was about to sit down, the passenger in front of me turned his head and said, "So, You're going to sit behind me are you?"

I looked closely at his face and asked, "I know you, don't I?"

"Yes, you know me."

"Sorry, I can't remember your name. Do you remember mine?"

He thought for a moment then said, "No, I don't remember." He moved over in his seat to make room for me to sit down.

I said, "I remember talking to you at the park in summer. Do you still go there? Does anybody go there, or is it too cold?"

He said, "I don't like to be with people. It's just me, myself and I. That's the way I like it.

"I was headed to an A.A. meeting. I got all dressed. I'm wearing three coats now. Something happened and I lost track of time. See that building up there on the corner. That's where I should have gone, but it's too late now." I could smell beer on his breath. That was the something that happened.

"Do you go to A.A? Have you ever?"

"No," I said, "I used to have a drinking problem, but I quit on my own. Now, I just have a beer every once in a while, maybe a glass of wine."

"Are you going home to have a beer?... It's okay, I won't charge you... I've been trying to get back into rehab.

"My roommate is pissed off at me for some reason. I don't know what it is. I used one of his onions. Maybe that's what it is. He's Jamaican. They eat that funny sort of food, but, he's okay. Maybe I had the TV on too loud last night. I don't know.

"Do you know if there's a McDonald's around here?"

I said, "I don't know the area very well. I've got a Tim Horton's card. Is that any good to you?"

"No, I'm not asking for money. Is that what you thought? No, I'm okay.

"This is a nice neighborhood we're passing through. I used to live around here. I had a sound system, three hundred watt speakers, a big TV. I got behind in my rent. I told my landlord, 'To hell will you, for all the trouble I've had to put up with.' I owed him two months back rent. He kept my stuff and changed the locks.

"This is my stop coming up. I'm going to visit a friend, to see if he's home. If he isn't home, I don't know what I'm going to do."

Brutal Winter

29 April 2015

Bearded Bruce was using the pay phone. I waited for him to finish. He said, "Hey bud, it's good to see you. It's been a couple of months now. It was a brutal winter."

I said, "I've been looking for some of my friends. Markus, I talked with yesterday. I've met with Magdalene and Native Nance. I've seen Greg and Luther. Little Jake I've talked to on the bus."

"You won't see Jake for a while. Three days ago was check day.

"We're still around. I pan on this corner then move on to the next block later on. I'm just waiting to hear about some work"

I asked, "What kind of work will you be doing?"

"Landscaping, the same as last year."

I remembered that Weasel and Bruce shared that job last summer. I didn't want to mention the controversial topic.

"Yeah, I'll be doing some work for Stella, as soon as the ground is dry enough."

I asked, "Have you seen Joy lately. Nancy was at her place for Easter dinner. Joy seemed to be doing fine then."

"Well," said Bruce, "she wasn't inclined to listen to the advice of her doctor."

"Yes," I said, "I'm well aware of that."

Bruce said, "I talked to Mariah yesterday, she hasn't seen Joy for three days and she's holding her check for her. She's knocked on Joy's door, but there's no answer. It's not like Joy to miss collecting her check. I'm going to drop by her place tomorrow."

I said, "It was great seeing you, Bruce. Take care."

"Take care, bud."

Joy, R.I.P.

30 April 2015

Two-four, the free newspaper vendor, took me aside and said, "I have bad news for you. Joy passed away." I was shocked. I said, "I haven't seen her since before Christmas, but she seemed fine then, apart from sore legs." He gave me a shoulder pat and said, "Sorry, man. I know you cared for her."

I phoned Mariah. "Hi, Mariah, I'm so sorry to hear the news about Joy. I know how close you were to her, like a sister. I just wanted to be informed when the funeral will take place. If you could contact Chuck or Metro — I see them every day."

"I will, Dennis, but I don't know when they'll be releasing the body. The coroner has ordered an autopsy. The police had all kinds of questions. I was up half the night."

I said, "I won't keep you any longer, Mariah. I just wanted to express my condolences to you and to let you know that I'd like to pay my respects at the funeral."

"Thanks, Dennis. Take care."

I was on a search today for Joy's friends. I wanted to commiserate with them and be informed of any funeral arrangements. In Weasel's old spot was Buck and his dog Dillinger, Bearded Bruce and a man using a cell phone who Bruce introduced me to as Mike the Medicine Man. Bruce said, "He really is you know. His grandmother is teaching him all the old ways. Now he's a young shit who doesn't know his arse from a hole in the ground, but one day he's going to be a wise man. I'm sucking up to him now so that when my time comes, there will be someone to say a prayer over my dead body.

"I'm a bit drunk today — just because I am. I've already finished a twenty-sixer.

"Buck, can you spare me six grams of weed? How much is that? Sixty bucks! That stuff grows in the ground. I don't think I have sixty. I have fifty-five, so I'll give you back a gram then you'll owe me five. Are you good with that?"

Toothless Chuck stopped by and bought two grams, then asked Bruce, "Have you got the forty bucks you owe me?"

Bruce said, "No, I don't have it. Do you want some pot in exchange? Take it or leave it."

"No, I don't want any pot."

Bruce said, "Well, move along then. You're standing in front of my cup. How do you expect someone to make a drop if they have to fight their way through you and a dog?"

A woman stopped and dropped a dollar into Bruce's cup. "Thanks, sweetheart," he said. How's your nose? You're not going to take another dive are you?"

"No, I don't think so. The doctor said he's going to up my pain meds."

"Well tell him to double or triple them."

The woman said, "I don't want to be falling asleep. I'd end up like I did last time." she shook Bruce's hand then walked away.

"Bye, sweetheart, take care." To me he said, "She's a really sweet girl. She has some kind of disease, like epilepsy, where she gets massive seizures. They come on all of a sudden. A few days ago she fell and hit her nose on a car mirror."

I asked, "Have you heard any news about funeral arrangements for Joy?"

"No, Mariah would be the one to talk to about that. She found the body. Wasn't it just last night that we were talking about how Joy hadn't been seen for a few days? Mariah got the landlady to open the apartment. Joy was lying on the floor, stiff as a board, her lips blue."

I asked, "Do they know the cause of death?"

"Suicide over a period of years! Her doctor told her to quit smoking and drinking but, you know Joy, she refused. I blame that bastard Jake, beating her and letting her kidneys bleed out. I know he went to prison for that, but the next time I see him, I don't care if he is in a wheelchair, I'm going to lay a beating on him. At home I've got a five pound hammer with a yellow cord that won't break. I'll carry that with me. I don't care if I do go to prison. I won't be in p.c. (protective custody) like Jake was. I'll be with the general population. Maybe I'll get a judge whose daughter or sister was the victim of spousal abuse. That's what I plan to do.

"We're partly to blame for not convincing Joy to leaving that guy. I just don't understand guys that are beaters. I don't understand women who stay with them. Generally, I think women are smarter than men, but not when it comes to choosing a partner. I know lots of gay men who are in relationships. I never hear of them being beaten by their spouses, they'd just leave.

"Anyway, I'm finished here for the day. At the grocery store they have their 'Dollar Days' sale, so I'm going to stock up."

I said, "Take care, Bruce. I'll see you soon."

Don't Mess with Joe

I was expecting to meet my friends at the park. They said they'd be there, but street people have a very flexible concept of time. Most of them don't wear watches (an obvious indication of wealth). One has a cell phone, but the screen is so shattered that viewing is nearly impossible. I continued past the park, towards the bridge, where I saw Joe in his walker. We both waved.

"It's good to see you," said Joe. His upturned cap was on the sidewalk in front of him. "Good afternoon, ladies," he said to some women walking by. "Don't mind me I like people and if I'm cheerful they treat me better.

"That one's Inuit from Baffin Island. Do you know how to tell the difference between a woman from the Northwest Territories and the ones from Baffin? The ones from the Territories have a nice round bum, the others have a flat bum. I'm part Cree, but I don't speak it. There are twenty-seven different dialects, that's a lot to learn. I'm fluent in French though. Bonjour, Madam." A grey haired woman turned and smiled. "I have a lot better luck with the older ones. The young ones are nicer to look at, but I only get one of those every six months or so. A couple of nights ago two women walked by. We talked for a while and I asked them, 'Would you care to join me behind the bushes for a little fun?' One of them said, 'Show us the tool you have between your legs, then we can decide whether or not it'll be worth our while.' I didn't mind, I stood up and dropped my jeans. 'It looks like you'll do,' one of them said. The three of us spent most of the night together.

"I sleep back there. Last night it rained for about twenty minutes. I thought, This will be a good chance to wash my beard. I went down near the water and the rain stopped. It's a good thing I wasn't all lathered. There's no way I'd wash in that water from the river; it's too polluted.

"I have a lot of nasal congestion, so when I go to a restaurant I grab a big handful of napkins. When I buy my beer I always ask them to put it in a bag. When I have to blow my nose I put the used napkins in the bag. Later, I'll dump it in one of the trash containers. I like to keep my place neat.

"The cops came back there one time. They said 'Joe, you really shouldn't be sleeping back here.' They looked around and found an injection needle. 'Do you know anything about this?' they asked as they picked it up with rubber gloves. I said, "Sure, I found a guy shooting up back here. With one hand I grabbed him by the shirt collar, with the other I grabbed him by the ass of his pants, then I tossed him in that dumpster there. It took him most of the night to get out. At about that time my brother — who is six foot nine — and twenty of his gang buddies rode up on their Harleys. 'Are these two pigs giving you a rough time, Joe?' my brother asked. They picked up the squad car and carried it to the railing of the bridge. He asked, 'Should we throw it over?' I said, 'Hell no, a shitload of grief would come down on me and I'd have to find another place to live.' They dropped the car on the pavement, it bounced a few times, the cops jumped in and drove away. It helps to have family and friends in high places.

"I've got ten brothers and six sisters — my mother was a nympho — I'm the shortest of the boys at six foot four. I teased my mom and asked, 'Before I was born, are you sure you weren't cheating on Dad?' I got out of there quick. Mom kept a sawed off shotgun in the kitchen.

"Another time, before breakfast, I took a carton of eggs out of the fridge. With a needle I made a tiny hole in the shell of each egg, then sucked the egg out of the shell. I filled the shells with water, put them in the freezer, just long enough so they would start to freeze. When my mom tried to crack one of the eggs all that came out was water. I nearly busted a gut laughing. Mom was alright, she could take a joke."

Home Invasion

7 July 2015

I walked towards the park and to my surprise, a group of my friends were sitting on the curb. I gave a wave and they waved back. I shook hands with Shark, Little Jake and Outcast. Mariah stood and gave me a hug.

Outcast said, "It must be a year since I saw you last."

"It could be," I said, "I don't remember. How did you make out through the winter?"

"I had double pneumonia. Mind you, I get that every winter, it's from working with asbestos when I was younger. Now I have a double hernia. It sounds like ordering a coffee, 'I'll have a double, double please, to go.' Thursday I go to the doctor for the operations. The idea scares the shit out of me. I've never had an operation before. That's why I've been putting it off. One I should have had done last year. Now the pain is so bad, I can't put it off any longer.

"Did you hear what happened to Shark? I'll let him tell you."

Shark said, "Irene and I had a home invasion last week by a motorcycle gang. They had the idea that I was cutting into some of their drug business. I'm a little fish, what you might call the bottom rung of the ladder, if I'm even on the ladder. I'm a junkie, I sell enough to get me through to the end of the month. I'm not any competition for them; I don't even sell near where I live. My customers are all from the suburbs."

I said, "Someone must have ratted on you."

"Yeah, that's what happened. This woman said I was stealing some of her customers. That was bullshit. They asked me, 'Where is your safe? Where's your stash?' I said, 'I don't have a safe. I got a few pills that's all.' I got a flashlight and showed them around the place, back to front, top to bottom. I asked them 'Do you see any safe?' It was Irene that gave up the money, four hundred bucks. The same thing happened the next night, another four hundred bucks.'

I asked, "Did either of you get hurt?"

"No, I guess we didn't look like we were any kind of threat. They kicked the door down. Irene was shitting bricks. I asked them, 'What are you going to do, kill us? I'm dying of AIDS, Irene has cancer, that's how we get the marijuana and the Oxycontin, we have medical prescriptions for them. Do what you want. I don't care.' "

September 2015

Little Jake

I nearly ran into Jake; I was walking along the sidewalk on my way to work, he was exiting a building. He was wearing his usual green cap, an orange and black tee shirt, beige shorts and sun glasses.

"Jake!"

"Dennis, sorry I nearly ran you over! I just stepped in here to use the bathroom."

"How've you been?" he asked.

"I've been fine. I haven't seen many of the regulars around. I've seen Magdalene and Adam, Chuck, Joe, Mary, a few others. I stopped and talked with them a while. Do you still meet near the bridge?"

"Yeah, I go there, Mariah's there nearly every day, Jacques, Wolf and Shaggy. Wolf slept out last night. He was wasted on something. He could barely walk. I was partying and stayed out as well. this morning I've been panning in front of the coffee shop, trying to get enough change for breakfast.

"You'll have to come by."

"I will, Jake. I can't make it today, but next week, for sure. The weather's been so unpredictable lately. One day is too hot, the next day it rains.

"Are you still living in the same place?" I asked.

"Yeah, everything is still the same."

Chili

25 November 2015

"Hi Chili, I haven seen you for ages. You're walking without a cane now."

"Hi Dennis. Yeah, I can even run and jump now.

"This is my friend Rocco. He's going to be attending school with me as soon as I can get him registered."

Rocco said, "Hi man, yeah, I'm looking forward to going to school. I'm off drugs, taking it easy on the booze. I saw too much of that when I was young. When my parents would get into the hard stuff, they'd sort of blackout. That's the only way I can describe it. They'd beat us kids, and wouldn't remember a thing about it when they were sober. Now that I'm older I tell them all the shit they put us through.

"My brother is in prison near Pembroke. He's done four of a twenty year sentence. When he gets out he's going to see a brother who's made something of himself."

I asked, "How are you doing, Chili?"

"Great, I've been off the drugs for three years now. I still go for methadone treatments but they've cut my dose down to almost nothing. In a little while I won't need it any more."

"How's school going?"

"It's okay. I got a teacher that doesn't like me. I don't like him either. It's high school and I don't really get along with the other students. When I walk past, I hear them talking about me and laughing. It's okay though. I can handle it."

Shaggy bit into Chili's pant leg and started pulling and shaking it. He hadn't bitten into her flesh, but she was obviously afraid. Wolf jumped up, attached Shaggy's leash to her collar and pulled her over to where he was sitting.

"I'm sorry about that," Wolf said to Chili. She doesn't usually do that.

"Bad dog!" he said to Shaggy. "You know better than that, now lie down."

Wolf said, "I'm sorry Dennis, I'm drunk, Shaggy's acting up. She's fourteen years old. Who knows what's going on in her mind.

"Did I tell you that Jake came over to my place last night? It was a mess, beer cans all over the floor. He picked them all up. The place looks great now.

"Did I tell you what I'm reading now?"

"Yeah, you said something about a European crime novel translated from French to English."

"No, not that one, that's finished. This new book is about a hooker who lures married men into an alley, kills them, then cuts their heart out. Can you imagine that; cutting into someone's chest, through their ribs, prying open their rib cage and ripping out their heart? That's not the worst part. She takes the heart, puts it into a plastic container, then delivers it to the man's family. She puts it on the door step, rings the bell and runs. What a shock for the family. They don't even know the guy's missing and they open the door to that. I'm going to try to finish reading it tonight. I'm anxious to find out her motive. Also, I probably won't sleep until the story's resolved."

Wolf had the loop of Shaggy's leash around his wrist. He was gesturing with his hands and accidentally pulled on the leash. Shaggy jumped and bit him above the knee.

"Ow, that hurt! You stupid dog! What did you do that for?"

Wolf let go of the leash to inspect his wounds. Shaggy slunk away and lay down with her back to the group. He pulled up his pant leg. "I thought she drew blood, but she broke the skin." He dumped her water dish, took her food dish and threw the contents toward the railing.

Outcast yelled, "Wolf, what the fuck are you doing. You threw dog kibble over the three of us sitting here."

Wolf replied, "I didn't throw it on you. I threw it over you. What are you going to do about it?"

Outcast said, "How be I ram this beer can down your throat. What'll you do then?"

"I'll yell at you, that's what I'll do."

Family Reunion

22 September 2015

Since hearing from Little Jake that my friends were meeting in the park again I wandered over at noon. The first to greet me was Shaggy, wagging her tail, pushing her head under my hand, moving further forward so I could scratch her back.

Wolf said, "See, she missed you, we all missed you. Jake mentioned seeing you the other day. Have a seat." Mariah offered me a cushion to sit on. "What do you think of those Blue Jays, they got a real streak going. Tickets are selling for three hundred and thirty-seven bucks, unless you want the luxury seats for seven and a half thousand. They've even brought seats out of storage. The others were sold out. Can you imagine what it's going to be like if the Jays win the Series over New York. There'll be riots in the streets. If they lose there'll be riots in the streets."

I said to Outcast, "The last time we met, you were going into hospital for a hernia operation. How did that go?"

"Yeah, I had a double inguinal hernia. The operation went okay, but I didn't listen to the doctor's advice. He said that I should take it easy for two weeks after the surgery. I was over at Jacques' place the next day horsing around. I pulled out some stitches. Now, the mesh that they used for the repair is scraping my intestines. Sometimes, I notice blood in the toilet. I'll have to go in and have it re-done."

"Nick," I asked, "didn't you need surgery the last time I saw you?"

"No, but I had a heart attack. Since that I 've had some memory loss. My brother, who was an alcoholic, passed away a couple of days ago. They're burying him today. I'm also supposed to see my doctor this afternoon, but to hell with it. I'd rather just sit here with my friends.

"I still make sandwiches and give them out to any homeless people that I come across. There are a couple of women staying at my place. They had nowhere else to go."

I asked, "Do you know Rhea, a small native woman, who pans up the street."

"Yeah, she's a sweetheart."

I said, "She is staying at a women's shelter, but isn't getting along with her noisy roommate."

"Yeah, noisy roommates are often a problem."

Outcast said, "Nick, how would you deal with a situation like that?"

Nick responded, "If it happened with women staying at my place, I'd read to them out of my bible. If that didn't work, I'd take them out in the hall. A bible can be used in many different ways."

"Wolf," I asked, "what are you reading now?"

"My ladies brought be some European crime books that have been translated from French to English. I like to read about what happens in other countries. They don't use guns as much. I like the descriptions of the towns and the countryside. When I'm not at my spot in the morning, or down here at noon, I'm at home reading."

Sirens

I was approaching Rhea when a fire engine drove by with sirens blaring. I said hello, but she held up her hand indicating that she couldn't hear.

"That's four that have come by. Sirens scare me. I hate to think of someone being hurt."

I asked, "Have you been sleeping better lately?"

"Yes, they moved me out of the room I was sharing and put me on a cot. I like it a lot better."

I said, "I've been having trouble breathing lately. I have asthma and they're renovating the building where I work."

Leah reached into her backpack and pulled out a blue puffer. She said, I use this a couple of times a day. When it gets too bad I take pills. My voice sounds a bit raspy due to an operation I had on my throat when I was eighteen."

"What operation did you have?"

"I fell off a fifty foot cliff. The last thing I remember was looking up and seeing purple, then I saw stars. Doctors had to do a tracheotomy. Now, my windpipe only has seventy per cent capacity."

"Where are you originally from?"

"Nunavut."

"Do you go back there often? I guess there aren't many jobs available?"

"No, there aren't, but I don't miss the place."

I left to visit my other friends at the park. Gaston was passing around a joint. He said, "This is the best weed you'll ever taste. I grew it myself, no chemicals, just water. I still wish that they'd decriminalize it. I'd lose business, but if I could buy it at a reasonable price it would take it out of the black market and customers would know what they're buying.

"There is a guy they call the four hundred dollar doctor. He'll give anybody a year long prescription for medical marijuana. You don't have to have anything wrong with you. He'll just make something up. You give him four hundred for the prescription and he'll say, 'See you next year.' The problem with medical marijuana is that the buds have stems in them. They also reduce the potency with fillers. It has a THC content of about nine percent. Of course, you can also take it by vaporizing, eating extracts, taking capsules or using oral sprays.

"You know, a while back, people were saying they were smoking hash laced with opium? It came with white powder on it. Do you know what that white stuff was? Mold, from coming in on ships from Viet Nam. It gave you an incredible high, but it was dangerous for your lungs."

Jacques' phone rang. He looked at the display and said, "Outcast, I think this is for you."

I heard Outcast say, "Yeah, I'll be coming home soon. I'm going to stop by the Food Bank for vegies. It's the once a month one. I'll be home in about an hour, or two, or three. No, I'm coming right home. Don't start cooking anything, because I'm going to make my soup. Bye.

"We don't have a relationship anymore, so we get along better. She does her thing, I do mine.

"Have you heard about the trouble between the uber drivers and the taxi companies. Yesterday a passenger was dragged out of an Uber car and forced into a cab. I can't remember the company name. I don't like the idea of Uber coming in, taking business away from the drivers who have to pay for a taxi licence. Also, I don't think they are insured if a passenger is injured. On the other hand, the taxis are charging too much and it seems to be arbitrary. My girlfriend took a cab to the airport, it cost thirty-seven bucks. For the return trip, exactly the same route, they charged forty-nine. Where's the logic in that?"

St. Nick

I stopped briefly to talk to Rhea. She was eating an egg salad sandwich from a plastic bag. Beside her was a juice box and an energy bar. I said, "It looks like the sandwich guys (volunteers from the Innercity Ministries Outreach Program) have made their rounds."

"Yeah, Shawn and Mike came by. They're good people."

"How have you been sleeping?" I asked.

"It's been good these past few days. I see a psychologist this afternoon. I really find it hard talking about my accident. It's hard to remember things. I remember riding in the ambulance, but I can't remember what happened immediately before that."

"Why were you up on a fifty foot cliff?"

"It was my eighteenth birthday. I was high on drugs with a couple of friends. When I was in hospital I asked one friend what happened and he acted all shifty like. So, I don't know whether I fell or was pushed. I had two breaks in my femur, throat injury, a fractured skull and some brain damage It was eight years ago now so there's nothing I can do about it. I have to be careful eating because of my restricted windpipe. If something went down the wrong way I could die."

I said, "So if your accident happened eight years ago, that means that you're twenty-six now. Is that right?"

"Yeah, I have a baby face and look a lot younger. It's a problem sometimes."

I said, "I promised Nick that I'd visit with him this afternoon, so I'll see you on my way back."

Nick was standing near the park railing. We shook hands and I asked him, "How is your health now?"

"It's okay, my blood sugar level is at about three. At one time it was fifty-six. That was when I was panning on the streets. I didn't take care of myself then. Now I'm careful. I may share a joint or a tug from a bottle, but it's only to be sociable. It's sharing.

"Diabetes is the reason I lost my job. I used to be a Tower Crane Operator. From where I was sitting a man down below looked like an ant. We communicated through hand signals and by radio. Sometimes I would lose consciousness, or I'd be at the back peeing. I had to pee a lot. After a few missed calls they sent me to the union doctor. He said that I should see my family physician. The doctor took some tests and asked me, 'Did you know that you are diabetic?'

"The union doctor knew what was wrong. He told my boss and that was it for working the Tower. They offered me another job operating a Shunt Locomotive to move rail cars around. It was a demotion and it was boring. I didn't like that, so I quit.

"I've had a few heart attacks in the past month and a half."
I asked, "Was it due to stress?"

"Yeah, sometimes when I come home my head is so full. People dying in my arms, beatings…you know what it's like. That's when I talk to God. I say, 'Please help me God. Lift this burden that is weighing me down. Please help the homeless people on the streets. I do what I can, but my resources are limited.'

"It was God who told me to stop panning. He said, 'I'll provide.' That's what I tell other people as well. There was a woman panning on the street. I told her 'You don't have to do this.' Maybe she had a drug habit to pay for. I don't know. While I was sitting there a woman dropped fifteen dollars into her cap. After she left the woman panning said, 'You're lucky for me.' I said, 'It's not me, but God who will provide.'

"There is a twenty-three year old woman who sleeps in doorways. I brought her back to my place and told her, 'Look,

I'm a fifty-six year old man. I have a daughter older than you. I'm not going to touch you. Don't worry about that. I have a spare bed, food. You can wash your clothes. I have others that you can put on while you're waiting for them to dry. I told her 'You can use this address to have your check delivered and you'll always have a place to stay.

"She slept there for a few nights, then last night I found her sleeping in a doorway again. I said to her, 'This is a dangerous place. You're young, you don't know how dangerous it is. Some of these people have been on the streets for thirty years. They know how to protect themselves, but if a man grabbed you and hauled you into an alley he'd either do you or he'd stab you — one or the other. I gave her my phone number. She wrote it on her hand. She didn't come by last night. I'm not going look for her. It's her choice. Soon the weather will be cold and I may not be around.

"Would you please sign my bible? As you can see I have signatures dating back to 2002. I also have church bulletins. I attended the Biker Church last week. I really enjoyed the service. It was down to earth guys. After the sermon I talked with the pastor. In some of the churches I've attended the pastor looked down his nose at me. When I told him about my outreach program he asked about my qualifications, what seminary I studied at. I've got a grade five education. I can barely read.

"Sometimes I'll wake up at three in the morning and I'll hear someone calling. I know it's time to go. I'll make up a dozen sandwiches and go to all the places that I know that homeless people will be staying, beneath the bridges, in alleys, behind dumpsters in back of the coffee shops. By the time I get downtown the sandwiches are gone. I'll load up with a couple of trays of coffees and I'll go back the way I came, passing cups out as I go. I receive a monthly pension. I spend about three hundred dollars a month to make the sandwiches and to hand out cards for coffee. It's all I can do. I can't help everybody."

October 2015

Mandy

8 October 2015

I was walking along a crowded sidewalk when I heard, "Dennis, down here."

Mandy stood up from the curb and gave me a hug. I reached into my pocket and pulled out a meal card and handed it to her. She misunderstood and said, "Okay we'll shake hands too. Oh, You're giving me a coffee card. Thank you, I can use that."

"How have you been?" I asked.

"You know, same old same old. My mom got her own place, finally. It's about four blocks from here. We're both so happy about it."

"Do you have a place to stay now?"

"Yeah, I've been in the same place for four years. It's a rooming house, costs me four hundred and fifty a month. After I pay my rent there isn't much left for groceries, or to feed my addictions.

"Did you near that Nick's was hospital."

I asked, "Was it because of his diabetes?"

"Yeah, he started drinking beer again. There is too much sugar in it. He went into diabetic coma. He's out now, but not feeling too well."

"That's a shame. I saw him less than two weeks ago. He looked great. He gave me the impression that he was off drinking completely. He looked healthy and happy, although he did say that he'd had a couple of heart attacks."

"Dennis, you've let your hair grow long. Why is that?" She reached up and touched my hair. "Sorry, I didn't mean to mess your hair."

"That's okay, it can't get messed up. Having it long is really low maintenance. I don't brush it, comb it or even bother drying it some days. If it gets in my eyes I run my fingers through it and that's it.

"The reason I let it grow was because I had Meningitis last February. The doctor shaved both sides of my head to perform temporal biopsies. They took two sections of blood vessels out to examine them under a microscope. I have two one inch scars at my temples, but they aren't noticeable now."

"Oh, I thought that maybe your hair was thinning."

"No," I bent over to expose the crown of my head, "my barber says that I'll never go bald. He says that he should charge me extra for the volume of hair I have. Many of his clients my age are bald, or close to it."

Mandy removed her cap, "See what I've done to my hair?" She had a buzz cut. I touched her hair. It felt like a brush, reminded me of when I used to wear my hair that way.

"It's nice," I said, "it suits you."

"I'll let it grow out over winter then get it cut off again. One haircut a year, that's all I need."

St. Nick Leaving

8 October 2015

I met Nick and Mandy sitting on a low concrete wall near the park. I shook Mandy's hand and Nick said, "Give me a hug, brother." which I gladly did.

"How are you doing, Nick? I heard that you've been in hospital?"

"I'm conflicted. I prayed to God all night long. I've had three heart attacks in the past two months. One left me in the hospital for eighteen days. I got a message saying that I should stay with my family in Blainville near Niagara Falls. Two of my brothers are anxious to carry on my work. Two friends here have said they would take over for me here. They'll be coming by later with pizza.

"I have a schizophrenic woman staying at my house also a twenty-three year old who is trying to get off crack. She's been clean for a while. Yesterday she told me she was going to her dealer for a fix. I said to her 'You're following the devil's path. When you suck on that pipe, you're blowing the devil.' She's an adult. I can't make choices for her.

"Another woman had asked me for a sleeping bag. I told everyone I know, about her situation and someone came through for me. I was given a brand new sleeping bag worth a hundred and fifty bucks. I gave it to her. Do you know what she said to me? 'I don't want it.' I asked, 'What do you mean you don't want it? I went to a lot of work to find this. Someone paid a hundred and fifty dollars so you could keep warm at night.' She said, 'I'll give it to someone.' So now some kid she pans with has a sleeping bag. These kind of things stress me. Because of my heart condition I'm supposed to avoid stress. How do I do that? I feel guilty abandoning these people."

I said, "You'll carry on your work where you're going. You'll be helping people there who otherwise wouldn't be helped. You can't be everywhere."

"You're right. Let's join the others at the park… Look, they're not at the park, they're on the traffic island. I wonder what happened."

I greeted everyone then sat next to Wolf. He said, "Nobody's talking to me because I yelled at the park maintenance guy. There he is with the yellow jacket. Yellowjacket, that's a type of wasp isn't it? It suits him. Anyway, we were all over there. This guy is standing not three feet away and he turns on the sprinklers. The rest of these guys jumped up and ran. I have a hard time getting up and I had Shaggy's wagon with Rick's stuff in it. Me and the contents of the wagon were getting drenched."

I asked, "Are you still wet?"

"Well, I've got a set of long johns under my pants and I've got a heavy coat on, but yes, I'm still wet.

"How are you?"

"I'm fine -- Same old, same old.

"Look I want to apologize for being so drunk the last time I talked to you."

"There's no problem, Wolf."

"I'm drunk now as well, but I haven't taken any of the other stuff. I got some weed for later, but that's all."

Rick announced, "This is my friend, Nathan, and he's brought two boxes of pizza."

Nathan said, "It seems odd celebrating the departure of a friend who we'll all miss. Before we eat I'd like to say a few words from Psalm Fifteen:

A Psalm of David

1 LORD, who may dwell in your sanctuary? Who may live on your holy hill? 2 He whose walk is blameless and who does what is righteous, who speaks the truth from his heart 3 and has no slander on his tongue, who does his neighbor no wrong and casts no slur on his fellowman, 4 who despises a vile man but honors those who fear the LORD, who keeps his oath even when it hurts, 5 who lends his money without usury and does not accept a bribe against the innocent. He who does these things will never be shaken."

Depending on weather, I'm hoping to see Rick and the others tomorrow. I said my goodbyes and shook hands with anybody who wasn't holding a slice of pizza.

Check Day

10 October 2015

As I neared the group at the park, Peter said, "Sit over here. They watered the lawn and this is the only dry place. Jacques offered me a plastic shopping bag, Mariah offered me a plastic cushion; I took the cushion.

I said, "Did you hear that Nick was in hospital?"

Outcast said, "Yeah, we heard, he's across the street right now. We moved from there when they finished watering the grass. It's too warm in the sun."

"How is he?"

"Who knows, one minute he tells me he has to go under the knife for something, the next minute he says we won't see him after a week because he's going to Niagara Falls. How's he going to do both?"

Mariah said, "He has a brother in Niagara Falls. That's probably why he's going, if he's going."

I said to Outcast, "He needed surgery last year and refused it. He said he'd place his health in the hands of God."

"I think he has a hernia like I had, but lower down. He's got a lot of health problems."

I asked Outcast, "How are you doing? Will you be having your hernia operation redone?"

"No, I'm not having it redone. The netting they used for the patch is rubbing on my intestines, so I see blood in the toilet. The doctor said he wasn't worried about it. If it's still bothering me after a year he'll operate.

"Little Chester was by earlier, drunk as usual. You can always tell he's drunk because then he drags his foot. He bought a bottle of sherry at nine thirty, by eleven it was gone. He's a small guy, he should know that he can't handle that amount. Then he peed in the middle of the sidewalk. He could have gotten arrested for that."

Little Frank walked up breathing heavily. He said, "I've had the morning from hell. I got my check today and went to Money Mart to cash it, since I don't have a bank account. I was standing in line behind an old woman who was trying to cash a check for seventy-five hundred. There was some kind of problem. They had to call in the manager. I waited an hour and a half for my measly ninety-seven bucks. So, Wolf here's the fifteen. I owe you. Outcast here's the five. I owe you." He was on the phone to someone and said, "You'll have to wait for your thirty until my next check, man. I'm cleaned out."

He continued, "You'll never guess what happened to me this morning. I went in to buy a pack of smokes and the owner was training a girl on the cash. Before she'd sell me the cigarettes she asked for proof of age. I said, 'Look, honey, I'm forty-four. It takes a long time to lose all these teeth.' Maybe she thought I'd been in a lot of fights before I was sixteen. There was a big biker guy standing behind me. He laughed and said, 'I bet that made your day.'

"Now I get to relax. I haven't even had a drink yet," he said as he pulled out a bottle of sherry.

"Jacques, can I borrow your lighter, and can you fill this one for me? Last night I was trying to light some weed from the wooden pipe that you gave me. Can you believe it? three lighters ran out of fuel at the same time. I nearly went nuts. I couldn't find anything to light my pipe, so I just went to bed."

Outcast said, "What you do is take a piece of paper towel and shove it in the toaster. When it catches fire you pull it out and you have a flame to light anything you want."

Wolf said, "Dennis, your hair is getting long. You're getting to look more like us every day."

"That's the whole idea, Wolf. I'm trying to look like you. You're my idol. Maybe next I'll grow my beard down to my belly like Jacques. I've had a beard like that before."

Wolf said, "Now my beard comes in kind of salt and pepper, mostly salt. When I was younger it came in red. Go figure.

"I'm still having trouble breathing through my nose, probably because I had it broken a few times. At night I use those Breathe Rite Strips. They work great, but they're expensive — Thirty two dollars for thirty strips."

Outcast said, "So that works out to be about a dollar a strip. You pay for those, or can you get them on prescription?"

"Okay, I steal them. I didn't want to say that, but they're almost a necessity. I don't use them every night. A box will last me maybe a couple of months or more."

Outcast said, "I figured that you stole them. I just didn't want to accuse you of something if you were innocent."

Election

Yesterday Canada held a federal election. The Liberal Party won by a landslide led by Justin Trudeau, son of a former Canadian Prime Minister.

I saw Leah sitting in her usual place, cap upturned on the sidewalk. I was still half a block away when she waved and yelled, "Hey, Dennis!"

"I'm so excited. When I woke up this morning and they told me that Justin had won I started cheering, jumping up and down. See what's written on my cap, LIBERAL on the peak and JUSTIN on the crown."

I asked, "What differences do you think you'll see with a new government."

"I think he's going to raise the O.D.S.P. (Ontario Disability Support Program). I've been on it for eight years, it's really hard getting by. I'd like to get a job doing labor, but because of the broken leg I got eight years ago, I think I'd have too much pain. I also have PTSD (Post Traumatic Stress Disorder)."

I said, "A friend of mine had PTSD after returning from Viet Nam. He was on a lot of medication. Driving a road grader he fell asleep and cleared twenty miles of trees before he woke up.

"Then he got a job as a house painter. It happened that he got a contract to paint the house next to his. He saw his wife in bed with another man. I thought he'd be angry, but he said, 'I just didn't bother going home there.'

I said, "I guess Justin will legalize marijuana. What do you think of that?"

"It will be good, he'll do a lot of good things."

Following are two of the party promises as reported in today's National Post.

3. Marijuana

The Liberals are promising to legalize marijuana, arguing that the current system "does not prevent young people from using marijuana and too many Canadians end up with criminal records for possessing small amounts of the drug." Trudeau has promised to get to work on the changes "right away" if elected, but he could not offer a firm timeline. "We don't yet know exactly what rate we're going to be taxing it, how we're going to control it, or whether it will happen in the first months, within the first year, or whether it's going to take a year or two to kick in," he said.

4. Missing and murdered indigenous women

The Liberal platform promises to "immediately launch a national public inquiry" into the killings and disappearances of indigenous women and girls. "We need to get justice for the victims. We need healing for the (families). And we need to ensure as a society, as a country, that we stop this ongoing tragedy," Trudeau told a town hall hosted by VICE Canada this month.

December 2015

Bearded Bruce

2 December 2015

Bearded Bruce, a hulk of a man, was sitting on the sidewalk, panning for change.

"Dennis, come down here. I want to give you a hug. Don't make me stand up. I'm a bit drunk today."

"Bruce, I haven't seen you for ages."

"Loretta said she met you a while back, so I've been hoping to see you. This isn't my regular spot. It's the first of December today, isn't it? I get excited about Christmas approaching. I'm going to stop drinking so I can save money for a big Christmas meal. Tonight I put up my tree, the little one foot tree that Weasel brought over last year. I miss him and Blackie too."

"How've you been?"

"I've been fine, Bruce, no complaints. Loretta mentioned that she'd been staying with you."

"Yeah, for a few days, for a few months, whenever she can get her legal troubles settled. They asked her if she had a place to stay and she offered my name. I was accepted. She takes care of me. She's a beautiful woman, but she can be a fierce bitch."

I said, "She mentioned that she'd been drinking and had gotten into a few fights."

"Well that pretty well sums it up. She's staying with me until her court date when she finds out what's going to happen. I was surprised that I'd been approved to be her guardian, but they checked me out and since I've been in my own place for three years they figured that I was stable. That's why I'm a bit drunk today; I'm celebrating three years with a home. I've paid my rent on time. That's another first for me.

"They cut me off Welfare, so I have to pan twice as long to get enough money to eat."

"Why did they cut you off?"

"I wouldn't go along with the silly things that they wanted me to do. For one thing, they won't accept that panhandling is a job. If I was a hooker, I wouldn't have a problem. That's considered acceptable work."

I said, "Have you thought of listing yourself as a hooker, but earn your living as a panhandler?"

"Believe me, I've given that a lot of thought, but it's just not me."

"The world is a crazy place," I said.

"Yes, it was Socrates that said, "The only true wisdom is in knowing you know nothing."

"I'm glad to hear that Loretta has a place to stay."

"Now, don't you go looking at her through rose colored glasses, like you did towards Joy. She's a beautiful woman, but an alcoholic, who has some serious charges against her and she can be a real bitch."

I said, "I can appreciate that. I haven't seen that side of her, but alcohol can turn the nicest people mean.

"Did you hear that Rick moved to his home town? I really admired him."

Bruce asked, "What did you admire?"

"That he made and distributed sandwiches to other homeless people."

"Yes, that's admirable. Did you also hear that he did two years in prison for stabbing a guy in the lung."

I said, "I hadn't heard that, but I know that he broke his hand while trying to strangle somebody."

Bruce asked, "Would you like to share a joint?"

I said, "Sure."

"Do you have any cigarette papers?"

"No."

"Well, I've got the pot, but no papers."

"In that case would you like a drink?" He pulled out a flask of vodka.

I looked around, saw that the coast was clear and said, "Sure." I took a swig. It tasted good. I handed it back and Bruce took a swig.

As people passed on the sidewalk Bruce would yell, "Hey, hey, can you help a fellow out. Have a good evening. God bless you."

A while later he asked me if I wanted another drink, "I said sure." I took a swig and handed it back to him. I said, "I could very easily become an alcoholic."

Bruce said, "You already are."

That jolted me a bit, but I said, "My father, brother and nephew were alcoholics. My niece was addicted to cocaine and her husband was on heroin. It probably runs in the family."

Bruce said, "I heard that you've written a book. Is that right?"

"Yes I have. It's about when I first met Joy about five years ago. I donate the proceeds of book sales to the Innercity Ministeries, Outreach program. I also continue to help street people on my own."

"That's great. I like those Outreach people. Writing about what people say to you is one thing, but to understand this life you have to live it. I don't mean for a week, but at least a month. I suggest from January fourteenth to February fourteenth. Bring a warm sleeping bag, three pair of heavy socks and anything else you can fit in one backpack. You can't rely on any money you have in savings accounts or credit cards. I'll help you find a place, I'll show you how to panhandle and I'll be across the street, if you have any problems. That's what I did with Loretta and now she's independent. That means a lot."

"I appreciate that, Bruce. I'm not ready to do that this year, but I agree that the only way to understand this way of life is to live it. On the street is real; it's immediate. Either you make enough money for food or you don't."

"What is real? Wasn't it Plato that asked that same question?

"For Plato, in order for something to be real, it had to be permanent and unchanging. Reality and perfection for Plato were closely related."

I asked, "Have you managed to find any jobs as a chef. I know you have the qualifications."

"Yeah, I worked as a chef for twenty-three years then I let alcohol and crack get the better of me. To tell you the truth, I don't want to work. I enjoy what I'm doing. When the sun is shining, this is the best job in the world."

February 2016

A Dying Breed

17 February 2016

Yesterday the city experienced a record breaking, twenty inch snowfall. Buses got stuck. Commutes that would in normal weather take thirty minutes took four hours. One hundred and twenty vehicle accidents further snarled traffic. I gave up on my regular bus. Some people had already waited two hours. I walked five blocks to take another route. On my way, huddled against a building, panning for change was Bearded Bruce covered in snow. I didn't recognize him at first and wearing two scarves over my face he didn't recognize me either.

I pulled down my scarves and asked, "Bruce, is that you?"

He said, "Hi laddie, how've you been. I looked for you a couple of times in some of the regular places, but didn't see you."

I said, "My asthma has been bad this year. With the extreme cold I haven't been out much lately. How have you been?"

"Not so good lad. They cut off my Welfare. If I can't make enough panning I won't be able to pay my rent and I'll be sleeping on the streets again. I could have lied to them, but it's just not my way. They said I should get a job. I said, 'I have a job panhandling. Sometimes I'm panning ten to twelve hours a day. Do you think that's easy?' They wouldn't go along with that; now if I was a prostitute, they'd consider that a real job, but panning — no. I'm an alcoholic, there's no way I can hold onto a regular job."

I suggested, "Tell them you're a prostitute."

"I just couldn't do it, man. I'd rather sleep behind the dumpster again.

"Shark died last Sunday. I guess you knew that he had cancer. The funeral is this week. I won't be going. I didn't like the man that much. I expect that Irene will will be dead by next Sunday. She doesn't look very good. There aren't very many of the originals left. We're a dying breed."

Bearded Bruce and Beyond

19 February 2016

"Matey, have a seat," commanded Bruce. "I've cleared a space, you can sit on my bag. It's okay folks, just a couple of bums, sitting, having a chat."

"Hi, Bruce, I notice that you've shaved off your beard. What inspired that?"

"She told me to do it."

"Who's she?"

"Loretta, my girl, she said that you were talking to her yesterday. I think I was talking to you a couple of days ago. I don't remember. I was too drunk."

"Yeah, she told me about you pounding on the door. When she opened it, you were rolling around in the snow.

"Is there any chance of you getting back on Welfare?"

"No, I don't want it. It's just a crutch. There wouldn't be any point in me leaving my apartment if everything is paid for. I still get my disability allowance, my ODSP (Ontario Disability Support Program). Part of that is paid directly to my landlord. I still have three hundred and twenty a month to make up. Loretta helps. She pans where you saw her yesterday and I'm just across the street in Weasel's old spot. I don't charge her rent, but she's been staying with me for the past five months. She's stayed clean and sober the whole time. She still has her weed.

"See that couple panning across the street? You know who that is don't you?"

"I can't see them very well."

"It's Shakes' daughter, I don't remember which one. I had a bit of a dust up with them earlier. I guess they had some sort of disagreement then he jumped up and started hitting her, really punching her. If there's one thing I can't stand it's a man who hits a woman. There were lots of people standing around, but nobody did anything. I saw some with their cell phones out. They may have been phoning the police — I don't know. Anyway, I pulled him off her and started pounding him. Then she jumped on my back and said, 'Stop hurting my boyfriend!' I can't figure these women out, just like Joy getting back with Big Jake.

"I've known a guy for about ten years. I just found out that he has nine kids. He's on the street because he doesn't want to pay child support. I said to him, 'Take some responsibility. Haven't you heard of condoms?' I don't have anything to do with him any more."

I saw Trudy, Anne's daughter walking towards us. I waved.

Bruce said to her, "Just keep walking." To me he said, "That's another one I avoid… Here come the cops! We better not be seen sitting here." We walked to the end of the block.

"Yeah, they're picking him up, throwing him into the squad car. I'm glad to see that."

Psycho Freak

15 April 2016

A man sat huddled on the sidewalk, an empty cup in front of him, his back rested against the outside wall of McDonald's. A half eaten hamburger was in his hand. He looked familiar, but without my glasses everything was a blur.

He stood up, "Dennis, man, I haven't seen you for ages."

"Hi Jake, how are you doing?"

"I've been here since five thirty this morning. It's taken this long to collect enough to get something to eat. Have you seen any of the guys around?" He was coughing, chewing and trying to talk all at the same time. I noticed that he no longer had any teeth, his distinctive green cap was missing, his complexion was grey and his face looked puffy. In frustration he threw the rest of the hamburger into the street.

"Yeah, I've seen Bruce, Trudy and her mom, Anne."

"I have bed bugs at my place, so I don't socialize much. I don't want anybody accusing me of bringing bugs into where they stay. Jacques has the same problem.

"I got to tell you what happened last night. It was right around here. I was by myself when I seen this psycho freak jump into the street and start banging cars. I ran out and grabbed him. He threw me down on the pavement. All of a sudden, almost as if he fell out of the sky, Bruce stepped in and took care of the guy. The bouncer from the club across the street seen what I'd done and gave me a dollar.

"Anne and some native guy were panning near here this afternoon. That's where I'm coming from. I'd never seen this guy before. They were sitting together with a hat out then he, all of a sudden, jumps up and runs away with the hat and all the cash. I'm looking for the motherfucker now. That's no way to behave with friends."

I said, "I'm just heading back to work so I'll be turning left at the next corner."

"That's okay, we can walk and talk, talk and walk. I'm not going anywhere anyway. Where would I have to go?"

Reunion

28 April 2016

I hadn't seen my friends at the park since last fall when the cold weather hit. Little Jake had told me that people were starting to gather there again, so I took a chance. Sure enough, from a block away, I recognized Hippo, Mariah, Chester, Jacques, Wolf and Shaggy.

I asked Hippo, "How was your winter?"

"I've been hibernating, playing with the TV remote, sitting in the middle of the destruction I call my apartment. I've got holes all over my walls."

I said, "When I talked to you last you were having a problem with a water leak from the apartment upstairs. Did they get that sorted for you?"

"Sort of. I don't have the leak, but every time the woman turns on her tap it sounds like a jack hammer, ratta tatta tatta tatta tat."

"Have you been staying out of trouble, not threatening cops with a hammer?"

"Oh, I've done worse than that. This guy had a guitar and a keyboard and didn't have anyplace to store them, so I said, 'I can keep them at my place.' My next door neighbor offered to teach me how to play the guitar, so I was walking down the hall to his apartment when the other guy sees me. He thought that I was going out to pawn it. I'd never do that. I'd never do that. I said to him, 'You want your guitar? Here it is!' and I threw it at him. I said, 'You want your keyboard?' I threw it down the hall. It ended up as a two piece. I saw him drive by, I picked up a hatchet and threw it, knocking out his back window. It just missed his head by inches.

"It's okay now though, we're friends again. We shook hands and I said, 'I love you, bro. Tomorrow I may kill you, but today I love you.'

I noticed that he was wearing a Jack Daniels jacket with logos all over. I said. "That's a nice jacket. Where did you get it?"

"I just got it yesterday. I was standing near the grocery store when a woman came by wearing this jacket. I said to her, 'Hey, I'll give you twenty bucks for that jacket!' She shook her head and went into the store to buy her groceries. I saw her when she came out. I said, 'I'll give you fifty bucks!' She thought it over and said, 'Okay!' So I gave her the fifty bucks, she gave me the jacket. It was cold yesterday and she was left with just a tee shirt, so I gave her my hoody."

I asked Wolf, "How was your winter?"

"It was a real hell of a winter, but the good news is that I'm now cancer free."

"I didn't know that you had cancer!"

"Either did I until after Christmas. I went to my doctor suffering from chest pain and difficulty when I swallowed. I also had a lot of indigestion, heartburn, choking and vomiting. He had a scan done and told me that I had esophageal cancer and my esophagus would have to come out. He also told me that I had to quit smoking. He's told me before to quit smoking but this time he said, 'Either you quit, or you die.' Well, I didn't want to die, so it's been nearly three months since I've had a smoke. I'll have the odd joint, doobie now and again, but that's different. I stay away from the pipe (crack). I can't handle that any more.

"I had the operation on the 2nd of February."

"Esophagectomy: Surgery to remove some or most of the esophagus is called an esophagectomy. Often a small part of the stomach is removed as well. The upper part of the esophagus is then connected to the remaining part of the stomach. Part of the stomach is pulled up into the chest or neck to become the new esophagus.

Minimally invasive esophagectomy: For some early (small) cancers, the esophagus can be removed through several small incisions instead of large incisions. The surgeon puts a scope (like a tiny telescope) through one of the incisions to see everything during the operation. Then the surgical instruments go in through other small incisions."

"So that's what they did, they made ten one inch incisions in front to put in their tools and cameras and a larger incision in my back. That's where they pulled out my esophagus. I've been in pain and haven't been able to eat for nearly three months. I lost twenty pounds. You can see by looking at me that I didn't have twenty pounds to spare. I even went back to the hospital to be fed intravenously. They did some kind of a botox treatment at the site where they joined the stomach to the remaining part of the esophagus. That helped. I had the odd beer, like today, but I don't drink a dozen at a time. Since Monday I've been back on solid food, but only an ice cream scooper of mashed potatoes and a scooper of minced hamburger." He placed two oranges on the sidewalk demonstrating the size of his meals. "If I eat more than that it'll all come back up.

"I thought that by quitting smoking my lungs would start to feel good, but they don't. They may not feel quite as bad as they did before, but they certainly don't feel good. I still have a bout of coughing when I first wake up. As you can imagine, coughing is very painful.

"I don't want to seem like an old granny complaining about every ache and pain, but that was serious stuff. I could have died.

"Jacques, how would you feel about going on a beer run for me?"

"Sure," he said, "how many do you want me to get?"

"Eighteen?"

"No, eighteen won't fit in my bag."

"Twelve then."

"Okay."

"Mariah said, "Jacques, wait, I'll go with you. I want to get some poutine."

"Poutine?" said, Hippo, "Did somebody mention poutine? I want in on that. How about you, Jacques?"

"I don't have money for that. I was going to come straight back here."

Hippo said, "That's okay, I'll buy your poutine."

"Well, if you're buying, I guess I can change my mind about that."

Timmy passed a joint to Wolf who carefully inhaled. "Hey, this is the brown hash that we used to get. It kind of bubbles up when you light it."

"I can get you some," said Timmy.

"Sounds good. We can discuss the details later.

"Timmy, tell me how you spend the last five months since I seen you last?"

"I was here, man. In the park all winter."

May 2016

Dirty Toes

Today was the first warm, sunny day of the season. I was walking toward the park when I detected the distinctive aroma of poutine (french fries, covered with melted cheese curds, topped with gravy). I felt a shoulder brush mine. That was odd, since there wasn't much pedestrian traffic. I looked to my right and saw the smiling face of Mariah.

Surprised, I said, "Hi, I'm on my way to meet you."

"I stopped at the Poutine Festival. I'm on my way back now to Jacques, Outcast and Loon."

As I approached the group Outcast said, "Get a haircut."

I said, "I'm trying to look more like Jacques."

"Nobody's allowed to look like Jacques," who was sitting cross legged, wearing green framed sunglasses and a white baseball cap. He pulled out a shiny, stainless steel pot pipe.

I said, "That's new isn't it, Jacques. What happened to your stone pipe."

"I still have the stone pipe, but it's heavy. I got this when Shark passed. It's good for one person. The other one was only good if I was passing it around to a group of about five. I'm going to make a new stone pipe as soon as they finish working on my balcony. I like to use my drill outside. I'm on the 8th floor so I get a nice breeze to blow the dust away."

Outcast said, "We're just waiting to see who's next to die. I was hoping it would be Jacques, but I'm probably next in line."

"You!" said Jacques, "I've got a tape at home I'm going to give you. It teaches you how to speak French. Then, I'll tell you what it's all about."

I asked, "How was your winter, Outcast?"

"Bad, I was in hospital three times, once for the flu, twice for pneumonia. I have a weak immune system due to lung cancer. I catch everything that's going around.

"Debbie was in Vancouver visiting her folks. I asked her to bring me back something. Look what she gave me, a Vancouver Canucks hockey cap. She knows I cheer for Montreal. What was she thinking? Wait until Fall, Loon, I'll give it to you. She'll have forgotten about it by then."

Jacques asked me, "Have you seen Chester with his neck brace?"

"Yes, what happened to him?"

"He wouldn't tell us at first. but we got it out of him. He had drunk a twenty-six ounce bottle of vodka, then passed out on his bed. He should have known better. We're too old for that sort of thing. Sometime during the night, he fell out of bed and broke his collar bone in two places. I guess he'd been lying on the floor for quite a few hours until someone went in to check on him. He was in hospital for a week and came out with that neck brace. He's been wearing it for the last four months. It's not healing. He's going to have to go back to hospital for surgery."

Outcast said, "He's never been the same since he fell backwards down that flight of stone stairs."

"Yes," said Jacques three of us were standing at the top of the stairs. We'd been drinking. I was talking to Candy, when I looked around he was rolling down the stairs. We found him lying in a big pool of blood.

"My two women neighbours got into a fight last night. They were kicking and screaming until the cops took them away. One of them has a walker. Maybe, if she goes to jail, I'll get to use the walker."

I asked, "Do you think it's the one with the walker who's going to jail?"

"You know how these things work. Whoever tells the best lies is the one who gets off."

Outcast said, "I went to the Salvation Army food bank the other day. After ninety days I'm usually allowed to get three bags of food. This time I got four cans. It's because of the refugees."

Jacques reached into his bag and pulled out a flyer for Giant Tiger. "Look, they have chicken pies for ninety-nine cents. I'm going to get some of those. They have canned peas on sale and avocados. Do you know what I make with avocados? I grind almonds in my food processor, since without teeth I can't eat whole almonds…

"Jacques," said Outcast, "if I'd known you had trouble chewing, I'd have lent you my teeth. I won't be needing them for a while."

"As I was saying," said Jacques, " I scoop out the avocados and mix with almonds, add tortilla chips and maybe a little salt. It's really good to spread on toast. You can use other kinds of nuts like cashews, but not peanuts. If you do it just tastes like peanut butter. I call it Dirty Toes. When it dries out I break it in pieces. Try some." He unscrewed a glass jar and offered me some. I took a pinch and tasted it.

"This is good!"

"Maybe it needs a little more salt."

He/She

"Hi Jacques," I said, "I see that the right neighbour went to jail and left you her walker."

"Yes, I get to use it until she gets out. So, now I have my own push along chair. It's very nice, better than sitting on the curb. It even has a pocket to put my beer.

How have you been?"

"I saw Bearded Bruce last night."

Outcast said, "Next time you see Bruce, tell him that Stella is responsible for the money she advanced him last year. They did it through a lawyer; Bruce was loaned some money for a job, Stella cosigned, then he didn't do it. Just tell him to contact Stella. He's been avoiding this place on Wednesdays, because that's the day that Stella visits.

"If he just talks to her they can work out something — twenty dollars a month, whatever. Wolf owed me some money, he came today to say that he couldn't afford to pay me, but we're good. This isn't finance we're talking about, it's friendship.

"I just realized that in the past three years twenty-three of my friends aren't here anymore. That's just the people that I know, that doesn't count all the people that these guys know. They've been around a lot longer than I have. It may be my turn next. I visited my doctor, he used this fancy new scanning machine to check the tumor on my lung. This machine works vertically, horizontally. Anyway, he said the tumor has only grown about fifty per cent larger in the past three years. What's fifty per cent of a quarter — an eighth of an inch?

"He said to just keep doing what I'm doing. He knows that I smoke cigarettes and weed, I'm an alcoholic, a crack addict. He said, 'Your lungs are never going to get better, but it doesn't look as if they are going to get significantly worse.' I take a green pill each morning for my heart — that'll probably go before my lungs."

Jacques said, "Shark didn't come around for a long time before he died."

Outcast said, "I saw him right up to the end. Irene is now staying at the same women's shelter where Joy was. She'll be there until her condition shows some sign of improvement."

Mariah said, "I can't believe it, but my son John is now thirty-two."

I asked, "Where is he staying?"

"He's still in the suburbs living with his childhood friend, Rick who said he now wants to be called Myra. He contracted HIV when he was eighteen. With all the drugs and hormones he's been taking he gradually started transforming. His breasts got larger, and he's come out as a woman. His outside plumbing is still male, but inside he feels female."

I said, "It must be hard on him to go through all those physical and emotional changes."

"He's accepted it now, and he's going through it step by step. Surgery is very expensive and it's not covered by medical plans. John said, 'He/she's such a bitch, now.' I've known him since he was a kid, she's still the same person."

Happy Birthday!

11 May 2016

Shaggy barked a greeting then Wolf said, "Dennis, it's good to see you. We're celebrating my birthday."

"Happy birthday, Wolf. How old are you?"

"I turn sixty today, but this is the last year I count. I'm feeling better today. Yesterday I bought two beers from Jake, took about two swallows from each, then had to dump them. My stomach just wasn't cooperating. Today, I had two eggs and toast for breakfast and I've been able to down three beer. This will be it for today. I'll pick up a six pack on my way home, but just because I have it, doesn't mean I have to drink it all at once. I've been off cigarettes for four months now and for most of that time I wasn't drinking. Except for what they gave me in hospital, I haven't had any pain pills either; no morphine, no percocet, no oxycontin. The last thing I need is another addiction. It's not that I'm religiously cutting everything out, like in AA. I still smoke pot, I've had the odd cigarette and today I'm drinking beer, but for ninety per cent of the time I've stayed away from those things and I'm feeling better for it."

"That's great, Wolf, just take each day as it comes. What are you reading now?"

"I'm into the Lee Child books, you know, Jack Reacher.

The author describes his character thus: "(He's) two things in one. On the surface, he is an ex-military cop who is suddenly dumped out into the civilian world. He doesn't fit in, and he spends his time wandering America, seeing the things that he's never had time to see before. He's trying to stay out of trouble, but masterfully once a year getting into trouble. He's also the descendant of a very ancient tradition: the noble loner, the knight errant, the mysterious stranger, who has shown up in stories forever... He is a truly universal character... I'm writing the modern iteration of a character who has existed for thousands of years."

"I've read The Enemy, it takes place while Reacher is still in the military. The Affair was the next one. It covers the end of Reacher's Military career, and leads into Killing Floor. That's the one I'm reading now. It's the kind of shoot em up books I like.

"How have you been?"

"Same old, same old."

"I wish I could say that. For me every day is different. It's still tender where they sewed my stomach to what was left of my esophagus. Sometimes I start coughing. I don't want to do too much of that or I'll puke. If I eat too much or drink too much the same thing happens. So, every day I learn something new."

I asked Outcast, "How are you feeling now?"

"I go to the doctor next week for a biopsy on my lung tumor. No matter what he says, I'm not going to change my life. I'm still going to smoke, drink beer. I'm not going to be one of those people who drags an oxygen tank around."

Outcast asked Wolf, "Have you seen Irene lately? The last time I saw her she had to be on oxygen for two hours a day. After that she'd go down for a smoke."

"Yeah," said Wolf, "she doesn't come out much since Shark died, but she's looking okay. She has what look like liver spots all over her face. I don't know what that's about. You'd think there would be some treatment. After all the years of drinking, her liver must be in rough shape."

I asked Jacques, "Do you know how long your neighbor will be in jail?"

"She's not in jail, at least yet. She has a restraining order against her boyfriend. That's who she had the fight with. He still comes around. I don't know too much about them."

Wolf said, "You'd think that with all the closed circuit cameras around he'd be spotted. Mind you, I have cameras all through my building. Half of the hookers are banned from entering, so I have to sneak them in the side door. I wonder if it'll make a difference if they totally decriminalize prostitution. With this Bill C-36 the government introduced, there seem to be a lot of grey areas. What the cops do now is pick up a hooker in one part of town and release her in a different neighborhood."

In Ontario, women arrested for offences related to prostitution are placed in a Streetlight Support Services program through the criminal justice system.[48] These women are required to take the program by court order[49] as an alternative sentence to imprisonment or a fine.[50] The program is composed of a one-day class on the subject of choices and an eight-week life skills-based course financed by the proceeds from a john school.

Protest

12 May 2016

"Dennis," said Outcast, "have you come to watch the protest?"

"Who's protesting?"

"Mariah," asked Outcast, "Who's protesting? I forgot."

"Pro-life organized the protest, but Pro-choice is here too. They clashed last night, there were a couple of arrests, that's why there are so many cops. There must be two hundred of them and they're wearing riot gear." By one o'clock RCMP estimated that about 10,000 protesters had gathered."

Outcast said, "If they're down there, they won't be bothering us up here."

Hundreds of pro-choice activists met at Confederation Park and headed down Laurier shouting 'my body, my choice'. Several group members said they hoped to meet up with the anti-abortion walk so that they could have a discussion.

Police officers worked to keep the two groups from coming face-to-face. Officers ran up and down city streets rerouting both sides away from each other.

Gnome rode up on an electric bicycle. He asked Outcast, "Where's Wolf today?"

"He's getting his dentures replaced and a bunch of other things. I didn't pay attention. I don't want to talk about him."

Gnome rode away. Outcast said, "I don't talk to Wolf. I'll be civil to him when he's here, but he screwed me over when he was in hospital. As far as Gnome is concerned, I'd like to punch him in the face, but I'm a lover not a fighter... not even a lover. The mind is willing, but the flesh is limp."

Jacques said, "That's a nice bicycle. I should get me one of those."

Outcast said, "You're to heavy for something like that. You'd never be able to ride it."

Jacques said, "Then maybe one of those motorized wheelchairs. I'd like that."

I said, "Those electric bicycles are expensive aren't they."

Outcast said, "He paid seven hundred, eight hundred with tax. Then he wrecked it and had to pay the insurance deductible of two fifty, so in fact he paid over a thousand.

"Jake isn't here, that probably means that his check didn't arrive. Mine didn't come either. I can't even afford a beer."

Jacques reached in his bag and handed Outcast a can of Molson Blue. "Can you see what's going on down there? I'm facing the wrong direction. If I turn to the left then turn to the right it's like one of those exercise machines."

Anne, R.I.P.

18 May 2016

A pair of Outreach workers in their bright red vests, pushing a sandwich cart, passed me on the way to the park. We greeted each other and shook hands. My friends were munching on sandwiches and wrapped candies. I hugged Mariah and said, "I'm so sorry to hear about Anne's passing. Her daughter must be very upset."

"Yeah, Trudy was here earlier. Of course she was in a drunken stupor, but what can you expect when her mother has just died. Anne is the second person this week who's died, Sharon passed away yesterday. The last time I saw her she was falling down drunk. Her husband said she was continually up and down — sober one day, drunk the next. It finally caught up with her. She died of cirrhosis of the liver."

I asked, "Do you know how Anne died?"

"No, she died at home, we know that. There was no violence, but they're performing an autopsy. When that's been conducted we'll know more about the cause of death."

I said, "I was talking to Bearded Bruce. He said, that she wasn't eating enough."

"You saw Bruce? I'm still pissed with him. Three times he phoned me asking for stuff, then didn't show. I wouldn't have minded so much if I had been around and about, but I was at home and didn't particularly want to leave. When I saw him last, I grabbed that long beard of his and pulled him down to my level. He asked, 'Are you pissed off because I still owe you money?' I said, 'I don't give a shit about the money. I just don't like being dragged out of my house for nothing.' I don't care how big he is, no man frightens me. That's just the way I am."

I asked, "Couldn't he have walked to your place?"

"No, no, he's Mister Big Shot, 'You come to see me.' He won't even come to the park."

Outcast said, "We all know why he won't come to the park. It's because he owes Stella for that landscaping work he didn't do. Toothless Chuck paid her his share, but Bruce is in hiding."

Chris rode up on his bicycle, lay it on the grass and sat on the curb. "Mariah, I want you to tell me what you think of this." He reached into his sock and pulled out a small object wrapped in tinfoil and passed it to Jacques to hand to Mariah. She unwrapped it and sniffed the contents. "It doesn't have much of a smell, it's yellow, maybe Lebanese or Moroccan. I think this is the stuff that bubbles up when you light it. Jacques, put some in your pipe and let's give it a try." The pipe was passed around. Mariah commented, "It's not bad. It's not as good as what I get from my guy. I don't want any more. How much did you pay?"

"Fifteen dollars, but I still owe him five. I'm going to buy a scooter off him. He's not allowed to drive anymore.

"Here comes Ralph. How's it going, Ralph?"

"Not so good. I just came back from hospital. I got forty stitches in my arm from falling down an escalator at the mall. The paramedics were called and took me by ambulance. I'm going to sue the mall for injuries."

Outcast asked, "Were you sober?"

"No, I was drunk as a skunk and high as a kite."

"Don't even bother with a lawsuit. The paramedics would have reported that you had alcohol on your breath. No lawyer would take you on. Even if you represented yourself, the case would be thrown out of court."

Sing with the Angels

20 May 2016

The sun was shining, but a pall of sadness hung over the park like a black cloud. I hadn't seen St. Nick for at least a year, but he was sitting in his walker and gave me a big hug when I arrived at the park. "How have you been, Nick? It's been ages since I saw you last."

"It's just been one bad thing after another. When I left here to live with my family I had cirrhosis of the liver. They put me straight into hospital. I didn't know where I was or what was going on. Eventually they were able to get that under control, then I developed colorectal cancer. I had to have to have two, three-inch sections of my colon removed. I've been staying at the Mission. They arranged for nurses to change my dressings daily. I'd just gotten over an addiction to Dilaudid and Morphine; after the surgery the first thing they did was put me on Morphine. I have it in pump form so I only take it when absolutely necessary for pain. The doctor will tell me next week if there is any change. I'm prone to infections due to immune deficiency.

"I came here to give support to Trudy. I talked to her on the phone yesterday and I know she's taking her mom's death really hard. The three of us used to live in the same house, so it's almost as if she's family. I called her Smiley because she always had a smile on her face.

"I had a hell of a time getting here. My sister gave me a check for two hundred dollars and it bounced at the bank. I was at the teller's counter, trying to get the guy to hurry up because I had a friend waiting outside. I said to him, 'I've been banking here for twenty years. I've never given you a bad check.' He said, 'There are two names on this check. Who are these people?' I said, 'One of them is my sister. I don't know who the other one is.' He said, 'Then you should talk to your sister, because we can't cash this check.'

"I was nearly going out of my mind. I went outside to see Charlie who had driven me to the bank. I told him the problem and said, 'I'm going to that funeral even if I have to hitch hike.' He said, 'Here's a hundred and fifty; pay me when you get back.' I really appreciated that.

"This morning I was going to have breakfast at the Mission, but as soon as I got inside, I had to leave. Once you've been in prison, all institutions seem the same. I saw guys guarding their plates of food. Everyone wore a scowl. I'd just like to go in there and see some gratitude. I know the place; I've worked there as a cook, as part of the staff. I even knew the woman who checked me in."

I saw Trudy walking towards the group. Her head was down, she had lost weight. I held out my arms, she buried her head in my shoulder and sobbed. "It's okay," I said, "let it all out." Following her was her brother and her uncle. I shook hands with them both. I didn't say anything, because words wouldn't convey my feelings. Everyone sat in silence and waited. Nick gave Trudy a twenty for transportation to the funeral home and anything else she may need. He also gave her a ceramic bear. "I've got a cross for you to put on your mom's coffin. That way she'll be looking up at it and she'll also be looking down on you and the rest of us, just as she is right now."

After they left he said, "I know she'll be drunk tonight, but what else is a person to do in a situation like this. I'll see them tomorrow and maybe we can go out for breakfast someplace.

"I attended a funeral last week. The minister said that the deceased would be going to a better place. I said out loud, 'You don't know that.' He said, 'Perhaps you'd like to conduct the ceremony.' So I did. I'm qualified. I placed a cigarette in the coffin, put the guy's guitar in with him and said, 'Go now, brother, and sing with the angels.' "

Memorial Service

24 May 2016

"Hey, it's Dennis!" Mariah shouted.

"Hi Mariah, Outcast."

Mariah said, "We were just saying that lately, fewer and fewer people have been coming here. We were going to wait another half hour, if nobody else showed up we were leaving."

Outcast said, "I know why Jacques isn't here. He's got no money for beer. He hates just sitting here drinking lemonade.

"It's a hard month for all of us because it's five weeks between checks. The government is changing a lot of the rules concerning pensions. I'm going to lose two hundred a month because I'm being cut off the Quebec Pension. I was born there and if I moved back I could collect it again, but I'm not going to bother. I'm settled where I am. If I get kicked out it might be a different story."

I asked, "Does anybody know anything more about Anne. Will there be a funeral service?"

"When I talked to Trudy last," said Outcast, "Anne was going to be cremated. Trudy, her brother and uncle were going to bring the ashes home by plane, then she was returning here."

Mariah said, "She's back already. I talked to her this morning. She's arranged a memorial service at St. Margaret's church down the street for Thursday at one o'clock.

"Here comes Loon. I'm not sure if I want to see him or not. If he's been drinking I won't know a word he's saying."

Loon asked, "Has anyone else been by?"

Mariah said, "Chester was here, but he didn't stay."

"Dammit!" said Loon, "He was supposed to wait for me here."

Mariah said, "He probably forgot."

Outcast said, "He used to be really sharp before he fell down that set of concrete stairs. He was found in a pool of blood at the bottom. He still beats the shit out of me at pool."

Mariah said, "When I play him sometimes he wins, sometimes I win. It depends on who gets to break. I can run the table, so can he. I use to be quite the shark in my day."

I asked, "Loon, have you heard anything lately about Irene?"

"Last I heard she was doing fine."

Outcast said, "I went to see her last week. She's not doing cart wheels, but she's okay. I met her in front of the Mission. She was having a smoke. After that she said she was going to the second floor for two hours of oxygen treatment. Sounds like a waste if she's still smoking."

Mariah said, "I heard that she was moved to the fourth floor. She wouldn't be getting oxygen there."

Outcast asked, "Loon, what happened to that fifty-eight inch tv that Shark had. Where is it? I want first dibs on it."

"Nothing's happened to it. It's in locked storage around the corner from Shark's old apartment. I may keep it myself, after all he was my brother."

Outcast asked,"Don't you already have a fifty-two inch plasma?"

"Yeah, I'm thinking of putting them side by side. Anyway, nothing's been settled. Irene may have something to say about it, if she gets out."

In Loving Memory

Anne was beautiful, gentle, quiet with a gorgeous smile.
fifty-eight years of age, but looked much older -- the street
does that. She would often be seen panning with her daughter
Trudy. Her memorial service was held at St. Margaret's
Anglican Church, a small stone building with a blue piano
outside inscribed 'Play Me I'm Yours.' The English-Inuit
congregation is ministered by Roger Briggs, a former Dean of
St. Jude's Cathedral in Iqaluit. Aigah Attagutsiak, an Inuk,
now serves both Anglican congregations as a licensed Lay
Reader.

The church was packed to capacity. Most of the service was
lost on me since the language used by most of the speakers
was Inuktitut, spoken by Inuit living in the eastern part of the
Canadian Arctic. One woman wailed the entire time, so even
some of the English parts were drowned out. That aside, it was
a very moving ceremony.

Many friends and family gave accounts of their memories
with Anne. Her ex-husband who had remained a close friend
was very emotional. He said, "I can see Anne and her best
friend walking in the clouds, stopping every once in a while
for a drink of wine. That raised a few chuckles. Another friend
recounted, "I remember talking with Anne, we were both half
cut at the time. I had very beautiful teeth back then. Anne said,
'You have false teeth!' I said, 'No I don't and pulled on them
just to show her. She didn't believe me, so she pulled on them
herself. Another time, again we were half cut, she said,
'You've dyed your hair!' I said, 'No I haven't.' I don't know
how we resolved that one."

Anne's son Daniel and brother Christopher also gave brief
presentations and thanked everyone for attending.

After the service the crowd moved to the reception hall, where food and drinks were served. The main topic of conversation was the large number of suicides in northern communities. There are more than a thousand attempted suicide calls each year in Nunavut, a territory of just over thirty thousand people.

The suicide rate for Inuit is eleven times higher than the national average and the majority of deaths by suicide are people under the age of thirty, according to Statistics Canada.

Little Jake in Hospital

31 May 2016

"Dennis," said Outcast, "we haven't seen you since last week."

I said, "Thursday, I was at the memorial service for Anne. Friday, it was too hot."

"Yeah, it was hot alright. We moved back into the shade of the trees. It wasn't too bad there. I saw Little Jake last night."

"Where was he?" I asked. "I haven't seen him in any of his usual spots."

"For the last two weeks he's been in I.C.U. (Intensive Care Unit). Someone from his building found him. He was passed out having a seizure. The guy called the cops and they brought an ambulance. He's been in for two weeks now. Actually, they let him out once, but he was right back in. To get into that place you have to use a telephone and give the first and last name of the person you want to visit. I've known Jake for at least ten years, but I didn't know his last name. Who calls anybody by their last name? I phoned Jacques, Wolf and finally Mariah. She remembered it, a French name, I've forgotten now.

"Anyway, he's in rough shape. He could barely talk they had him so high on meds. Because he was drying out he was hallucinating. I've been through that when I'd been on scotch. I was seeing bugs — it's okay now that I just have a few beers. Jake was seeing spiders all over his walls. He said to me, 'When they open that main door, I can see the zoo. Did you see it?' Like I said, he was in rough shape. Before I left I took a look at the chart at the foot of his bed. They've booked a meeting with his family. That doesn't sound very good. He's only forty-three.

"I didn't see Shark before he passed. I'm glad that I got to see Jake."

Maria said, "When, Louis, my ex was in there, he was seeing all kinds of strange things. It was scary. One time he saw me as some kind of monster and tried to strangle me. I didn't stay around after that."

Outcast said, "Did you hear that they caught the guy who pulled women's pants down in the park. Police laid twenty-seven charges against a twenty-five year old man, including seven counts of sexual assault, eight counts of mischief, eight counts of breach of probation and one count of criminal harassment. He's also to be designated as a dangerous offender which means he may never get out of jail. He's fucked."

Broken Bones

1 June 2016

"Hi Dennis," said Hippo, "How're you doin' "

"Same old, same old. How about you?"

"I broke up with my girlfriend."

"I didn't know you had a girlfriend. Why did you break up?"

"I don't know. She drank a twenty-six ounce bottle of vodka then started beating on me. I held her away and said to her, 'You go your way. I'll go mine.' Before she left she kicked out all the windows in my apartment. Now, I've got an air conditioner with no window to put it in. Six cop cars pulled up outside. I was sober, so there was no problem with the cops, but I'm responsible for replacing the windows. I don't know how I'm going to do that."

Jacques, pushing his walker with a full backpack said to Rhino, "You want this sherry?"

Rhino said, "Sure! Ten bucks?"

"Yeah, you give me the bag of rice and jar of peanut butter. I'll give you five bucks and the sherry."

I was sitting on the grass beside Chris. I said, "I don't know what happened before, but Rhino seems to have gotten a good deal. I wouldn't mind a bottle of sherry and five bucks."

Chester started shouting at Jacques. Since most of it was in French I don't know what that was about, but Chester picked up his plastic crate and moved beside me. He was wearing a neck brace. I asked him, "How is your neck feeling?"

"Sometimes it's good, sometimes not so good. I've been wearing this now for five months."

I asked, "Did you fall? Is that how you injured your neck?"

"Yes, it was on December twenty-ninth. I'd been drinking beer. I was feeling depressed, I take pills for that. I drank a twenty-six ounce bottle of vodka. I started to feel dizzy and was going to lay on my bed. When I got in the bedroom I passed out and hit my head on the dresser. I woke up and saw carpet. I thought to myself, I don't have carpet in my living room. I must be in the bedroom. I got up, walked a few steps and passed out again. When I woke up I dialed nine one one and the ambulance came. They took me out on a stretcher, then to hospital. They did some scans. The doctor said I'd broken two vertebrae in my neck. He said if I'd broken three, I'd be dead. I go back to see him sometime in June. It doesn't seem to be healing properly. If I'm lying in bed I can take the brace off, but if I sit up I feel the compression and pain."

Chris, sitting on the opposite side of me said, "Have a look at this." He rolled up his pant leg, rolled down his sock, where he'd stuffed a twenty and said, "I ran into a bus while on my bike. This bone is broken, but I didn't go to hospital. I put a can of beans in a sock, put it behind the break and pulled on the sock. The broken bone popped back into place. I bet you didn't know that could be done. I haven't even been to a doctor.

"I wasn't drunk at the time. I stay away from vodka and hard liquor. It's too hard on my system. I mix my sherry with apple cider. That makes a real nice drink."

June 2016

Addiction

3 June 2016

"Hi Dennis," said Outcast. "It's only me and Loon today, everybody else had an excuse. Hippo and Mariah were partying at Jacques place and didn't make it home. Hippo doesn't have any windows and Mariah said that her mattress was leaking."

I said, "I've slept on waterbeds before, but I've never owned one."

"She doesn't have a waterbed, she has an air mattress. Have you seen how small her apartment is? The kitchen is larger than her bedroom. When she's not using it she leans the mattress against the wall so she can have some living space. It was probably fat Louie who caused the leak. I told her to go to the hardware store and buy a bicycle tire patch, but she can't find where it's leaking."

I said, "Putting the mattress under water in the bathtub will show her where bubbles are coming out.

"I visited Jake in the hospital yesterday after work. They've moved him from I.C.U. to the 5th floor. His mother, brother and cousin had been by. The nurse had him shaved and bathed, so he probably looked better than when you saw him Sunday."

"I was thinking of maybe taking him outside in a wheelchair. Is he still hooked up to tubes? When I saw him. he had a piss tube, a diaper, an I.V. in one arm and wires hooked up to a machine in the other."

"He's using a catheter and has an I.V. hooked to his arm. The nurse was giving him shit about pulling out the I.V.

because she had a problem locating his veins. I thought she was cute, but he said she's wasn't too bright."

"How about his lips? Are they still dry and scabbed?"

"Yes they are. I don't know why the nurse doesn't apply some kind of lip balm. He's been limited to eating ice chips for the last five weeks. The ice chips are for nausea. The initial symptoms of liver failure are usually nausea, lack of appetite, diarrhea, and exhaustion."

Outcast said, "You saw the fight between Jacques and Chester on Wednesday. Do you know what that was about?"

"No, I heard Chester call Jacques a pervert."

"Yeah, all kinds of things were said. It started four years ago. Jacques had a credit card — why anybody would give him a credit card, I don't know. Anyway, he used it to buy Chester a pair of hundred dollar shoes. Jacques never paid off the credit card, so Chester doesn't figure he owes Jacques the money. Mariah and everybody has explained to Chester that if you borrow money, you pay it back. It doesn't matter where the other person got the money. That fall down the concrete stairs and the booze have really messed up his mind. There's no reasoning with him.

"I remember what it was like when I was heavy into scotch. Each day I'd drink a forty pounder and go through five grams of blow. I was seeing spiders and hallucinating all kinds of things. Now that I'm on beer and weed I don't have that problem.

"Did Jake tell you that he's sworn off sherry?"

"He mentioned that he hadn't had a cigarette in five weeks. I asked if he planned to give them up. He said, 'I'm not saying that I will. I'm not saying that I won't.' "

Outcast said, "That's what people don't understand about addiction. I've got three spots on my lung, but I won't give up smoking. Some things just go together: If I have a beer I need a cigarette, if I smoke weed I need a cigarette, if I do some coke I need a cigarette."

Wolf

6 June 2016

I walked past a park bench and thought I recognized the
man seated. I looked closer and said, "Hi Wolf, I almost didn't
recognize you. You're shaved, you've had a haircut and you
have new teeth."

"Yeah, all that. I've just come from my denturist and now
have upper and lower plates. Having a lower plate is a real
treat. I'm on my way to an appointment with my doctor. It
was supposed to be last week, but that didn't happen. I
haven't been drinking — I did some lines, smoked a lot of
weed, stayed up late. That's the way I am. That's the way it is.
That's not going to change. Anyway, that was last week.
Another thing, I took Shaggy to the spa to be clipped, have her
toe nails done, same as I do every year around this time.

"I still have trouble eating. My favorite food is now a large
egg, scrambled, just one mind you — two would make me
throw up. I have that with a piece of toast about three times a
day. I also take a lot of pills. One of my regulars asked me how
I was feeling. I said, "I feel weak, tired, exhausted. This
woman has never given me money, but she came back with all
kinds of vitamin pills. I even take a greenie, which is
compressed vegetables in pill form.

"The doctor will probably want to do something about my
sinuses. Every night I use one of those Breathe Right Nasal
Strips. That's thirty strips a month — thirty bucks. If I didn't
use them my mouth would get dry. It's especially bad with all
the pills I take, they also cause me to have a dry mouth. I think
that if someone held their hand over my mouth for a long
enough time, I'd suffocate.

"I'm just waiting here for the bus to take me to my doctor
appointment. It's supposed to arrive at about twelve thirty,
give or take five minutes. I hope the driver doesn't give me a

problem with this transfer. I think it should be good. You don't happen to have a couple of bus tickets do you? I didn't get my pass this month and I'd hate to pay an extra three dollars cash for each trip.

"Here comes my bus now. There's Outcast. Outcast, hello!"

Outcast said, "No, I don't say hello to people who ignore me! No, I don't want to hear it and don't follow me!"

Coke

11 June 2016

"Hi," said Outcast into a cell phone, "Do you have any smokes... Yeah, but I didn't want to go into your purse. I'll have to call around. Oh, remember that doctor appointment I had this morning to see about the three spots on my lungs?... Yeah, well I left my brain behind in the waiting room. So what am I going to do?... Another thing, that noose hanging over the balcony, don't use it! I'll be needing it for tomorrow evening.... Yeah, I'll see you later.

"Chester, do you have any smokes?"

"Yeah, I got some."

"Do you have a carton to sell?"

"I have one carton, but I'll be needing them for myself. I can give you a smoke if you want."

Outcast said, "Is it brown or white?"

"It's brown. Do you want it?"

"No, if it was white, I'd trade you (brown refers to native cigarettes that are untaxed by the federal government)."

Cigarette packages with a peach-coloured federal stamp may be sold at authorized duty-free stores. Some on-reserve retailers are also authorized to buy, from authorized wholesalers registered under the Tobacco Tax Act, limited quantities of cigarette packages with a peach-coloured stamp. These packages are to be sold only on reserves to First Nation consumers who are Indians as defined under the federal Indian Act, for their own use.

To Mariah Outcast said, "Did you hear, there's a new noise bylaw. No construction noise before seven in the morning or after ten at night."

"Yeah, they know they're not supposed to start before seven, but if they don't get a complaint, they'll start earlier and earlier. They were at my place at seven yesterday. Today they were there at six forty-five banging around. I opened the door and said, 'Get the fuck out of here! You're blocking my hall, you're blocking access to my trash can and you're leaving your garbage in my yard. So, get the fuck out before I throw you out!' I was so mad I was shaking. He got out quick."

Outcast said, "It's really bad for parents with infants or toddlers. At my place they're using jack hammers. The kids can't get to sleep. They start crying. That keeps the parents up. Next day everybody is in a bad mood. I hear it from my neighbours all the time."

Jacques said, "Did you see it? I think it was a hawk or an eagle. It flew behind that building. Maybe, it'll come round again. There it is!"

Mariah said, "That's an eagle. It's too big for a hawk."

Jacques had filled his plastic drinking bottle with beer. He said, "The beer store has been out of my Old Milwaukee for over a week. I think they did it on purpose. They don't want people like us in there. I checked every day. It was on sale too, a twelve can pack was selling for seventeen forty-seven, usually it's twenty-two seventy-five and that's five and a half per cent alcohol. Five dollars is a big saving."

In his haste to see the hawk he dropped his bottle. It rolled and foamed until he was able to grab it and stop the flow with his mouth.

People wearing red tee shirts appeared from every direction. The annual March for Life demonstration took over downtown as activists protested not only abortion, but also doctor-assisted dying. We heard loud speakers advising where buses were waiting to take the protesters to their destination.

Outcast said, "I can see why some people are against abortion. I don't have an opinion one way or another. I'm never going to get pregnant. What's the objection to doctor-assisted dying. I've told my kids and family that if I'm ever on life support Do Not Resuscitate. I've filled in all the forms."

Michel said to Outcast, "I've been having trouble breathing lately. I'm wondering if it's allergies. Do you have a problem with allergies?"

Outcast said, "My nasal passages are fucked from using coke. I was a snorter."

Michel asked, "Did you ever inject it?"

"No, the only needles I've ever had were from nurses in the hospital."

Where's the Weed?

16 June 2016

"Dennis," said Wolf, "here's a blanket, sit yourself down. That's my blanket not Shaggy's. It was cold this morning, I had to wrap my legs with something, otherwise I'd have had to go home. I didn't work the first three days of this week so I figured I'd better get out. Of course I wanted to see my friends, Jacques and Outcast. Also, I'm out of weed.

"As you can see, I started smoking cigarettes today. I was off them for nearly six months. Old habits die hard. That reminds me, I paid twenty bucks for a hooker the other night. I wanted a blow job, but couldn't get a hard on. This is her tee shirt I'm wearing."

Outcast said, "Is it the hooker I'm thinking of, the one I've seen you with before. I wouldn't be able to get a hard on either."

I asked Wolf, "How is your eating?"

"So, so. I tried to eat two scrambled eggs this morning and about half an egg came back up. I knew I should have only tried one, but I was hungry and I was going out to work. So, in total, I had one and a half eggs and two slices of toast. I'm never going to gain weight. See how skinny my legs are? I'm down to a hundred and fifteen pounds.

"When I'm down here and my friends are drinking I have to have a drink or some weed. That's just the way I am. I found this Vox vodka, the same color as the old Listerine we used to drink. It even makes me burp. That's a good thing. I remember forty years ago — I was in bad shape then, worse than Little Jake — a buddy and me were drinking in an alcove, or an entrance way, just down the street. A cop came along and grabbed our bottle. He said, 'This stuff isn't for drinking, it's for rinsing your mouth.' I started drinking when I was twelve so that's forty-six years. Can you imagine that? It's no wonder I can't quit."

Outcast said, "I was the same age when I started, so for me it's forty-two years."

I asked, "How are you feeling Outcast?"

"Not so good. The doctor found another spot on my lung. That's four in total. I won't be able to get it checked until September. I said to him, "What's the point of telling me now?

I've got all summer to stew over it before I get the results.' It doesn't really matter, I'm still smoking. I can't quit that.

"Hippo is homeless again. He has to be out of his apartment by next Tuesday. It must be because his girlfriend kicked out the windows. You should see that place, he's got holes in the walls. The kitchen is ripped out. It'll cost a couple of grand to make it liveable again. It's no wonder they want him out. If he'd used his head, he probably could have worked out an arrangement with the landlord to pay for the damages.

"Jacques, let me use your phone. I got a phone number for a guy at the Mission who may be able to get us some weed. He's usually there from eight in the morning until noon.

"Hello, is this Q? I can barely hear you. Where are you now? That's no good. Thanks anyway old friend.

"He's in the west end, he won't be coming downtown. Is Buck coming down, or Mariah? She has good weed. What about Gnome, he lives near the Mission. He's in the same building that Jacques used to be in. Remember, Jacques, that place with the tiny balcony where we had six people standing. He lives in the basement. It's too bad that Roller Blades isn't around."

Wolf said, "He phoned me from prison. As soon as the operator asked if I would accept charges for a call from Millhaven I knew who it was. He was always grinding me. I took the call. He wanted me to make five phone calls for him. There's no way I was going to do that. If he wants to be a drug dealer, make a thousand bucks on a good day and risk going to prison, that's his choice. I choose to panhandle for a few hours each day and collect enough cash to enjoy myself. He's the one that broke my jaw a few years ago. The next time he called, I didn't answer."

Dancer

"Eighty-nine cents a pound," said Jacques, "that's the best price for chicken legs. It's at Walmart. They open each morning at seven, so I'll be there fifteen minutes early and stand in line. There's something else. They have ice cream sandwiches, the kind I like, for three ninety-seven. That's for twelve."

Outcast said, "You're wrong, Jacques, you keep saying it's for twelve, but it's for eight. You keep getting it wrong."

Jacques said, "You've been trying to start a fight with me all morning. Why is that?"

"It's probably because we started drinking at nine instead of ten."

Mariah said, "It's the same with my Louis. When he drinks he wants to fight. Yesterday he started getting ornery. I said to him. 'Are you really sure you want to do this. You hit me, you're out the door. Do you remember last time?' 'Yeah,' he said, 'I remember.' He sat down and was good after that. He knows that I'd punch him in the face if he tried anything. I don't fight like a girl. I prefer to fight a man."

I said, "Women are probably more vicious. Is that it?"

"Yeah, it's scratching and hair pulling. I don't go in for that shit.

"It's just two weeks until Margarita time."

"What is the occasion."

"July first is my birthday. I was a Canada Day baby. My mother used to say that the fireworks were to celebrate my birthday. On that day I don't do any dishes or cooking. I get taken out to eat and I have my Margaritas."

Outcast asked, "So, Mariah, how old will you be? Is this the big six five coming up?"

"No, I was born in 1955, so you figure it out."

Outcast said, "When I was born you were already pole dancing."

I asked, "Were you a dancer?"

"Yeah, for twenty years. It worked out well when I was bringing up my son. I could pick my own hours and be home when he got back from school. The first club I worked at was in Oshawa. They were really strict, no drinking, no drugs in the club. I didn't mind that. When I was off work I could do anything I wanted. They paid us in tickets. At the end of the week we'd cash in the tickets and a guy would give me an envelope. In it were four browns (hundred dollar bills) and another envelope (cocaine) for me. He also had two tequilas waiting. He said, 'These should calm you down a bit.' I lost that job for punching a customer in the face... he pushed his finger up my twat!

"Then I moved to Montreal. We didn't get a salary just tips. I could make a couple of hundred a night doing stage and table dances. That was before lap dancing came in. It changed after that."

Can you fly?

23 June 2016

Joe looked contented sitting in his walker, in the shade of a tree, listening to a blues band playing in the park. One of his regulars said to him, "Joe, you've got the best job ever, perfect weather, beautiful women walking past and you're listening to great music. How do I get a job like yours?" He bent down and put a two dollar coin in the paper cup at Joe's feet.

"You're right," said Joe. To me he said, "I like to watch the women, but that's all. I'm sixty-eight years old. I've been married three times, twice to doctors and once to a nurse. My daughter is now a nurse. She lives in Vancouver and keeps saying to me. 'Daddy, you should come here and live with us. I could take care of you.' I like to visit them, but I don't want anybody taking care of me. I take care of myself. I've been on this bridge for ten years. A couple of guys tried to set up close to me. I asked one of them, 'Can you fly? Can you swim?' I grabbed him by the scruff of his neck and the seat of his pants and threw him over the railing. The other one ran away."

A man and woman in military uniforms walked past and waved to Joe. "I've known those two for a long time. They're both in special forces. They do a lot of spy work for the army. They travel all over the world.

"I've got a granddaughter in Vancouver. She's eight years old. Every month I send her a thousand dollars. When she's eighteen it'll pay for her education. I've been doing that since she was born. I don't need much. I stay at a hospice, one room with a hospital bed. It has those buttons to raise, lower or tilt the mattress. There is a nurse who checks on me. I'm allowed three beer a day, because I'm alcoholic. She labels my bottles. I asked her, 'Why do you do that? I'm the only one who uses that fridge.' She said, 'It's our policy and you may want to drink these outdoors.' I said, 'If I wanted beer outside, I'd buy it outside.' I have special food in there as well. I have a lot of allergies, diabetes and other medical issues.

"I told her that I'd be coming in late tonight. One time I was visiting a lady friend and I stayed away three days. We were watching the news on TV and saw my picture. The announcer said, 'If anyone has information about this man, please call the station. He uses a walker, is bald and was last seen wearing a red shirt. He's been reported missing by medical staff.' We laughed at that, but now I always leave a note if I'm going to be away.

"I use the walker because of Parkinson's and because of my knee. The plastic has worn away and it gets stiff on me. I also have diabetes. I'm thinking of getting one of those electric wheelchairs. They're so expensive. They range in price from twenty-two hundred to twenty-six hundred. If I hold off sending money to my granddaughter for a few months I can put that towards a wheelchair.

"My mother left me a lot of money, but I only use it for special circumstances, like if I fly to Vancouver. I have ten brothers and six sisters. When my mother was sick in hospital not one of them came to visit her. When she died I made all the arrangements and none of them came to the funeral, so I don't have anything to do with them any more.

"Do you have the day off?"

"No," I said, "I work in that tall building over there. I'm on my lunch hour. I'll have to head back soon." I reached into my pocket to check my watch. It read twelve fifty.

"You carry your watch in your pocket just like I do. I've had this a long time. It never needs batteries, it's self-winding. As long as I'm active, it keeps running. It tells the time, the day of the week, the date, has a compass and an alarm that can be set. Unlimited is etched on the back. I got it from a guy who wanted to borrow fifty bucks. I said to him, 'Leave me your watch and your wallet, take your identification out. I'll return them when you pay back the money.' He never came back. I checked the wallet and although it looked empty, I found a secret compartment with a fifty dollar bill bill tucked out of sight. So, I got the watch and my fifty bucks."

She Bit Me

As I was approaching the group in the park I heard Little Jake yell, "Dennis, how've you been, man. I haven't seen you since I was in hospital."

Outcast said, "Jake, do you remember what you told us in the hospital, that there was a zoo in the waiting room?"

"Yeah, I saw kitties and tigers. The kitties were cute and cuddly, but the tigers...ROAR. I thought they were going to claw me to pieces. My arm was strapped to the bed, because I was flailing about trying to fend off the tigers. I thought it was just a wire that I could undo with my free hand. A couple of weeks later I realized that it was some kind of black nylon double zip tie that the police use for handcuffs."

I said, "You had some cute nurses."

"Yeah, I was scared of them at first. I thought they were going to gouge me and take my internal organs."

Outcast said, "Jake, Remember in the hospital you said you were never going to drink wine again?"

I asked, "How long did that resolution last?"

Jake laughed and said, "Until the day I got out of hospital."

Mariah said, "Frank still has to build up his strength. When I saw him in the hospital he was just skin and bones. I've been telling him to eat molasses. Blackstrap molasses contains vital vitamins and minerals, such as iron, calcium, magnesium, vitamin B6, and selenium. Frank bruises easily. That's usually a sign of anemia — a condition where your body doesn't have enough red blood cells — he often feels tired and weak. One type of anemia is caused by a lack of iron in the diet.

Blackstrap molasses is a good source of iron. About five tablespoons of molasses contains ninety-five percent of your daily allowance of iron. I keep telling him to eat lots of bananas for the potassium. I had to learn that stuff when I hit bottom as a crack addict. I had infection in my ears and when I finally went to the doctor he said that without medication, I had about twenty-four hours to live.

"I don't know if you know it, but Weasel proposed to me. I knew that I had to get away from Louis because he would get so violent with his PTSD. I said yes to Weasel because then I'd be committed. I wouldn't be able to go back to Louis. It was a rough time. If I drank like these guys I'd be dead. I dilute my vodka with water and only take small sips at a time. A twenty-six ounce bottle will last me a week."

Wolf shouted, "Dennis, don't you see what's going on. You've been ignoring Shaggy and she's getting upset. You're not doing your job." I turned to pat Shaggy and scratch her around the ears."That's better, now she wants a treat. Look at her she's trying to get right into the bag. Here girl, this is what you're after?" Wolf handed her the bacon flavored dog treat. She chomped the treat as well as Wolf's finger. "Did you see that, she bit me."

"Shaggy," I said, "you shouldn't bite the hand that feeds you. That's an official doggy rule."

Wolf said, "It's not that bad. She didn't draw blood like she does sometimes."

Bologna Stew

27 July 2016

The regular group was at the park. Jacques handed me a tarp. I sat beside Theodore — bushy beard, baseball cap and a teardrop tattoo below his left eye.

> *The teardrop tattoo or tear tattoo is a symbolic tattoo of a tear that is placed underneath the eye. The tattoo can have various meanings: it can signify that the wearer has killed someone[1] or has spent time in prison; that the wearer was raped while incarcerated or it can acknowledge the loss of a family or fellow gang member. Sometimes, only the wearer will know the exact meaning of the tattoo.*

I didn't ask him the meaning of the tattoo.

He immediately started talking, "Hi, man, great weather, eh? We got a nice breeze here. It's hot in the sun. I'll be going back out there later with my paper cup, but now I'm enjoying it here. Some nights, I sleep across the street at the heater. Last night I slept by that tree over there. It's cool in the shade. When the sun moves, I move. They don't piss there, that's further down."

I said, "The park workers don't know that. Last week a guy wearing a construction vest was sleeping there. Mariah walked up to him and said. 'Hey, man, I thought I should tell you that you're lying in a place where a lot of the guys piss. The reason is that between this brick wall and the bushes there's a bit of privacy. You're okay further down, but suit yourself.' The guy packed up and walked away."

Jacques handed me a copy of the Metro newspaper. He asked, "Do you want to read this? It has all the flyers in it. They've got packages of bacon on sale for four ninety-nine."

I asked, "Do you still make your bacon stew? Joy said you used to make that."

"No, I have to be careful what I eat because of my heart. I'm supposed to cut out animal fat."

Theodore asked, "Have you ever tasted bologna stew? It's really good, My mom used to make it for me when I was a kid:

Newfoundland Bologna Stew:

Ingredients:-
1 lb. bologna, thickly sliced and cut in quarters
Salt and Pepper to taste
1 medium onion sliced
some celery, diced
Carrot, Turnip and Potatoes; cut as for any stew.
Water
2 to 3 tablespoons ketchup (optional)

Method:-
Fry bologna until lightly browned. Place in a pot and add salt, pepper, and vegetables.

Add enough water to just cover. Let boil slowly until vegetables are tender.

Add ketchup, if desired, for flavour and colour.

Thicken slightly with flour and water OR cornstarch and water.

"That's my lunch over there, in the bag tied to the fence rail. I want to keep it away from the ants. Yesterday, I left the bag on the ground and when I went to eat my sandwiches, they were covered in ants. I had to throw the bag into the trash container. I don't eat ants."

I asked, "What do you have for lunch today?"

"I've got three sandwiches, tuna, egg and ham. I've also got a container of pudding. Do you want a sandwich?"

"No," I said, "but thanks anyway. I've just eaten my lunch." I remembered that, this being Wednesday, the Innercity Ministries would have stopped by with their sandwich cart.

Theodore continued, "Did you hear that Hippo ripped off Wolf again for his last thirteen bucks. He was supposed to meet Wolf across the river with a pack of smokes and three cans of beer. He didn't show. Wolf is really pissed off. You don't treat a friend like that."

I said, "I remember the last time he did that he went into hiding for about two weeks. When he showed his face again he apologised and said, 'I'm sorry, Wolf, I fucked up'. Wolf said, 'You're damned right you fucked up. That's serious shit, man. We're family. You don't treat family like that. Now fuck off.' Nobody trusted him for a long time after that."

Theodore said, "If he keeps ripping people off he's going to get into big trouble; like, buried under the ground trouble."

Finish the job you started…

28 July 2016

The park was much the same as usual and the usual gang was there. Theodore was asleep on the cedar chips between the wall and the grass. Mariah said, "He says he sleeps there because he's out of range of the sprinklers that turn on every so often." She handed me a plastic crate with a folded newspaper on which to sit.

"Thanks, Mariah, I'm really being treated in style."

I asked her how her day was going. She said, "Don't even ask. It started at six thirty this morning and never quit. Just don't ask."

I asked Wolf, "What books are you reading now?"

"A lady gave me some of those Spencer and Hawk books, the ones we like. I can't remember the name of the author (Robert B. Parker). You know the ones I mean — easy reading. Apart from that I got a good bill of health from my doctor. I weigh a hundred and fifteen pounds. He asked me, 'How many meals do you eat a day? five?' I said, 'It's more like ten.' For breakfast I had one egg. I'm not supposed to eat heavy bread like rye or pumpernickel. It's too hard to digest. If I eat any bread it should be toasted. I'm stuck with that for the rest of my life. Donuts are a no-no. That's what I used to look forward to on Sundays. I've cut my smoking back to about five a day. I don't buy them I just bum one every so often."

Loon threw over a lighter. He said, "There's not much fuel left. You should use it soon."

Outcast said, "Loon will sell you a cigarette for 60 cents. He's even got the white ones."

Wolf said, "What are you guys talking about. Did I ask for a cigarette? If I wanted a cigarette, I'd ask for one. I don't even want your damned lighter." He threw it back to Loon.

To me he said, "Now where was I? Oh yeah, I've been drinking these little bottles of Vox vodka. I like the blue color. After about four of these, I still feel fine. Yesterday, Blaine stopped by with a bottle of sherry and asked me if I wanted a drink. We were sitting right on the sidewalk. I said, 'Sure!' and I took a big swig. Later he asked me if I wanted another — well, you know how I am. I said, 'Sure, I'll have another.' So, by the time I got here I was fairly wasted."

Outcast said, "I heard a joke today: I've got Alzheimer's and Parkinson's, but I forget to shake."

Loon said, "That's not a very nice thing to say."

"What!" said Outcast, "It was a joke. Nobody around here has Alzheimer's or Parkinson's. At least, not that I know of.

"Okay, it was a bad joke. I'll remember not to repeat it again." Shaggy started barking. Wolf said to me, "You started scratching her and then you stopped. She didn't give you permission to stop. Now, finish the job you started."

Daytona 2008

29 July 2016

For the past three days Theodore has been wearing the same Daytona 2008 tee shirt. It certainly had eight years worth of cigarette burns. We met on the sidewalk as I was walking to the park. "Hi, Dennis," he said, "they're all up there, a few of them at least. It's payday so some aren't around."

"Thanks, Theodore, maybe I'll see you up there."

I sat next to Little Jake on a blue tarp that was spread on the grass. Mariah handed me a cushion. She was seated in Jacques' walker. I said, "I just saw Theodore heading west."

Mariah said, "He just got a call on his cell phone and said, 'I have to head to Chinatown.' so it must have been good news. I've been trying to call Wolf but he's not answering."

Outcast said, "He's probably high. His check was deposited in his bank account at midnight. I'm guessing that he's been stoned since twelve fifteen."

"Dennis," said Little Jake, "take a look at what I'm drinking. It's Bacardi with iced tea. Do you want a gulp?"

I said, "No thanks, not right now. Is that better for you?"

Mariah said, "Oh yeah, sherry will rip your guts out. That's why I drink vodka."

Jake said, "The only problem with iced tea is that it's so damned good. I'm going to be drunk in no time. Maybe I should have bought Coke. I guess what I could do is buy another iced tea and dilute what I got in this bottle. That would work.

"I may visit with my family this weekend. My brother's going up there but I can never get hold of him. When I try to call him on a pay phone. I'm told that it's a long distance call, because he hasn't changed his phone plan since he left Winnipeg. He delivers for the post office, so he gets off work at about three. I could call him on my landline at home. If I had his phone number with me I could call from here on somebody's cell phone. Maybe he'll drop by my place. It doesn't matter. It's not that important.

"Since my mom died, he's doing some repair work on her house. I signed my share over to him.

"Do you know what?"

"What, Jake?" I replied.

"I lost my wallet."

"What did you have in it?"

"Just identification. I don't need it right away. It was just a thin wallet. Maybe it is in the shirt I was wearing yesterday. I felt something stiff, maybe it was my wallet."

Jacques said, "I just felt something drop on me."

Outcast asked, "Is it white?"

August 2016

Shaggy

"Dennis have a look at this," said Wolf. "Shaggy's got a boo-boo. This morning I found her licking her hip. There was a red spot the size of a dime. When I got out of the shower it was the size of a quarter. At my corner people had all kinds of theories as to what it was. Some said it was caused by a tick that she chewed off, others said it looked like a spider bite. I've got a plastic collar for her — she hates it. Any time I'm not nearby I'll put it on her. It's going to mean a trip to the vet. That's going to cost me."

Outcast said, "It's too bad the Bondi Vet isn't closer."

Wolf said, "Do you watch that program? It's amazing the operations that guy can perform. He could probably cure her limp as well. That's what fourteen years brings on. She's an old dog.

"By the way, did you hear Donald Trump's criticism about the Muslim parents of a slain American soldier? That's an all time low. I support all vets and their families, especially those who have lost loved ones. My son is a vet. I don't know where he is now, but I'm proud of him."

Outcast said, "I'll be scared if Hillary Clinton becomes president, but there's no alternative. Trump called her a devil, but they're both devils."

Little Jake ambled up the hill and joined the group. "I was just talking to Bearded Bruce. He still doesn't have the twenty he owes me.

"Now Loretta's under sixty days house arrest. She has to wear one of those electronic ankle bracelets. The maximum range of is three thousand feet from the base unit. I think it was because she had some assault charges against her. She's a feisty one when she drinks. Bruce has taken on a lot, but now he has a way of controlling her — if she wants beer, he's the one who has to get it.

"Wolf, did Hippo pay you the money he owed you?"

"No and I don't expect to see it. Three days after payday he was broke."

Outcast said, "His worker was looking for him yesterday. She has an apartment viewing lined up. I can't see that working out — the apartment is above a family with little kids. Can you imagine Hippo stomping up the stairs, putting his fist through walls and kicking out windows. He's not a neighbor that I'd like to have."

Fumigating

3 August 2016

"Dennis," said Jacques as he handed me a folded, blue tarp, "here's something to sit on."

Outcast said to me, "I tried to phone Wolf this morning, but he didn't pick up his phone. I wanted to ask him how Shaggy was recuperating after her appointment with the vet yesterday. I was also curious to know what caused that sore on her hip. He's probably got that plastic cone around her neck, so she wouldn't be very sociable today."

Theodore said, "I had to be out of my apartment this morning at eight. They were fumigating for bed bugs. I was up all night preparing for them. They didn't give us much notice.

Bed Bug Fumigation Preparation (Structural Fumigation):

1) Bring as few items as possible when leaving the residence, fumigate everything possible. Bed bugs are known hitch hikers and can harbor in suitcases, backpacks, boxes, clothing, bedding and pet cages. This is the most common way they are being introduced into buildings. They have even been known to infest small electronic devices.

2) For all fabric items that will not be fumigated, wash in hot water and dry on high heat in a dryer, no less than 140 degrees, before moving back into the residence. This includes any clothing, bedding, pillows, stuffed toys and pet bedding.

3) DO NOT use boxes, suitcases, backpacks, gym bags or any similar items from the infested residence/dwelling, to pack the items that will remain with you. The items you take with you should be packed into a light colored or clear box or bags that have not been stored into the infested residence/dwelling.

4) DO NOT fumigate anything that requires oxygen to breathe such as plants and animals.

5) Medicinal items need to be removed, especially if they are over-the-counter medications. Prescription medications, while commonly distributed in airtight containers, should also be inspected then removed from structure/property for safety's sake. Precautionary step.

6) You can fumigate all topical toiletries; however, toothpaste and mouthwash need to be removed as they can be ingested in their use. Precautionary step.

7) All items that are open and digestible need to be fumigated and discarded after fumigation this is done to ensure that bed bugs are not spread by simply tossing out the items. This includes items in the refrigerator, freezer and pantry.

8) Baby mattresses or plastic encased mattresses that have been fumigated CANNOT be placed back into the home. If the encasement can be removed, we can fumigate the mattress and you can place it back into your home.

9) Pet Cages and bedding should be included in your fumigated items. Pet cages can contain small gaps in which bed bugs could harbor. Pet food needs to be removed. Your pet needs to be transported in a new pet carrier or placed in a bed bug free housing prior to the fumigation. The pets bedding should not accompany the pet unless it has been washed, dried and packed as previously described.

10) Use cardboard boxes when packing for the fumigation. DO NOT use plastic crates or containers. The fumigant cannot penetrate the plastic.

11) We require 20% of air space when loading the container/truck to ensure proper circulation of the fumigant.

12) Be sure you have your pest control operator apply an intense, residual application of the residence prior to moving back in. The gas will kill all stages of the bed bug in the stored items, however it provides no residual and therefore no permanent control or continuous protection and the items fumigated could be subject to infestation. Please have the pest control operator treat the premise with a long lasting residual application.

Theodore continued, "When everybody was out they drilled a hole and blasted the chemical into the building. We aren't allowed back until noon which is about now."

Outcast said, "Theodore, I hope you covered your bed before you left."

"I don't have a bed."

Outcast said, "They say you can go back in after four hours, but with my lungs I'd wait six. That's a powerful chemical they use." He then began coughing. "This is what cancer and asbestosis will do to you." Jacques handed him a small stainless steel pot pipe and said, "Have some of this. It will fix you up."

"Thanks, Jacques," he said, then began a renewed coughing fit.

Jacques said, "The problem with fumigating is it only kills the bugs that are in the apartment. The bugs also attach themselves to animals. When people bring their dogs and other pets back in they're also bringing the bugs. Even if you have some on your pant leg it only takes a couple to create a whole nest of them."

Outcast said, "Also, it doesn't get the ones in books or behind the walls. They fumigated our building for cockroaches. It got rid of them, but when they started jack hammering at the building next door the roaches came to our place.

"Jacques, remember when we were living at the Central Towers? There were three thousand people under Ontario Housing staying in that building. It was all single rooms, so they could pack in a lot of people. Tenant rent is based on income. Tenants pay their share of the rent directly to the landlord, and the Rent Supplement Office pays the balance directly to the landlord. We'd get our checks on the fifteenth and at the end of the month. Can you imagine how many people would be hanging around the lobby waiting for the mailman to bring their checks?

"That building was full of bed bugs and roaches. I had white tile floors. One night I came home, turned the light on, the floor was black with bugs. What they did was gut the whole place leaving just the shell. Then they rebuilt from the ground up. Of course, that left us with nowhere to live. I think it's all condos now."

Jacques said, "I like where I'm living now. It faces north so I never get the sun shining on my windows to make it hot."

Outcast said, "Yeah, Jacques, you have also have a great view of another building."

Jacques said, "I think I'm going to hire a contractor to blow the top off that building, then I'll have a nice view."

Hippo

9 August 2016

From a distance I recognized Hippo standing bedside a group in the shade. "Hippo," I said, "I haven't seen you in ages. How are you doing?"

"Hi, Dennis, I'm sleeping outside again. This morning I was shoeless. I had this cheap pair of flip flops, but a guy grabbed them, 'cause I'd stolen, or borrowed them from him. In my bare feet I walked to the baseball diamond. This guy came up to me and asked, 'You're not a cop are you?' I said, 'No, I'm not a cop.' He brought out a joint and we shared it. He said, 'Wait here a couple of minutes. I've got something for you.' He went away and came back with these nice sandals. When I came to the park Jacques had these sneakers for me."

I asked, "How do they fit?"

He said, "Well, it took me about three hours to get them on. These are size ten and I take a twelve, but they're better than nothing. Do you have a smoke?"

Outcast said, "Hippo, you know that Dennis doesn't smoke."

Loon threw him a cigarette.

"Jake," said Hippo, "give me a drink."

"Fuck off, man." replied Jake, " I don't have anything, so keep out of my face."

Hippo said, "I filled your bottle twice yesterday."

Outcast said, "Hippo, yesterday is yesterday, this is today. You can see that Frank's bottle is empty. He can't give you what he doesn't have. Why don't you go out and pan for a while. That's what Jake did."

"I don't pan."

Outcast said, "Neither do I. I've tried it but people say, 'You're too well dressed,' or 'You're too fat,' or 'You're too good looking.' What can I do?"

Hippo said, "I can't leave here because my worker is coming here to see me. Hopefully, she has keys to my new apartment. It's furnished; I don't have to buy a thing. The people who were there before were evicted for not paying their rent, so all their furniture was confiscated. I'm not going to use the bed that's there. I have my furniture in storage and my papers and stuff are at my mom's place. I've got a thousand dollar mattress that I got from a guy at my old building. It's about two feet thick. He was going to throw it out. He'd only used it for about six months, so I asked him if I could have it. He said, 'Sure.' So, I'm all fixed up."

I asked, "Do you have a television?"

He said, "No, I don't believe in them. I watch the odd movie, but I go to the theater. I've got a radio. That's all I need."

Jacques turned on his antique looking radio. Jake said, "Turn it up, I like that song."

Jacques said, "You may like it, but I don't think Hippo does. If I turn it up too loud we can't hear each other talk."

"Damn it, I hate waiting," said Hippo. "Buck was supposed to come here with some money and smokes. My worker was supposed to come with my keys. **FUCK!**" He picked up his backpack and stormed off." Five minutes later his worker arrived.

Outcast said, "You just missed him. He walked up the hill."

She asked, "Was it long ago? Do you think I can catch him? Is it worth trying?"

I said, "He was walking slow. At the top of the hill you'll probably see him."

Outcast said, "I don't think it's worth chasing him. I wouldn't bother."

Jacques said, "That Hippo, I heard that he got six hundred bucks from someone. He never came around then. He comes here when he has nothing and bums from us. That's not right."

Court Appearances

19 August 2016

"Dennis," said Jacques, "I have a crate with a tarp for you. Have a seat. You'll be sitting in style today."

"Thanks, Jacques, I appreciate that."

Wolf said, "Dennis, I'm so glad to see you. A lot has been happening, most of it bad. I've been charged with cruelty to Shaggy. The cops came to my door and handed me a ticket. The ticket read, that I wilfully caused unnecessary pain, suffering, injury or death to an animal. I cried when they said that. You know me, Shaggy has been with me for fourteen years. There's no way that I'd hurt her in any way. The SPCA was there as well. In their instructions it said to only approach the owner with a police escort. That's because I yelled at them and tore the ticket up the last time they came.

"Apparently there are two witnesses, one from my building and one from downtown. One said that I ran over Shaggy with her cart. She jumped out while she was riding in it, but I didn't run over her. The other woman said that I kicked Shaggy up the ramp to the apartment building entrance. I didn't do that. I may have nudged her with my foot because she's fourteen years old. Sometimes she doesn't want to move.

"This is my second charge. I went to court last Spring. I brought my mental health worker with me. One witness said I was rough putting Shaggy in her cart. The other said that she thought she saw me kicking her, but she wasn't sure. When they asked me I said, 'I was drunk. I don't know what happened.' The judge said, 'We have two witnesses who don't know each other and have no reason to lie. You say you can't remember because you were drunk. The only judgement I can reach is guilty. You'll have to pay a three hundred dollar fine over the period of one year.' So, here we go all over again."

Little Jake asked, "Did you hear what happened to me? I was panning in front of the pharmacy. This fat woman panhandler told me to move. Lots of people pan there. It's not her spot, so I waved her away and said, 'Fuck off, get out of my face. Anyone can pan here.' That was one day. The next day when she saw me she flagged down a cop. She said that I had verbally assaulted her then stood up and kicked her in the stomach. I didn't lay a finger on her. Now I have to go to court. Can you imagine that, a panhandler calling the cops on another panhandler. That's just wrong."

Outcast said, "Well I'm homeless again. Debbie and I haven't been getting along so well lately. Her daughter is pregnant and wants to move in. They got together and wrote a really nasty letter about me and sent it to the Housing Authority. I'm fucked."

Wolf said, "I told you about the problems I'm having with my stomach, or the part of my stomach I have left after the surgery. This is the first beer I've had since Saturday. I can't smoke because if I start coughing I'll throw up. I can eat a May West cake coated with chocolate. The other day I had some chicken and the most delicious ice cream. It comes in packages of six assorted flavors. I know I can't eat the vanilla fudge chunk, but this one had bits of caramel in it. I thought I'd be okay, but after an hour I started getting these intense pains. I put up with them for another half hour then I had to go to the bathroom to ralph it, but the taste of that ice cream was worth all the discomfort that came later. Next time, I'll just eat half a container, maybe I'll be able to keep that down. Each day I try something different. I know I can eat flaky stuff, but I don't like flaky stuff. I want donuts."

The Sally

23 August 2016

As I walked toward the park, Loon staggered towards me. "Hi Dennis," he said as he shook my hand. With no teeth he mumbled something I couldn't understand. After three tries I gathered that he was saying, "Hippo and Outcast are up there. I bought beer and vodka. Now, nobody will even give me a drink."

Outcast stood and offered me the crate on which he was sitting. He said, "You're only going to be here a short time. I can stand." He wouldn't take no for an answer. He said, "I have to get home soon anyway to guard my groceries."

I asked, Does that mean that you and Debbie are back together?"

"No, I'm sleeping on Big Chester's couch — not the guy from Newfoundland. I got a big bag of groceries yesterday from the Food Bank. I said to him, 'I'm going to take a nap. Don't eat all the treats. We'll share them later.' When I woke up he'd eaten all the cookies, chips and candies. I was pissed. I said, 'Jesus Christ, you could have left something for me! After all, I got the stuff.' I cooked him a nice omelette with veggies on the side."

I said, "Joy had the same complaint when she was staying with him. Has he still got bed bugs?"

"No, I wouldn't be staying there if he had."

I asked Hippo, "How are things going with your worker. Has she found you a place yet?"

"Yeah, I'm just waiting for the keys. They have to change the locks and do some other things, but I should be able to move in this week. It's five seventy-nine a month, more than I was paying at my last place. I hope it doesn't have electric heat. That would be expensive."

Outcast said, "Your worker was by this morning. I didn't tell her that you were at the police station being fingerprinted. I didn't know if you'd want her to have that information."

"It's okay. She knew where I went. I told her."

I asked, "What were you being fingerprinted for?"

"It's because I had this bicycle lock that curls up. I was trying to pull it off my bike and it slipped out of my hand, crashing through the window of the apartment behind me. They have it all on closed circuit TV. I don't know what the judge is going to say. I may have to pay a fine. I may go to jail."

I said, "If it was an accident, I can't see you going to jail."

Outcast said, "No, you're not going to jail."

I asked Hippo, "Where are you staying now?"

"I'm at the Sally, but I'm not getting much sleep. The guy in the bunk above me tosses and turns all night, all I hear is creak, creak, creak, creak, creak."

Outcast said, "You two are a good match. You snore like a chainsaw, he makes the bed creak."

"Yeah, I snore like a Husqvarna, roarrrr, roarrrr, roarrrr.

"I ate breakfast there this morning. A giant cockroach climbed onto my table and was heading toward my sausage. I slammed him with my fist. Pow! A guy behind the counter yelled, 'What's all that banging about?' I yelled back at him, 'I just killed a big mother fuckin' roach! D'ya wanna see it? I should call the Health Department!' That shut him up."

Louis wandered up. He was meeting Mariah at one. Outcast said, "So, Louis, how's the new job working out."

"Good, I'm doing landscaping. For the first couple of hours we sat waiting for supplies. My first job was raking cedar chips. I thought to myself, for fourteen seventy-five an hour, I can do this."

October 2016

BROKE BUT SEXY

28 October 2016

Overnight snow had turned to rain. Sidewalks were slushy and I was wearing my awkward, heavy overshoes. Beside the church was a man with a cardboard sign around his neck that read: BROKE BUT SEXY. There was an upturned cap in front of him with a few coins. I'd seen this man several days in a row and always greeted him. I don't carry cash of any kind so, previously, I had nothing to give him. I was prepared today and had stopped at Tim Horton's (similar to Starbucks) and purchased ten five dollar meal cards. I said to him, "Good morning, my name is Dennis, here's a five dollar card to help you with a meal."

"Thanks, Dennis, I appreciate this. My name is Bernard."

I said, "You must be new in town. I know most of the street people in this area."

"Yes, I'm from North Bay, but I've been a lot of places. I've applied for Welfare, but I can't receive anything until I have an address, so for now I'm sleeping under a bridge."

I asked, "Have you tried staying at one of the homeless shelters?"

"No, those places are terrible!"

I said, "My friends have told me about noise, bedbugs, theft and fights. I also know a woman who was raped there. I don't blame you for your decision to sleep under a bridge."

"Yeah, it's quite a way from here. I have privacy and I prefer to be alone. I've been single for fifteen years and I intend to stay that way. Women always want money and control. I've had enough of that. The government wants all cash transactions to be by debit or credit card, that way they know where you're spending your money."

I said, "I do all my transactions by plastic, that's why I haven't had anything to give you."

"I can understand that, but you always greet me, acknowledge me; most people ignore me and have a frown on their face. I don't ask for money. If people care to drop a quarter, I appreciate it. If everybody dropped a quarter I'd have enough for a day's food and other expenses."

I said, "I've noticed that as well when I'm sitting with panhandlers. Even my co-workers ignore me."

Bernard continued, "Some people say I'm too well dressed to panhandle. These are just clothes I've been given. I've been really lucky. What I could use is a shower. The YMCA used to allow people to shower for two bucks, but they don't do that anymore. I thought they were supposed to help people. I use wipes and clean myself as well as I can, but it isn't as good as a shower."

I said, "I've read that some communities are providing outdoor toilets and publicly accessible shower facilities. It would be even better if they provided accessible housing and rooms."

Under the Bridge

"Good morning, Bernard."

"Good morning. It's good to see you. My problem with being broke and so sexy is that I'm stuck with this face and the beard. This is Halloween, most people get to take off their masks at the end of the night, but not me. In another week I'll be reaching the big six zero."

A woman stopped and handed him a half pack of cigarettes. "Thanks darlin'. That's awfully sweet of you."

I asked, "How old were you when you started smoking?"

"Six years old. I'd go to the store and say my dad sent me to buy him some cigarettes. I don't know if they believed that, but they always gave them to me. Back then, a five-pack of Export 'A' was twenty-five cents. I started drinking when I was nine and hard drugs when I was thirteen.

"A woman said that she had a surprise for me this evening. She wouldn't say what it was, but she rents rooms. She was disappointed when I told her I was looking for a place. She said she just rented her last one. So, I don't know what the surprise is. It could be socks or underwear. I don't know. I'll just have to wait and see."

"Awaiting a surprise gives you something to look forward to. Life can be full of surprises," I said.

"Oh, I know all about that. I had a massive heart attack when I was still a young man. Died three times on the operating table. Now, I have a pacemaker installed. That got me off the hard drugs. Then I was diagnosed with cirrhosis of the liver. That got me off the booze. Then I got the cancer — leukemia — that put me in a wheelchair. In a couple of weeks I dropped from two hundred and thirty pounds to one forty. It took all my effort to wheel that chair around. I went back to school and trained as a drug and alcohol counsellor. I worked at that for over ten years."

"Working as a counsellor must have been an emotional experience. You must have seen some sad situations."

"Yes, sometimes it was heartbreaking. It's not always the young people who are to blame, sometimes it's the parents. I counselled a teenage girl who was a crack addict. I got her off the drugs. She went back to live with her mother, who was a nurse. One time, the mother returned unexpectedly and found her boyfriend trying to sexually assault her daughter. It was only after actually seeing it that she believed what the girl had been telling her. We have to protect our young people. They're our future.

"I've been clean and sober for twenty-seven years. I still use marijuana, but I don't smoke it in public."

"Do you have a doctor's prescription for that?"

"Yes, I'm registered and have a licence to purchase. There are some new weed shops that have opened up. They don't even ask me for my licence. They're operating illegally, but the cops haven't started charging them with anything. The government may come through with legalization like they have in Colorado, Washington state and Oregon. These stores charge tax. I have to pay twelve bucks per gram, when on the street I could get the same amount for ten, but I don't mind paying the extra two dollars. On the street you never know what you're getting. Crack dealers usually add speed. They've changed the name from crack to 'more', because once a customer tries some he want more. Sometimes, they mix in household cleaners, laundry detergent, boric acid, laxatives, local anesthetics: procaine, tetracaine or lidocaine. That can be deadly.

"In the pot dispensaries you can buy different flavors, different doses, candies, brownies, cookies, gummy bears, cannabutter or cannabis oil for cooking."

I said, "It's getting colder each morning. Do you have a good sleeping bag?"

"It's adequate. I'm putting money aside so I can get a warm room for the winter. Welfare will pay the first month's rent, but I have to come up with the last month. Something good happened this morning. A young woman who I'd talked to a few times handed me an envelope. Inside was a note that read, 'Dear Broke and Sexy, here is a token of my esteem for you.' Also in the envelope was a hundred dollar bill."

I said, "That will go a long way towards your last month's rent."

"Yes, I've put it away."

November 2016

Shitty, if you want to know the truth!

1 November 2016

"Good morning, Bernard. It's below freezing, how did you sleep?"

"Shitty, if you want to know the truth. I got to sleep okay, but I was freezin' by morning. I guess I'm not supposed to talk that way. Most times if people ask me how I'm doin' I just say fine. They don't give a shit anyway."

"You mentioned yesterday that you were expecting a surprise last night. How did that work out?"

"The woman told me that she would put up my last month's rent if I was able to find a place. I went to my bank this morning expectin' to find three hundred bucks, instead I found that I'm seventy in the hole. Welfare must have cut me off."

"Do you have a worker you can contact?"

"I can never get through to anybody. I may need to get a new worker. There is a two week waiting list for appointments. I talked to a Street Outreach Worker. He told me I had to be registered with the Salvation Army. The Salvation Army won't help me unless I'm a resident there. I'm not going to stay there. I'd be robbed."

"I've heard that from my friends. Boots were stolen from lockers with a padlock on them. How does that happen? You don't need a permit to buy a chain cutter. They sell them at most hardware stores."

"Another problem I have is my shoes. These are leather summer shoes. They aren't going to do me any good in the slush and snow. My feet are cold right now. If I had a gun I think I'd shoot myself. Mind you, I don't need a gun, just some rat poison. It would be a painful way to go, but it would be over."

"Take care, Bernard. There are some people who have your interests at heart."

Illiterate

2 November 2016

"Good morning Bernard, how's your morning going, any better than yesterday?"

"Yeah, I got over that. Remember that lady that stopped by yesterday? She was by today and dropped me five bucks. She walked away with her child then turned back and asked me what boot size I wear. I said, "Ten." So, maybe I'm going to get some winter boots.

"I saw one of the outreach workers this morning. He said that he'd been lookin' for me under bridges. I said, "You must have looked under the wrong bridge, because I was there." He wrote my name down, apart from that he didn't do anything."

I asked, "Have you talked to Welfare to find out why your benefits were cut?"

"Yeah, I found out what the problem is. My file's in North Bay and I'm here. It hasn't arrived yet. I don't fill out my own applications because I'm illiterate. Hopefully, it will come soon, but my benefits will only start when they've received the file and registered me. I've been eating well though. I have a friend who is manager of a Tim Horton's; she won't let me pay for anything. She's even told her staff not to charge me. I've never eaten so well in my life.

"Another friend owns a hotel in Carleton Place. I'm going to phone him and ask what he'll charge me for two nights this weekend. He always gives me a good rate. If he has something available I'll hitchhike. It'll be great to have a shower and a warm place to sleep.

Rain, Rain Go Away

3 November 2016

The rain was doing what rain does. Most people on the sidewalk were carrying umbrellas. Bernard was standing with his sign in the shelter of a doorway. "Hi Bernard, did you manage to stay dry last night?"

"Yes, I'm always dry under the bridge, unless the rain comes in sideways. When I came out this morning it hadn't started raining, so I was sitting on the sidewalk, then it started spitting, then pouring."

"I see you're using your cane. Is your leg sore?"

"Yes, that's why I'm rocking back and forth. I'm trying to relieve the pressure on my hips. I also have degenerated discs in my lower back. The only thing that relieves the pain is marijuana."

"Yesterday you mentioned that you were illiterate. How did that come about?"

"I just didn't like school and I missed as much as possible until I was eighteen, then I was allowed to quit. They passed me from grade to grade even though I couldn't read or write. If I try to complete an application I can read some of the questions and the words are flying around in my head, but I can't put them on paper. Now both my long term and short term memory has gone. I don't remember what happened last week. When I left this mornin' I knew I had forgotten something, but couldn't figure out what it was. Then it came to me -- rolling papers. Sometimes I'll go into a room and forget what it was I went in for.

"I'm just waitin' for my little French girl. I think she has some money for me. Then I'll call it a day and go back under the bridge."

Bernard's Birthday

4 November 2016

Bernard turns sixty on Sunday. He has that written on his cardboard sign, hoping to stimulate generosity. I asked him, "How did you sleep last night?"

"Well, I got to sleep alright, but around three thirty I had to get up to go to the bathroom. I was too cold to sleep after that so I walked to the nearest Tim Horton's to have a coffee and get warm. I was out here on the street by six thirty. There's a religious guy that comes by and says to me, 'You got to get out of the cold, man. May God bless and keep you. You're in my prayers.' I wanted to say to him, 'The only way I'll be able to get out of the cold is if people like you give me some money. I can do without your prayers. It's in the bible that we're supposed to help our fellow man, not just walk past someone in need.' Of course, I didn't say that. I just smiled at the stupid fucker."

As I sat with Bernard several people dropped two dollar coins. He took them out of his upturned cap and put them in his pocket. He said to me, "I always take the big ones out and leave the quarters. I've had my hat grabbed by other panhandlers or kicked over."

I asked, "What is the worst that's happened to you when you've been panhandling?"

"I've had my tent set on fire when I was in it. I was camped on native ground. I guess they thought I was a hunter or somebody up to no good. When they realized that I was homeless they felt really bad. They bought me a new tent, invited me to eat with them."

I said, "One of my homeless friends was doused with gasoline and set on fire. Another had his teeth kicked out while sleeping on a park bench."

"University students are the worst. They'll get drunk and walk around the parks looking for homeless people to beat on. They think it's funny."

"Have you arranged to stay in a hotel on the weekend?"

"Yes, I phoned my friend and asked how much he would charge. At first he said one sixty for two nights, plus tax. I asked him, 'Do you know who's calling? It's Bernard, the old guy with the cane and beard. It's my birthday Sunday.' He said, 'Bernie, it's good to hear from you. In that case, it'll cost you seventy-two per night without tax. Maybe I can do better than that. Come by and see me.' So that's taken care of. I'll have a warm place to sleep. I'll take a bunch of showers and watch TV all weekend. I'll be down here tomorrow morning. Around one I'll take a bus to the outskirts and hitchhike from there. I won't be able to do any panning in a small town. It's against the law. Here, the cops haven't bothered me, so far"

I said, "Some of my friends here have been ticketed, but it's always thrown out of court. It's obvious that they have no money to pay a fine. They don't own anything so there's nothing to repossess. They've been told that if they ever apply for a driver's licence their fines will have to be paid. There's no chance of that.

"Has anything happened with your Welfare application?"

"No, It'll probably all come in one fell swoop. After turning sixty I'll be eligible for the Canada Pension Plan. They'll have to fill out forms for me. When I'm there I'll ask them about the Welfare."

Sit on My Face

9 November 2016

"Good morning Bernard, how was your weekend?"

"It was great. My friend got me a nice end room at his motel. Smoking was allowed. The first thing I did was to take a shower. It felt so good. Then I lay on the bed and watched tv. I fell asleep and when I woke up I couldn't get out of bed, my back was so sore. I had another shower to loosen up then spent most of the weekend watching tv.

"I got back yesterday and went to the Welfare office. They asked me what the problem was and I told them, 'My file is in North Bay and I'm out on the street. I need my file sent here and have to find a warm place to sleep. He asked,' Have you tried the shelters?' I asked him 'Have you tried the shelters? I don't want to put up with bed bugs, fights and forty men snoring and farting all night.' He put me on a list for subsidised housing. There are three people ahead of me. He said that when I've been accepted they will cover two fifty a month of my rent. Of course I'll have to contact my French girl, who's promised to pay my last month's rent. They'll need her address and phone number.

"Later on an outreach worker came by. He took all my information and said that he'd check on me tomorrow. He said they might be able to arrange something."

I asked, "Have you been following the US election at all?"

"Yeah, I knew Trump would get in. People are looking for a change. They don't care what kind of a change it is, just something different from what they have now."

I said, "I read a headline in The Independent newspaper 'Former KKK leader David Duke: 'We won it for Donald Trump' That's scary."

"Well, there are a lot of people he's going to have to answer to including Putin."

I asked, "Do you have any family?"

"Nope, it's just me, nobody else. Mind you there's an old lady at the courthouse now that I've been talking to. She asked, 'If you get a place can I move in with you?' I said, sure, 'I won't charge you rent but you'll have to pay for the groceries.' She seemed to think that was a good deal. I call her granny, like from the TV program, The Beverly Hillbillies. She calls me Jed. We laugh about that. She brought me a coffee this morning. That was nice. I said to her, 'There's another thing you could do for me. My nose is cold. Would you sit on my face to warm it.'"

Affordable Housing

10 November 2016

"Good morning, Bernard."

"I'm thinking of making a really big sign and taping it to the church wall. It'll read, IGNORANT PEOPLE PLEASE WALK ON THE OTHER SIDE OF THE STREET. **I hope I said that loud enough for the guy to hear that just passed, he's one of them.** I've been sitting here every morning for three weeks. I smile, say good morning to people, very few people say anything. Some even turn their heads so they won't see me. I remember when people were a lot more friendly. It's not so much the Baby Boomers, but the Millenials. I don't expect everybody to give me money -- although a quarter isn't going to hurt anybody -- but I would appreciate being acknowledged."

"So you have your appointment today with Welfare?"

"Yes, one o'clock. I hope they have good news for me. I haven't seen my little French girl for a while. If Welfare finds me a place I'll need the last month's rent guaranteed. I guess she'll be able to arrange that with her bank. She also said that she had a surprise for me, but that was a week and a half ago. She has a good heart. I just hope she can come through."

I said, "I remember when I was a salesman in northern Saskatchewan. If I visited a farm near lunch time I would always be invited to share a meal with them. It didn't matter whether or not they were interested in what I had to sell. I was their guest."

"Did you know that Lethbridge, Alberta has no homeless problem. They did at one time, they recognized and addressed it. Now they have affordable housing for everyone."

5 Year Plan To End Homelessness

https://buff.ly/2mSr6KX

"Bringing Lethbridge Home is Lethbridge's Plan to end homelessness in Lethbridge. Homelessness is a complex issue and one of the most critical issues facing our community. We believe we can end homelessness and we're taking action!

Looking forward: The achievement of the targeted goals and alignment with Bringing Lethbridge Home: Plan to End Homelessness. Our goals for the 2015-2019 are:

1. Prevent people from becoming homeless

Focus on the prevention of the root causes and pathways into homelessness
Strengthen support for young families and children experiencing trauma and mental illness
Implement healthy transitioning from public services such as health care and treatment centres, foster care and corrections
Increase access to Diversion programming and strategies
Strengthen diversion programming, eviction prevention and rapid re-housing
Increase access to affordable and attainable housing
Support the prevention of family violence
Support poverty reduction strategy and employment opportunities
Strengthen social and community integration programming
Strengthen positive landlord tenant relations

2. Develop and increase affordable permanent housing options

Complete the Housing Action Plan based on need and projected demographics

Increase housing options by 1000 units to include innovative permanent supportive housing and affordable housing options (such as inclusive neighborhoods, laneway housing and container housing)

Build landlord relations through recruitment and retention

Identify options for affordable home ownership

Increase rent supplement funding and programs

Universal design for increased accessible housing options

Engage Elders in the design of affordable housing options for indigenous people

Engage the community in dialogue

Reduce NIMBY in neighborhoods

3. Strengthen and sustain a systemic Housing First approach

Increase awareness of what Housing First is and isn't. Fully implement Standards of Practice including integrated System of Care

Keep it simple while maintaining the fidelity and integrity of Housing First

Flexible mandates to meet the needs of the client.

Review the eligibility criteria for Housing First and provide quick pathways to get people housed

Ongoing leadership, team and community education and development. Include understanding and support of vulnerable populations.

Review recruitment and retention strategies for Housing First teams. Include coaching and mentoring strategies

Support and options for people that are not eligible

Evaluate impact of the Housing First programs including service participant's involvement in policy direction

Strengthen the collaboration and inter-connectedness of the
Housing First teams
Housing First for women fleeing abuse and family violence
Team building
Fully integrate the Housing First Standards of Practice

4. Strengthen coordinated access to integrated community
support services

Intensive Case Management to prevent eviction
Continuously improve referral time for client centered
housing
Accessible transportation
Increase follow-up services
Intox and Detox services
Increase physician access
More collaboration providing housing to people with
disabilities
Continue to strengthen community partnerships

5. Provide shelter in emergency situations and quickly
move people to permanent housing

Complete the implementation of the Shelter Visioning
Increase funding for damage deposits and first month rent
Strengthen access to stabilization units
Strengthen diversion and rapid re-housing programming

6. Increase community awareness and education

Actively participate in Building a Welcoming and Inclusive
Community and Vibrant Lethbridge initiatives. This includes
building welcoming and inclusive neighborhoods
Develop and implement curriculum opportunities in
schools

Involve people with lived experience in policy decisions
Increase data analysis and communicate information
Involve community to reduce the impact of NIMBY"

Prisons

14 November 2016

"Good morning, Bernard. How was it sleeping under the bridge last night?"

"Not too bad. It's been worse. Now the sun is shining and we're expecting a warm day."

"Have you heard from Welfare yet?"

"Yeah, everything is set up. I'm on the list for housing. I just have to wait for the Outreach people to come visit me."

"Do they come by on a regular basis?"

"No, I've only seen them once in this month, but they know I'm here. I'll just have to wait."

"Trump was elected President, just like you predicted and they've legalized marijuana for recreational use in California, Nevada, and Massachusetts. That should send a message to the Canadian government to go ahead with the legalization that they've planned for next spring."

"That's a good thing. The American prisons are full of people convicted because of drugs. I wonder if in the states where it's become legal they'll release the prisoners that have been convicted of minor marijuana offences? It's the same case in Canada. That's why we have so many prisons in Ontario. There's Joyceville, Collins Bay, Millhaven, Kingston and the Prison for Women..."

I said, "I think the POW is now closed and has been turned into a museum. Joy told me that. She'd served time there. Inmates were moved to the Bath Institution and the Grand Valley Institution for Women."

"Yes, I think that the Kingston Pen. has been turned into a museum as well. It was falling apart. They now give tours there, but I'll bet they don't show people the dungeon in the basement where they had the torture chambers."

I said, "It costs taxpayers a lot of money to incarcerate people."

"Yeah, it would be far better to put some of that money toward affordable housing."

Doing Time

15 November 2016

"Good morning, Bernard."

"Good morning. I had a good day yesterday, seventy bucks. I bought a fleece hoodie, the one I'm wearing now. When I woke up this morning I was too hot. With my winter coat, my sleeping bag then my leather over top of me, it was quite a job to fight my way out. The next thing I need is winter boots."

I said, "I've found that Goodwill or Value Village has good prices on used boots and clothing."

"Yeah, Value Village is good. I've bought a few things there.

"You know, when I leave here to go to the bathroom, my backpack, sleeping bag, even my cap with some change in it stays here. I take out the big coins, all that remains are dimes and nickels. People ask me why I don't take everything with me. I figure if somebody needs a sleeping bag that bad they can have it. I can always get another."

"Yesterday we were talking about prisons. Do you mind talking about that?"

"No, I've been in a lot of them: Joyceville, Millhaven, Collins Bay and I finished out at Drumheller. They gave me early parole. I was supposed to go to a halfway house, but as soon as I got out of the prison I just kept walking. They caught up with me in Calgary. I had to go back for five months to finish off my sentence."

"What kind of things were you charged with?"

"Well, I was a pretty rowdy kid. I pulled a string of b and e's (breaking and entering) and car theft. When I was in prison I got into a fight and hit another inmate with a weight lifting bar. Back then, in the seventies, when you got in a fight you had to make sure the guy wouldn't get up, otherwise he'd come after you. I wore a pair of cowboy boots with steel toes. A swift kick in the ankle would put a guy out of commision for quite a while and he'd always have a weak ankle. Another time, I threw a guy over a four story balcony inside a fridge."

"How did that come about?"

"Well, I had a can of pop in the fridge and I'd put my initials BT on the can. Later, when I came to get the coke it was gone. There was only one guy sitting at a table and he was drinking a coke. I walked over to him and asked, 'Is this yours?' He said, 'Yeah.' I picked up the can and showed him my initials on it. When you're in prison you have to protect what's yours or you're really in trouble. I pulled everything out of the fridge, stuffed the guy in and pushed it over the balcony. That added five years to my sentence."

I said, "The guy must have been in rough condition."

"Yeah he was, he was in hospital when I was charged. He died later. If he died earlier I would have been charged with murder instead of assault and battery. That was a long time ago. I learned a lot in prison. I even got my cook's papers. If I'd stayed in longer I could have qualified as a chef."

"Did you work as a cook?"

"Yeah, I did, until the first heart attack. You've heard the phrase 'If you can't stand the heat, get out of the kitchen.' That's what I did."

Sleeping in the Cold

16 November 2016

"Good morning, Bernard, how did you sleep."

"Oh, it was okay. There was a bit of wind, but the temperature wasn't too bad. Next Monday we're going to have snow. I usually go to sleep at about eight. I wake up at ten to go to the bathroom and again at twelve and one. When three rolls around I'm so sore from sleeping on the hard concrete that I say. 'To hell with it.' and walk down to McDonald's for my first coffee. Tim Horton's isn't open that early.

"A guy came by this morning and said that he's got a really, really thick blanket for me and some fleece pajama bottoms. I'll wear those all winter. He couldn't believe that I was still sleeping outside. Saturday a guy is going to bring me a pair of winter boots. He came by today to check my size.

"Another guy said, 'I nearly didn't see you in this doorway, usually you're farther down the wall.' I said, 'Well, I'm so sweet that if I stood out in the rain I'd melt. He asked me why I was so happy I said, 'It's raining, not snowing, so I don't have to shovel.'

A woman walked past then came back. She said, "I love your sign, BROKE AND SEXY, it made me laugh." She dropped a five into the upturned cap. Leonard quickly pocketed the bill saying, "I'm putting this away for socks. At Giant Tiger they have ten pairs for eight dollars, or is that at Walmart? I'll have to check. A man on a bicycle stopped and said, "A woman asked me to give you this." He dropped a twenty into the cap.

Bernard said, "This is my lucky day. It's probably from a woman who didn't want anyone to see her giving me money. Probably works for the government. They're the worst. I can always identify them because of the white, plastic security passes dangling from their belts.

"My friend came out of court and was so happy because her case had been dropped. Then she said, 'I'm going to pan to get enough money for smokes and some weed.' I said, 'I'll get it for you.' For both of us it cost eighty bucks I said to her, 'You're expensive.'

"I'm going to have to stretch my legs. I can only sit so long before my hips stiffen. It's from arthritis. I have it in my fingers as well and have degeneration in my lower spine. I usually wrap my hands in those tensor wraps. I like the ones with the hole for your thumb, but I haven't been able to find them lately.

"Sometimes people ask me, 'Why do you keep saying 'Good morning' to people when they hardly ever say it back?' I say, 'I figure I'll wear them down eventually. After they start saying, 'Good morning' it may take them a couple of weeks to decide to give me money. It starts with them looking at me and acknowledging me. That's the hook.' "

Led Astray

18 November 2016

I was bundled up in my winter coat, scarf over my face waiting for my bus. I was approached by a woman with long blond hair. She asked, "I know you don't I? Pull your scarf down so I can see you. I'm grieving now. My family was recently killed in a car accident. I only had one mother and one father, they were with the underground. I was led astray. Perhaps you'll pray for me." I said, "I will." She walked away from the bus stop, but ran to catch the bus at the next stop. She paid her fare in small change, rode for about six blocks then got off the bus. It's a mystery.

When I arrived at Bernard's spot he asked, "Have you got a minute to sit here while I go to the bathroom. I won't be long."

"Sure," I said, "I'll get to be BROKE AND SEXY."

"Yeah, that's right. I'll be back soon."

While I was waiting his little French woman stopped by. She said hello and asked, "Are you holding Bernard's place for him?"

"Yes, he's gone to the bathroom." Bernard returned shortly after. The woman commented, "Look at all those empty coffee cups. No wonder you had to go to the bathroom." She laughed, put some change in his cap then said goodbye. Bernard collected the cups and walked them to the trash container.

He said, "You did a good job, but you have to smile more."

I replied, "Perhaps I should also have been waving my arms."

"Well, Housing visited me and told me that my name was near the top of their list. They asked if I'd consider staying at a shelter. I said, 'I'd rather freeze to death under the bridge, than stay at one of those noisy, dirty, bed bug infested places. I've got enough problems without adding bed bugs to the list.' 'In that case,' they said, 'we'd better find you a place fast.' I don't know how long it will be, hopefully soon. Tomorrow, a guy promised to bring me a pair of winter boots. I'm looking forward to that. Right now I'm sitting on both of my blankets, but with my feet on the concrete they get cold fast. Soon I'll have to wrap them in one of the blankets."

Summer Shoes

22 November 2016

"Good morning, Bernard, do you have your winter boots yet?"

"No, the guy who said he was going to get them for me didn't show. I sat out here all day Saturday in a snowstorm and all day Sunday. I've only got leather summer shoes that get wet in the snow. My feet are freezing! It really annoys me when someone says they're going to do something and then they don't. Better they didn't offer, then surprise me, rather than getting my hopes up for nothing.

"There is this religious guy who comes by every day. He says to me, 'You've got to get out of the cold. You've got to get out of the cold,' yet he doesn't drop any change into my cap. How does he expect I'm going to get out of the cold? I thought the idea of religion was to help people in need, not just walk by."

"Did Outreach come by?"

"I tried to call them on the weekend and I got a recorded message saying they were closed Saturday and Sunday. What kind of emergency service is that? If I'm going to freeze to death do I have to do it on a weekday? I guess I'm a bit down today. One good thing happened on Sunday. The Santa Claus parade came by. I didn't get anything during the parade but after the crowd started to disperse a lot of people dropped change. I made seventy bucks that day."

Destroyed

23 November 2016

"Good morning, Bernard, are you enjoying your new winter boots?"

"Yeah, the boots are fine, but I had some bad luck yesterday. Remember I told you that I was sleeping under a bridge and I'd stored some of my gear there. Well, I went back there fairly early in the evening, about six thirty. I could see from the footprints in the snow that somebody had been there. They'd slashed my sleeping bag inside and out. I don't know if anybody pissed on it. They'd cut up my rubber sleeping pad. I had a big umbrella that I used as a bit of a windbreak, they destroyed that. It won't even open. I think it was maybe construction guys. They've been doing some work on the bridge. It could have been kids, but the footprints were big. If somebody had wanted me out of there they could have just left a note. I would have left. As it was I gathered up all my gear and took it under one of the downtown bridges. I had to sleep in my boots so they wouldn't get stolen. I'll have to find some glue that they use to mend fabric to deal with some of the rips. Duct tape wouldn't work, it'd tear off."

I said, "I can't understand why anybody stoop so low. It would have been obvious that you didn't have much if you were sleeping under a bridge."

"Yeah, well it can't be helped. I hope that Housing comes through for me. They say I'm near the top of the list, but what does that mean? I've heard of some people being on these lists for years. It's going to be raining this weekend, so I'll have to find some kind of shelter with a roof on it, even if it's a doorway. When we get the really cold weather I'll have to find a place near a heat exhaust vent. There are a few I know of around the city, but then I'll be out in the open. Stuff will get stolen. I could get kicked and beaten while in my sleeping bag. That happens a lot. Cops and Security Guards will be patrolling. If the cops get me they'll confiscate my weed and maybe lay charges."

"I'm sorry to hear that, Bernard, I hope that Housing comes through and some good luck comes your way."

No Room at the Inn

24 November 2016

"Hi Bruce!"

"Dennis, I hardly recognized you all bundled up like that. You look more like a homeless person than I do. Here, let me shift over, you can share my cardboard. It'll insulate you from some of the cold of the sidewalk."

"How is Loretta?"

"She's doing great. She has her own place now, but generally comes to my apartment to sleep. Now she's off at some First Nations conference in Thunder Bay. She's been sober for a year and no drugs, except marijuana. Did I tell you they closed my weed store last week. That's so stupid. I don't know why they don't legalize all drugs, including heroin. The people who use it are still going to use. That won't change, but there will be a lot fewer incarcerations. They should also have free injection sites so AIDS and Hepatitis don't spread like they do."

I said, "I've read a book, In the Realm of Hungry Ghosts: Close Encounters with Addictions by Gabor Mate M.D. He ran a free injection site in Vancouver. His recommendation was that heroin and other opiates be available with a doctor's prescription. That way addicts could be weaned off the drugs with supervision. Also there would be clean drugs available. Three addicts a day are overdosing on drugs laced with illicit fentanyl.

A total of 433 people have died in British Columbia due to overdoses from January to July this year. A huge proportion of these deaths—62 percent—was associated with fentanyl, a powerful opiod that is mixed with drugs like heroin

Bruce continued, "The government is going to start the process of legalization this spring, but then it has to go through the Senate. Who knows how long that will take."

I asked, "What do you think about the political situation in the US?"

"When I saw the front page of the Sun, the day after election, I laughed my head off. This is a guy who's going to shake things up. Nobody knows where the pieces are going to fall. Maybe we'll have a third world war. That's a possibility. It's just like Brexit, that certainly shook things up. Now, Scotland is going to have the chance to hold a referendum to seek independence from Britain. That'll be a good thing. The vote last time was within two percentage points.

"A politician that I respected was Margaret Thatcher. I didn't agree with most of her policies, but when she said she was going to do something, she got it done, no matter how unpopular. She was honest. I admire honesty in a politician, there's too little of that in the world."

I said, "I talked to Bernard this morning, his sleeping bag was slashed inside and out, his rubber sleeping mat was cut in strips and his umbrella that he uses as a windbreak was broken."

Bruce asked, "Was he there at the time?"

"No, he had his stuff stashed under a bridge. By the footprints he thought it might be construction workers, because there were some in the area."

"I don't think construction workers would do that. I've had lots of dealings with them and had no trouble. I think it's either personal, somebody who's had a run in with Bernard, or someone who just doesn't like the way he's living. It's probably university students, they have the reputation of hobo bashing. Bernard is lucky he wasn't in his sleeping bag when they came. It could have been serious.

"A guy asked me today what the solution was to the homeless problem. I said, 'More affordable housing. See those empty offices across the street — housing; empty houses and apartments — housing; empty hospital wards — housing; empty military barracks — housing. The solution is obvious, implementing the solution is what government can't seem to come to grips with. There is a poverty industry. It cost the government twelve hundred dollars per month to keep one man in a shelter. Do you know why I'm on the street? I broke my leg and couldn't work. I couldn't pay my bills so I lost my apartment. Welfare pays me six hundred and ten per month in income assistance — three hundred and seventy-five for shelter and two thirty five for a support allowance that includes food. Try to find a room in this city for three seventy-five per month, the average cost is four hundred to four fifty.

"If every one of these people passing by dropped me a nickel I'd have enough money to cover my living expenses.

They don't realize that most people are only one or two checks away from being homeless.

"The waiting list for emergency mental health care is eighteen months. So, if a guy walks in saying he has suicidal thoughts. They'll say, 'We can schedule an appointment for you in May, 2018.' That alone is enough to tip him over the edge. If he keeps the appointment, fine. If he tops himself off they'll say, 'We didn't know that he would actually kill himself.' Go figure!"

New Winter Boots

25 November 2016

"Hi Bernard, I see you have new winter boots. Are they keeping your feet warm?"

"They're okay. I'm standing on a patch of ice. If I stay still my feet are going to get cold, so I slide from side to side. I just hope that I don't slip and break my nose. My cane is of no use on ice. If my leg gets too sore I can sit on my backpack.

"My hands are cold. These leather gloves are wet from the rain. When I go to the bathroom I hold them under the hand dryer for a while, but since my gear is outside I don't want to risk having it stolen.

"Do you hear those sirens? It seems I only hear them on days when it's rainy and wet. Yesterday there was a house fire where four people were forced out on the street.

"I saw two cop cars pull around the corner. They got out of their cars and walked toward me. I thought to myself, 'Oh, oh, I wonder what's going to happen now.' They just walked by. One said hello and laughed at my sign."

I said, "I've heard from some of my friends that unless there has been a complaint made against you by a pedestrian for harassment, or by a store owner, if you're on their property and they think that you're discouraging customers, the police don't get involved. In any case they usually just ask you to move along, or if they charge you it's a misdemeanor. The courts will throw it out."

"I never harass people. Here, I'm standing on church property. If I was on the sidewalk it would be a different story."

"Have you had any complaints from the church?"

"No, they're fine with me being here. They say hello when they pass by.

"I tried changing my sign instead of having it read BROKE AND SEXY I was going to print BROKE AND SEXY IN THE COLD, but I couldn't remember how to spell THE. The letters were floating around in my brain but they wouldn't come together."

December 2016

Welfare

2 December 2016

"Good morning, Bernard, have you heard any news since I talked to you yesterday?"

"Well, I went to the Welfare office, talked to my worker, apparently they haven't had time to process all my information, but she said a check will be waiting for me Monday morning. With that I'll at least be able to get a hotel room if the weather is really bad. We've been lucky so far. This is awesome for December. I feel sorry for the folks in the prairies and in the maritimes. They've got a foot of snow now."

I asked, "Has Housing been by to see you?"

"No, they're supposed to be checking on me every day, but I've only seen them the once since I've been here. I don't expect to get anything before Christmas, but you never know something could happen. I can always hope."

"How have you been sleeping? Are you staying warm?"

"Oh yeah, I'm warm enough. It's just the pain of getting up in the morning. I stood all day yesterday because of the rain, I'm sure paying for it today. My leg gave out entirely on my way here. Even my cane didn't save me. I went right over."

Bernard was sitting cross legged. In trying to straighten his legs I could see the pain and difficulty he was going through. A few people dropped quarters into his cap. He picked out a dollar coin and put it in his pocket. "I don't like to have these showing in case someone grabs my cap. Every once in a while I go to the grocery store where they have a change sorter. It costs eleven per cent, but I can get all my change converted to bills — a lot lighter in my pocket.

"My little French girl is leaving today to visit her father in Quebec City. She's going to visit him for his birthday, he'll be eighty-six. He has no idea that she'll be coming; It'll be a complete surprise. All my regulars are leaving."

Merry Christmas

1 December 2016

"Dennis, man, where've you been? I looked for you Monday, Tuesday. I thought maybe something had happened to you."

"I came by yesterday, Bernard, but didn't see you."

"Oh, yesterday, I was feeling so sick I didn't get up until about two in the afternoon. I ached all over, I couldn't even stand. I rolled over and unzipped my sleeping bag to take a leak then went back to sleep. I came downtown later in the day to check my bank account. There was sixty-six cents in it. I'm going to the Welfare office to check on things. I think they issue checks at eleven o'clock, so I'll wait until then to visit with my worker, otherwise they may tell me to come back later to get my check. The Ontario government hasn't raised social assistance rates since cutting them by nearly twenty-two per cent in 1995, although the cost of living has risen thirteen per cent. The shelter allowance for a single person it's three hundred and twenty-five a month. If your shelter costs are over the max, you're dipping into the province's basic-needs allowance, which is one ninety-five a month for a single person. Until then I don't even have enough money to buy a pack of smokes.

I asked, "Has Housing contacted you?"

"No, I haven't seen them around. Since it's past the first of the month, I probably won't have a place to stay for Christmas. It's bad enough being alone for Christmas, standing alone outside in the cold makes it even worse."

Sleeping in the Snow

10 January 2017

I was walking along the sidewalk expecting to see Ted standing beside the church. I couldn't see him. I saw his upturned cap near the sidewalk and thought he may have left to go to the washroom. I thought of putting a meal card in his cap, but feared it might be stolen. Behind a snow drift I saw a man lying next to the building. He was huddled with his hood pulled tight around his face, no sleeping bag, no blanket, nothing separating him from the frozen concrete.

Freezing to death is a real concern, especially when wind chill temperatures hover around minus thirty degrees. In Toronto, Canada's largest city:

"The only group that even attempts a full accounting is the Homeless Memorial project, a volunteer-run initiative that compiles a list of street-involved people who have died every month. The list stretches back to 1985 and is now over 740 names long. The project recorded 18 homeless deaths in 2014, down from 31 in 2013, and well below the all-time high of 72 in 2005. (Ben Spurr, Now News,Toronto, January 15, 2015."

I walked over to him and saw that his eyes were closed. I said, "Good morning Ted, are you okay."

He responded, "Hi, Dennis, it's good to see you. I haven't been sleeping well due to this cold weather. I thought this might be a good opportunity to catch up on my sleep."

"Take heart, Ted, tomorrow will be warmer."

"Yes, but that's twenty-four hours away. The weather forecast is for snow this afternoon turning to freezing rain."

Beet Juice and Road Salt

11 January 2017

Walking a dimly lit stretch of sidewalk between street lights, I noticed a man sitting cross legged with his back against a building. I squinted my eyes wondering if it was one of my friends or a stranger.

He said, "Hi, Dennis, old man! Come have a seat on my extendible couch." He stood and separated two folded boxes, kicked snow away and set them back on the concrete. "These are plasticized, a butcher saves them for me. I guess I shouldn't have called you old man, but I meant it in a good way. Have a seat, let's talk awhile."

I said, "Bruce, you can call me old, I just turned 70, so there's no other word that would adequately express my age."

He continued, "How've you been? How was your Christmas?"

"I'm great, Christmas was great! I've been on vacation for the past month, so I'm relaxed, contented. How about you?"

"It's been mostly good, only one problem. I got a bill today from Hydro. I'm on an equalized billing plan. I've paid my December bill. This bill they send once a year to make up any differences. I phoned them and said to the guy, 'Come check my meter. There's got to be something wrong.' He came and checked everything. I've got a draft at my front door. There's nothing I can do about it, but the guy said he'd cut my bill in half. That was decent of him."

I asked, "Have you seen any of our friends around. I've lost contact over the last month."

"Yeah, I've seen most of the guys. There are fewer all the time. Little Jake stayed with me for a couple of weeks. He had pneumonia, like he gets every winter. Because of HIV/AIDS his T cell count is down. That affects his immune system. Anyway, I cooked his meals, gave him a place to sleep and said, 'Just take care of yourself and get well. You don't need to go out and pan. I'll pay for the groceries.' He kept forgetting to take his medication. Now, a person doesn't die of AIDS, they die from some other disease that their immune system isn't able to fight. I really worry about him. He'd given me fifty dollars to keep for him until the end of the month. I gave it back to him and said, 'Jake, use this to buy your bus pass.' The next day he was asking me for bus tickets. He didn't buy his bus pass he went straight to the wine store. It's not as if he's got extra weight to draw from. He's skinny as a rail. I invited him for Christmas dinner, but he got drunk instead.

"I guess you heard that Shark died. I don't know how Irene is doing."

I said, "I'd heard about Shark and the last thing I heard about Irene was that she was staying at the Salvation Army Hospice."

"Well, you know what that means. That's the last place they put you before you die. You don't get out of there alive. It was the same with Longjohn.

"These are really crazy times. The weather is up and down, freezing one day, rain the next. Ice melting from the roof of the building in front of where I pan has been dripping on my back all day long. I'm really getting stiff. I'd rather have snow. I've been helping a guy who plows driveways. I have a steel shovel and clear show away from cars and other areas he can't reach. He pays me fifteen bucks an hour.

"When it rains I don't collect any money panning. When pedestrians have a coffee in one hand and an umbrella in the other there's no way they can reach for change.

"See these boots I'm wearing. A friend of mine at the Salvation Army gave them to me. They're size fifteen, I usually wear thirteen, but I can wear two extra pairs of socks. They keep me really warm. The guy said they were too small for his son. Can you imagine how big his feet are if a size fifteen is too small?

"The butcher I mentioned also saves me knee joints, chicken and turkey carcasses, necks, feet, tripe, offal. He gives me a good price since it's all stuff that's little demand. If it gets too old it would go in the trash. I put it in a big soup pot, let it boil on low heat for about twelve hours, then add potatoes, carrots, peas, anything I have in the fridge. It makes a delicious stew. It's good if you can make something useful out of another's waste.

"Listen to what I read in the newspaper about beet juice:

The government is mixing it with road salt to melt ice on the highways. It cuts down the use of salt by thirty percent and there's also a side benefit: Sugar beet juice lowers the effective temperature of road salt to around minus twenty-five from about minus ten. The juice also doesn't cause cars to rust."

Ted Talks

14 January 2016

"Good morning, Ted. I must have missed you yesterday."
"No, with the strong winds I decided to rest instead. I have a place to stay now. I've had it for twelve days, but only slept

there three. I have to transition into sleeping inside. I leave the windows wide open. I don't have any furniture, but that's not a problem. I haven't slept in a bed for seven years. I talked to my worker yesterday. I get a welfare allowance of seven hundred dollars. My rent is four eighty-five. That doesn't leave much to spare. I think I'm going to buy a bed today. I can get one at the Salvation Army for fifty bucks and they offer free delivery. I'd like to get a television. My landlord gave me a television aerial that attaches to the wall. He said I'd be able to get thirteen channels. I'd be happy with two.

"I was a trapper up north for twenty-nine years. I was married, had two kids, but that kind of a life is hard on a family. I'd be away for seven months at a time. Eventually my wife moved in with my best friend. That really hurt. It only lasted for six months before he threw her out. We had a family gathering at Christmas, but I couldn't bring myself to look at my wife. My daughter, who is short and round invited me into the bedroom. I thought that was odd, but she opened the closet door and there were seven years of Christmas presents that came tumbling out. Then she reached up and smacked my face. She said, 'Don't you dare go away again without letting us know where you are.' I've promised her and my son that I'd keep in contact with them.

"My worker has arranged for me to take a course in social skills. I've lived alone for so long I've forgotten how to talk to people. I sometimes say things that sound right to me, but others take offence. I often think that my way is right and that's all there is to it.

"Do you know Bernard?"

"I haven't seen him since the first week of December. He was hoping that his worker would find him a place to stay before Christmas. I haven't seen him since then."

"Well the last time I saw Bernard we were standing here together. I'd loaned him two hundred bucks, then lay down and went to sleep. When I awoke Bernard was gone and I was short another hundred that had been in my pocket. This is the only place I've seen him, so I've been standing here everyday hoping that he'll return. That isn't looking very likely."

"I'm sorry to hear that, Ted. Bernard seemed like such a friendly, happy person. I'm disappointed in him.

"I noticed that you were reading a newspaper, do you enjoy reading?"

"Yes, I read all the time. It comes from living alone for so long."

"Here's a copy of my book Gotta Find a Home: Conversations with Street People. The names and places have been changed, but you may recognize some people. I hope you enjoy the read."

"Thanks, Dennis, I really appreciate this.

"After I leave here I'm going home to take a shower, maybe I'll take two."

Just For Men

16 January 2017

I was looking for Ted, but he wasn't in his usual spot. I passed a man standing on the corner who looked vaguely familiar.

"Hi Dennis, it's me Ted. I tried some Just for Men hair color on my beard. I was supposed to leave it on for five minutes to get rid of some of the grey, but I passed out and when I looked in the mirror this is what I saw. I scrubbed and scrubbed, but I couldn't lighten it, so I'm stuck with a black beard for a while.

"They got me last night."

"Who got you?"

"Three Inuit guys. I was drunk. I went to the liquor store, from there I turned left into the alley and they jumped me. I can usually defend myself pretty well. I was able to protect my face but I had to give in. They got all my money. I'm aching all over, especially where I landed on my backpack.

"It's not the first time I've been attacked. One time I was sitting near the mall reading a newspaper. A guy came along and tried to kick me in the head. I'm always aware of what's going on around me, so I was able to duck. He tried to throw two more kicks then ran off. A security guard came along and showed me a cell phone picture. He asked, 'Have you see this guy?' I told him what happened and said, 'That's the guy. I'll be willing to testify.' The guard told me that the guy tried to grab a woman's purse as she was leaving the hotel. He didn't get it but he punched her in the face. Her teenaged daughter was standing beside her screaming, 'Don't hurt my mom!'. He punched her as well. I'm usually reluctant to inform on anyone, but this guy was crazy. He needed to be taken off the street."

"Did you get your bed?"

"No, I'm going to do that Friday. A guy is going to bring me some sheets and blankets, so I'll be all set. The problem is I got an eviction notice, so did everyone else in the building. There's a new owner, he wants to tear the place down and build a highrise.

"I've been enjoying your book. I'm on page thirty now. Joy was one tough woman. How did that guy, Big Jake get away with abusing her for so long?"

I said, "Eventually, he was charged and sentenced to eighteen months in Millhaven Penitentiary, but she took a lot of beatings before that. She was worried that if she called the police they'd be kicked out of their apartment. When neighbors called the police Joy got into a fight with one of the the cops and he broke her cheekbone. She said he was taking a beer out of her fridge. I'm sure there's a lot that she didn't tell me."

"I was married for twenty-nine years, but never had problems like that. The last place I was living was Tofino, on the west coast of Vancouver Island. It was like paradise there. I sent a letter to the fish-packing plant. I just wrote that I've been trapping for twenty-nine years and wanted to learn how a fish plant works. He had me do a lot of different jobs there. I really enjoyed it."

I asked, "What brought you back here?"

"I got a call from my mother, she's eighty-three. She said, 'Ted, get the fuck back here.' So I spent three hundred bucks on bus fare. She has a huge five bedroom house with a fish pond, waterfalls. I stayed there five months, but she worked me nearly to death. First of all she wanted me to unclog the fish pond. I had to dig about a dozen holes just to find the water connection. I drained the pond then used a five gallon can to get rid of the sludge. Finally I'd had enough. My dad died at sixty. He was a tough son of a bitch. Worked in a battery factory. He could hoist two batteries in each hand into the bed of a truck. Every once in awhile I'd ask him for money. He'd say, 'Go fuck yourself!' Later on he come to me and ask how much I needed. He was always good for it.

"He had diabetes and kidney problems. He was going to the hospital for dialysis. Eventually, it didn't work any more. The doctor told us that he was only expected lo live another three days so we took him home. The hospital wanted us fill out all kinds of forms, but we couldn't be bothered. We just took him."

Real Men

18 January 2017

Ted was sitting in the snow rocking back and forth. I approached him and said, "Good morning Ted, how was your night."

"Not good."

"Has your worker arranged a new place for you?"

"She's going to start looking in March. The building is scheduled for demolition, so I've got a place to stay until the end of February. That's not my only problem."

"What other problems do you have?"

"I told you I was jumped the other night. The same guy confronted me last night and asked for my money. I said to him, 'I'm not going to give you my money.' He's a big guy. He punched me. I said, 'I'm still not giving you my money.' He punched me again. It was a good punch. I laughed at him and asked, 'Is that the best you can do?' He said, 'You're crazy, but I'm going to see you again tomorrow. I'll get your money.' So, something is going to happen. The guy doesn't understand. I walked right through him. That should give him some indication. The judge told me that I'm not allowed to get angry. He said real men aren't controlled by their emotions. I'd blown a guy in half with a shotgun. I spent thirteen years in prison. I was ordered to take anger management classes. Everybody gets angry. I can get angry several times a day, but I'm not allowed to act on my first impulse.

"I could avoid this guy, but I refuse to let him dictate where I go. If you show weakness they'll tear you apart."

I said, "I guess that's something that you learned in prison."

"Yeah. I'm not afraid of this guy but whatever happens it's going to be bad. I'll try to make friends with him, but I don't see that happening. If I take him on I'll go back to prison. I don't want that. I've been out too long. So, I didn't sleep too well last night, thinking about what could happen. I'll think on it today as well."

"You told me that you had been doing some writing. Would you share it with me?"

"Sure, I've got about fifteen notebooks. I stopped because Big Daniel got mad. He thought I was writing about him, so I stopped."

I said, "I could help you. I could type your notes, maybe even get them published. It wouldn't cost anything."

"Thanks, Dennis, I'd appreciate that.

You're Not My Friend!

19 January 2017

"Good morning Ray. I was worried about you. You mentioned that you might see the guy that beat you."

"I saw him alright, but nothing happened. I said to him, 'I don't like you. I don't want to be your friend. I don't want to see you.' he said, 'I'm sorry you feel that way.' then he left.

"I was talking to a bicycle courier this morning. He told me about a guy who worked for their company. The guy had an appointment with his doctor. The doctor said, 'You're too fat. You're going to die of a heart attack if you don't lose weight.' The guy changed jobs and became a walking messenger. He'd walk all over the city. The next time he went to his doctor he was told that his heart was in perfect condition.

"There was this other guy who hated his job. He bought two lawnmowers, wrote his own flyer offering to cut lawns for ninety-nine dollars. He had three hundred and fifty printed and had the post office deliver them to every house in a certain neighbourhood. He got about a hundred and fifty replies. Now he's making about six thousand a month and he only works Mondays and Tuesdays."

I asked, "Have you been writing?"

"No, but I got out all my old notebooks. What a lot of memories they brought back. I used to work for a courier company, but I fucked the owner's wife. That didn't go over very well. It's not as if I meant to. She invited me to her place. I should have said no, but I was thinking with the wrong head."

I said, "It's not something that you can take back."

"No. Then there was this older woman, very nice looking. some guys said I was cruel, but I didn't think so. Tell me what you think. I sent her a dozen red roses every week. I didn't leave a card with them and I asked the florist not to give any indication of who I was. She was dispatcher and would ask over the microphone, 'Did any of you wonderful guys send me flowers?' She nearly went crazy trying to figure out who the sender was. Do you think that was cruel?"

"If she thought the sender was wonderful, I'm surprised that you didn't let her know that you were sending the flowers."

"That would have been awkward, since she was the mother of the other woman I told you about."

I said, "That would have been awkward if the daughter came over when you were with her mother."

TRUMP HATES KIDS!

25 January 2017

"Good morning, Ted. I missed you yesterday."

"Yeah, I got here late, around eleven. I had a bad night. Do you want to hear something funny? Friday night a guy came by and asked me if I wanted a flat screen TV. I said, 'Sure!' He said, 'Are you going to be here tomorrow?' I assured him that I would be. The next day he came carrying a big garbage bag; in it was the flat screen TV, a DVD player and 10 movies. I was so excited I wanted to go straight home to plug it in. I'd had a bit to drink and was rushing. I slipped on an ice patch and my feet went out from under me. You can see I'm a heavy guy. I landed on the TV and heard a horrible crunch. Sure enough the TV was smashed to pieces. I could have cried." he shrugged and said, "Easy come, easy go.

"I was sitting at the corner when the Trump protest started. One woman was carrying a sign that said TRUMP HATES KITTENS / TRUMP HATES KIDS. I thought, *that's a bit presumptuous. Is she God or somebody who can see what Trump likes or hates?* I asked her, 'Isn't that sign politically incorrect?' She walked over to me and said, 'How would you like to be grabbed by the balls?' She was tough looking, I said, 'No, ma'am!' I just sat there and waved. On her way back she asked, 'Now, do you get the point?' I said, 'Yes, ma'am.' She put five bucks in my cap."

He asked me, "Do you know what the protest was about?"

"Yes," I said, according to the newspaper:

"Thousands of women, with a strong representation of men and children, descended on the Human Rights Monument near City Hall Saturday morning to march in support of sister organizations in Washington and around the world. The marches were to protest the new administration of President Donald Trump, with a focus on

protecting and advancing women's rights. The protest march was to promote equality and equal rights for all people regardless of race, sexual orientation, or ability."

Ted continued, "Someone gave me this new backpack full of stuff, bubble bath, pads, women's stuff, nothing I can use. There's a young girl who comes by every day at noon. I'll give it to her." A man stopped and handed Ted a shopping bag. He responded by saying, "Thank you very much!" The man walked on and Ted said to me, "This is the comforter and sheets that I mentioned someone was giving me. I got my bed Saturday so I'm all set.

"I went to the pipeline protest, just to see what was happening. I was there for about an hour when a chief came up to me. He said, 'Take these, you need them.' I opened the package and saw a beautiful pair of Inuit mitts. I said to him, 'This is too much. I can't accept these.' He said, 'In my culture, to refuse a gift is an insult. Are you going to insult me?' 'No, No they're beautiful. I don't know what to say except thank you.' Ted pulled a package out of his backpack, unwrapped it and showed me a pair of white leather, decorated, gauntlet type mitts. "I wore them on the weekend and got them dirty, so I've put them away for now. I asked an Inuit friend of mine about them. He said they sell for about two hundred and fifty dollars.

"I want to show you something else. There is a couple named Dawn and Doug who have been really kind to me. They're religious people. They do missionary work all over the world. Doug said to me, 'You have work to do. There are a lot of kids on the street who need help. You have a responsibility to them.' I don't know what he expects me to do. I hadn't seen the couple for about four months, but they stopped by on the weekend. In one of the rich districts, I had picked something out of the garbage that I thought they'd like. What do you think?" He handed me a copper, stylized figure of Jesus on the cross. On the back was engraved to Dawn and Doug from Ted. "Do you think they'll like it? I don't mind telling you that I go through the garbage because I know that you understand."

I said, "I understand, Ted. A lot of people go through garbage. If I see something I can use in someone's garbage I'll pick it up. What's one man's trash is another man's treasure."

"Yeah, but this morning I found a half eaten container of yogurt. It looked alright. Now I'm feeling a bit queasy. I think I'm going to have to find a place to barf."

Deer Hunting

30 January 2017

"Good morning, Ted."

"Hi, Dennis. I had a good day yesterday, collected about seventy bucks. If today goes well I'll be able to buy a TV this week. It was nice to come home to the sheets and comforter that were dropped off. I get my check next Wednesday. That's February 1st isn't it? The government holds on to our money until the last second to collect as much interest as possible. It's deposited directly to my bank account.

"Now that I'm a bit settled I want to look for a job, maybe washing dishes. I'd like that. I'd be off in my own little corner and I'd get the leftovers that diners leave on their plates. If I wasn't waiting for that couple I have the present for I'd be job hunting right now. Did I tell you about the first time I met them? I was panning on the street and they came by with a hot roast chicken and fries. That was quite a surprise. I've gained about forty pounds since I've been here. People are always giving me junk food. When I was trapping I'd eat healthy all the time.

"Even with all the experience I've had, survival courses that I've taken, I've done some pretty stupid things. Bow hunting season opened in September. I'd gone into this wooded area of about a thousand square miles. Being *mister know it all*, I didn't bother taking a phone, a GPS or even a compass. I saw deer tracks so I climbed a tree. I waited about an hour when a doe and buck came into view, but I wanted to wait for the perfect shot. My legs got numb and I fell out of the tree, broke my ankle. The bone was sticking out and I was losing a lot of blood. I knew If I stayed there I'd drain out and die. I didn't know where I was, but I could hear the far off sound of traffic, so I crawled towards it for about an hour. I finally made it to the highway. I was lying at the side of the road waving my arms. A lady stopped, she pulled out one of those pocket flashlights and shone it at me. I said, 'Lady, I'm injured. I need to get to a hospital.' My face was nearly white from loss of blood. She was afraid to come near me. I said, 'I'm not going to hurt you. Look at my ankle. Please call for help.' The police arrived, they called for a helicopter to fly me out. Before the helicopter arrived I asked the cops, 'Would someone, please, go back for my bow?' One cop asked, 'How are we going to find it?.' The other cop said, 'Just follow the trail of blood.' When a person is crawling they leave an obvious path.

"There was something funny that happened on the helicopter that I gotta tell you about. I placed a phone call to my wife. I said, 'Hello, Dear, I'm afraid that I've had an accident and I'm being taken to hospital. The sounds you hear are the blades of the chopper.' I used to play lots of tricks on her and she thought this was one of them. She said, 'I'm glad you had an accident. I hope you're in lots of pain and that you die in hospital you son of a bitch.' Then she slammed down the phone. Because of the noise they had me on speaker phone. You should have seen the look on the faces of the rescue team when they heard that. I told them it was just a joke and everything was fine.

"There were three doctors waiting when I arrived at the hospital. First they gave me a blood transfusion. The doctor said I was minutes away from death. I had a very complicated fracture. I have pins and plates in there holding everything together. I was in hospital for a week when I told the nurse, 'I've got to get out of here.' She took me to the physiotherapy room where they had a flight of ten steps. The nurse said, 'If you can go up and down using crutches we can let you go.' I was determined to climb those steps and I did. I was in a cast for about a year, then a brace for another six months. It still gives me problems. I was on oxycontin for about six months. I hate taking pills. The bottles started piling up. I finally gave them to my brother. I'm still on medication. I haven't been taking it. Yesterday I started crying for no reason. I found a doctor who will give me an injection once a month, so I won't have to take pills."

Bear Hunting

31 January 2017

"Good morning, Ted."

"Hi, Dennis. I had a good day yesterday, collected about seventy bucks. Have you heard what Trump's doing now? He's building his wall."

"Yes, I heard that. I can't see how that is practical. He could use that same money paying for additional border security officers. If he's trying to keep out the drug cartels they have access to planes and have been using tunnels for years."

"He's also going ahead with the oil pipelines. That's got to be good for Canada. It will provide jobs and perhaps cheaper fuel."

I said, "A lot of my First Nations friends are upset because it will violate sacred burial grounds and will increase the possibility of oil polluting the land and the water. For some in British Columbia fishing is their main source of income. An oil spill could devastate them."

"Yeah, I've heard that as well. I just see it as providing jobs and hopefully, cheaper fuel. I don't drive a car now, but as soon as I'm able I'd like to buy an old beater to get me around. I wouldn't mind having the same access to hunting and fishing that aboriginals have. They're even allowed to spear pickerell in the shallow spawning beds. They also spear more than they can eat. I've often been offered pickerel for sale when I'm near a reserve. I only shoot as much as I can eat and I eat every part of the animal. I've dragged a three hundred pound bear out of the woods. Mind you, I was pretty stupid about it. I'd left my hunting platform and my ammunition. I was watching a bear cub reaching into a container of donuts. There was a roar nearby, a bigger bear was in the area. The cub ran away. A large male may kill and eat a cub. The bear spotted me and came running. I had my shotgun lined up, but instead of squeezing the trigger I pulled it and the shot tore off his front foot. I only had two shots left The three legged bear was enraged and chased me up a hill. I found a crevice in the rock where I was protected. I fired another shot, but still didn't kill it, only made it more angry. I got out in the clearing and as the bear came closer I took careful aim and brought him down. I'd never leave a wounded animal in the bush. If I had to track him ten miles I would. Now I stick to bow hunting. It's more of a challenge and the season is longer.

"I need to get back on my medication. Last night I found myself crying for no reason. I felt foolish. My worker has all my paperwork sorted now, so I'll be able to go to a doctor.

"There's a pizza place where I pan in the evenings. Restaurants don't give food away, something to do with health regulations. At nine o'clock, just before they close up they walk right past me carrying about ten boxes of pizza and throw them in the dumpster. I wait until they've gone then dive in after the pizza. I freeze most of it, so it can last me about a week. I don't know why they don't phone one of the shelters, they'd send a truck over to pick up food that would otherwise go to waste."

February 2016

A Dying Breed

Yesterday the city experienced a record breaking, twenty inch snowfall. Buses got stuck. Commutes that would in normal weather take thirty minutes took four hours. A hundred and twenty vehicle accidents further snarled traffic. I gave up on my regular bus. Some people had already waited two hours. I walked five blocks to take another route. On my way, huddled against a building, panning for change was Bearded Bruce covered in snow. I didn't recognize him at first and wearing two scarves over my face he didn't recognize me.

I pulled down my scarves and asked, "Bruce, is that you?"

He said, "Hi laddie, how've you been. I looked for you a couple of times in some of the regular places, but didn't see you."

I said, "My asthma has been bad this year. With the extreme cold I haven't been out much lately. How have you been?"

"Not so good lad. They cut off my Welfare. If I can't make enough panning I won't be able to pay my rent and I'll be sleeping on the streets again. I could have lied to them, but it's just not my way. They said I should get a job. I said, 'I have a job panhandling. Sometimes I'm panning ten to twelve hours a day. Do you think that's easy?' They wouldn't go along with that; now if I was a prostitute, they'd consider that a real job, but panning — no. I'm an alcoholic, there's no way I can hold onto a regular job."

I suggested, "Tell them you're a prostitute."

"I just couldn't do it, man. I'd rather sleep behind the dumpster again.

"Shark died last Sunday. I guess you knew that he had cancer. The funeral is this week. I won't be going. I didn't like the man that much. I expect that Irene will will be dead by next Sunday. She doesn't look very good. There aren't very many of the originals left. We're a dying breed."

Un-bearded Bruce

19 February 2016

"Matey, have a seat," commanded Bruce. "I've cleared a space, you can sit on my bag. **It's okay folks, just a couple of bums, sitting, having a chat.**"

"Hi, Bruce, I notice that you've shaved off your beard. What inspired that?"

"She told me to do it."

"Who's she?"

"Loretta, my girl, she said that you were talking to her yesterday. I think I was talking to you a couple of days ago. I don't remember. I was too drunk."

"Yeah, she told me about you pounding on the door. When she opened it, you were rolling around in the snow.

"Is there any chance of you getting back on Welfare?"

"No, I don't want it. It's just a crutch. There wouldn't be any point in me leaving my apartment if everything is paid for. I still get my disability allowance, my ODSP (Ontario

Disability Support Program). Part of that is paid directly to my landlord. I still have three hundred and twenty a month to make up. Loretta helps. She pans where you saw her yesterday and I'm just across the street in Weasel's old spot. I don't charge her rent, but she's been staying with me for the past five months. She's stayed clean and sober the whole time. She still has her weed.

"See that couple panning across the street? You know who that is don't you?"

"I can't see them very well."

"It's Shakes' daughter, I don't remember which one. I had a bit of a dust up with them earlier. I guess they had some sort of disagreement then he jumped up and started hitting her, really punching her. If there's one thing I can't stand it's a man who hits a woman. There were lots of people standing around, but nobody did anything. I saw some with their cell phones out. They may have been phoning the police — I don't know. Anyway, I pulled him off her and started pounding him. Then she jumped on my back and said, 'Stop hurting my boyfriend!' I can't figure these women out, just like Joy getting back with Big Jake.

"I've known a guy for about ten years. I just found out that he has nine kids. He's on the street because he doesn't want to pay child support. I said to him, 'Take some responsibility. Haven't you heard of condoms?' I don't have anything to do with him any more."

I saw Trudy, Anne's daughter walking towards us. I waved.

Bruce said to her, "Just keep walking." To me he said, "That's another one I avoid… Here come the cops! We better not be seen sitting here." We walked to the end of the block.

"Yeah, they're picking him up, throwing him into the squad car. I'm glad to see that."

March 2017

Harrassment

9 March 2017

When I saw Ted he looked dejected, "I really got myself in shit with my worker yesterday. You know how it is when you meet someone and she's overweight and not that attractive, but you can't help having strong feelings for her? I bought this woman a dozen red roses."

"How did she like them?"

"I didn't include a card saying they were from me. I sent them to my worker's boss. My worker said, 'That verges on harassment.' I just thought I was doing something nice, giving something to brighten her day.

"Anyway, I have another appointment today. Since I'm being evicted and they're demolishing my building there are some legal details that she wants to discuss with me. I don't know why she didn't just tell me over the phone. I hope she's not still pissed off.

"I had a pretty good weekend. I watched about seven dvds. Some of them I watched twice. I don't have cable service so I buy dvds from the pawn shop. They have good prices.

"I got so drunk on Friday that I couldn't stand. I had to sit here a couple of extra hours while I got sober. I haven't had a drink since. This big cop poked his fingers in my face and said he could charge me with panhandling. I said, 'I'm not panhandling, I don't have a sign, I don't ask people for money. I'm just sitting here. Go ahead and charge me.' I didn't get a ticket. He eventually just walked away."

I said, "Bernard used a sign saying I'M BROKE AND SEXY."

"Yeah, that guy still owes me two hundred bucks, but something funny happened, a little girl came up to me and handed me an envelope with fifty dollars in it, so I guess he's trying to pay me back. You never know about people."

"Did you hear about the cop who was charged with manslaughter. They had this guy on the ground and the cop kept beating him with his baton. It was all caught on video. The guy died."

Eviction

16 March 2017

"Good morning, Ted, how's it going with this bad weather we've been having?"

"Not so good. Yesterday with the blowing snow nobody wanted to stop. I was up near the hotel all day and made about thirty bucks. Today's a bit better; I collected enough to get one of those big breakfasts on a bun. The sun is out, the weather will be warmer."

"How about housing. Do you have that sorted?"

"Well, I don't know. They gave the seventeen residents a hundred and twenty days notice. That will take us 'till May sixteenth. I talked to a legal advisor. She said the company is required to pay is first and last month's rent, but in some cases they've been able to squirm around that. She said, 'Don't' give them your key until the check is in your hand. Don't listen to any of their excuses. Make sure your rent is paid in full so in court they won't have a leg to stand on. Give them one of my cards so they know that you have representation.' I'm not exactly sure what they're planning to do with the building;

they may gut it, they may demolish it. If they have tools in there they won't want a lot of disgruntled tenants with keys to the side door."

I said, "By May sixteenth the weather will be warm, no matter what happens."

"Yeah, my worker is supposed to find me an apartment, but I don't mind sleeping outside. I've done that before. We'll see what happens."

St. Patrick's Day

16 March 2017

The temperature has been hovering around the freezing mark, but the sun has been melting the ice on the sidewalks making the walking less treacherous. "Good morning, Ted, it should be a good day for you especially when the sun starts shining on you."

"Yeah, last night was really bad. I came this close (indicating a space of about an inch) to getting into it with these two big guys. I'm six foot and I was looking way up into their faces, but it all worked out the end. Lately I've been talking to this native woman, Fay. She's about forty, nice looking. Anyway, I was going into McDonald's as a friend of mine was coming out. He had a massive black eye. I asked him, 'Have you been in a fight?' He said, 'Yeah, a woman punched me in the face.' I laughed and said, 'A woman punched you?' 'Yeah,' he said, 'the one you were talking to last night.' I saw my woman friend at the bus stop talking to these two big native guys. I walked up and started talking to her. One of them says to me, 'Are you some kind of a fuckin' weirdo?' I stood right up to him and said, 'Do I look to you like I'm some kind of a fuckin' weirdo?' He backed off because he could see I was ready to get it on with him. I talked to Fay for a few minutes. I said to her, So, you punched my friend in the eye.' She said, 'Yeah, I punched him. He was being an asshole.' Everything was cool. I wandered away, but kept an eye on them. Soon after she starts yelling at these guys and stomps off. I breathed a sigh of relief because now she was walking alone."

I said, "So you had a chance to talk to her."

"Yeah, you could say that — 10 bucks. It's the way I am."

I changed the conversation. "Happy St. Patrick's day."

"Is that what today is? There are a lot of bars on this street aren't there?"

"Yeah, Irish bars, Scottish bars, any kind you want."

"I think I'll be panning in front of an Irish bar. They'll all be full tonight, the jails too."

Man Eating Snake

30 March 2017

Good morning, Ted."

"Hey, Dennis, I was just reading about a snake who swallowed an Indonesian farmer. The snake was twenty-three feet long. Reticulated pythons can grow as long as thirty-two feet. They've been known to eat small animals even cows. Then there was a case in Campbellton, New Brunswick where an African rock python escaped from a reptile store, bit and strangled two kids. I've had some experience with king snakes. I found one when I was camping. I fed it minnows attached to a monofilament fishing line. They're not venomous, but can give a nasty bite. They're called king snakes because they feed on other snakes even rattlers and copperheads. They have an immunity to the other snake's venom. A guy camped beside me; it was a public campground. One morning I saw him swinging a stick and beating the water. He'd killed my snake. I asked him to leave then kicked his truck as he was driving away. I was charged for that. I don't like to see any animal harmed for no reason. I was a hunter and a trapper, but that was for food and to earn a living. I used every part of the animal. I didn't waste anything."

I said, "The other day you introduced me to your friend Marcia. She seems very nice."

"Yeah, she's nice sometimes, at other times she can be nasty. She's a crackhead and an alcoholic. She also has some mental issues. Most people on the street have mental issues. She gets injections once a month because she can't remember to take meds on a daily basis. I'm not sure what her problems are. She may be schizophrenic, bipolar… I don't know. Her family kicked her out so she stays at the Shep. They control her medications. I have her over to my place sometimes, but she has a very short attention span. She'll say 'Let's watch a movie.' Ten minutes into it she'll say 'Let's watch something else.' I can remember being like that as a kid. They had me on ritalin, but my mom didn't like the way I reacted to to it. I was like a zombie, so she cut it off. I didn't do well in school, but I eventually learned to read and it really settled me down. I read all the time.

"Marcia is thirty-three years old. She had a baby three months ago but it was taken away by Children's Services. She has no permanent address, no income except for a disability pension. She was using drugs and drinking all during the pregnancy. She'd ask me to buy her energy drinks. I said to her, 'You can't drink those!' I'd try to get her to drink beer with the lowest alcohol level, but she'd get mad. She'd say, 'Why do I have to drink this shit?' I'd explain it to her but it would just cause a fight. She wasn't allowed to breastfeed because of the drugs in her system. The baby has been adopted by a family in the suburbs. She's allowed regular visits arranged by Children's Services.

I asked, "Have you thought of having her move in with you? It would save on expenses."

"Yeah, I thought about it, but it's the commitment. I counted the months back to when she got pregnant. I don't know if I'm the father, but it is a possibility. I'd support the baby -- I'm not irresponsible, but I'm going to be evicted soon. I'm still waiting to get on O.D.S.P. (Ontario Disability Support Program). It's been five months now since I applied. It's been approved but hasn't taken effect yet. I have nothing to offer that she doesn't have already.

"You're not recording this are you?"

"Ted, I have never worn a wire, and I never would. You can search me. The reason is, I'm afraid of being killed. I know that would be a real possibility. I'd never take that chance."

"Hey, I've been visiting my mother for the past week. She's been sick. She's eighty years old. Anyway, I walked into the house, she said, 'Ted, you're a bum.' I said, 'I know, Mom.' She said, 'I love you just the same.'

"Remember that Inuit I told you about. The one that tried to kick me in the face while I was sitting in front of the hotel. He never actually made contact because I kept dodging. I saw him the other day, he said, 'I know you from somewhere, don't I?' I said 'You're damned right you do. You're the mother fucker that tried to kick me when I was sitting down. What was that about?' He said, 'Maybe I'll do a better job next time.' I said, 'I've issued a statement against you. I'll be seeing you in court. Let's see what you have to say then.'

"I don't understand these guys. I'd never hurt anybody without a good cause. I was talking to a guy from the Shep this morning. His knuckles were all bloody, there was blood on his shirt. I asked him, 'What happened?' He said, 'I got angry with my girlfriend.' I said, 'So you got angry with your girlfriend. Did you hit her?' He said, 'No I hit this other guy.' I asked, "What did this other guy do?' He said, 'Nothing. Now I'm banned from the Shep for five years.' I said, you hit this guy because you were angry with your girlfriend. Christ, I get angry ten times a day but I don't hit anybody. Do you have any charges against you?' He said, 'Yeah, three for assault.' I said, 'You stupid fuck. A judge is going to look at your record and he's going to put you away for a long time. You're not fit to be on the street.'

"I applied for a place in the country. I'm sick of what I see here everyday. This Japanese guy has a farm with animals. He's offering it for free, he just wants someone to care for the place and his animals. He said, 'Absolutely no killing of animals.' I wrote an application where I mentioned that I've spent thirty years in trapping and want to give something back. He liked that. We'll see what happens."

I asked, "Have you seen Marcia lately?"

"Yeah, I was with her this morning. She stopped into McDonald's to use the bathroom. She asked me to wait, but I walked away."

April 2017

Mother of all Bombs

"Good morning, Ted."

"Hey, Dennis, I'm freezing here, just waiting for the sun to come over that building… I gotta stop drinking, man. I thought I could stop, but I keep getting drunk. This is the last week in my apartment. My worker is going to come by to let me know what's available. It'll probably be across the river, rent is lower there."

"That's where I used to live, near the strip club."

"I got hauled out of that strip club on my wedding day."

I asked, "How was your weekend?"

"It was bad. I'm too embarrassed to even talk about it… I was pretty drunk… They called the police on me… Okay I'll tell you what happened. I was panning in my usual place in front of the hotel. A woman came by. I've met her before. She sat down and asked if I had a beer. I pulled out two beer and we drank them. Then she asked if I had ten bucks. I said, 'Sure.' and gave her the ten. She said, 'Come up the steps with me.' So I did. She dropped her panties and lifted up her little black skirt. I said, 'I can't drop my pants here. There are people around.' She was backed against the wall, I unzipped my fly and we were going at it. An old couple stopped and said, 'Don't do that in public, you pig. I'm calling the police.' Cars were at the stop light honking their horns; guys were giving me the thumbs up. The police never came, but I felt like a shit. I saw her again the next night. She sat down and asked if I had any speed. I gave her two tabs. I usually buy four at a time. I only take a half, but she popped two at once. She said, 'Thanks, but no sex tonight.'

"The panning has been slow. I was out ten hours and only made fifty bucks."

I said, "I was talking to Bearded Bruce. He was out eleven hours and only made sixty. It must be bad for everybody. I've heard that Mondays and rainy days are bad, summer is slow. Bruce prefers it when it's thirty below."

Ted continued, "Trump is sure shaking things up. Did you hear that the *mother of all bombs* was dropped on Afghanistan. The 21,000-pound bomb had a blast radius of one mile. It broke windows three miles away and knocked out all of the tunnels used by the Taliban. Scarier than that is the aircraft carrier the US sent to North Korea. Neither of the leaders are known for backing down. We may be looking at the start of World War Three.

Sleeping in the Cold

18 April 2017

"Good morning, Ted."

"Hey, Dennis, it's my birthday today, I turn the big six zero."

"Do you have any plans to celebrate."

"My mom wants me to phone her. I may visit her. I was supposed to see my worker last week but I didn't show. It's the twenty-fourthth today; I have to be out of my apartment by the end of the weekend. I'll wait for her today, she should come by. She's a real porker, big and round. I call her M&M,

you know like the candy? I imagine her with two little arms and legs sticking out. I'm being mean. I've got to stop that."

I said, "It's a good idea to be nice to the people who can help you. How was your weekend?"

"I don't know, a drunken mystery. I can't remember what happened. Do you remember the guy I told you about, sleeping in front of the mall. I'd given him a sleeping bag, he lost it. Outreach gave him another one, he lost it. I saw him last night sleeping on the sidewalk in just his clothes. He was shivering. I figured he'd die if I didn't do something, so I draped him with my parka. He didn't even wake up. He won't last long, he can get hypothermia even if the temperature doesn't go below freezing.

"I did something stupid last week. I found a rope and made a hangman's noose. It took a while to figure out how to do it, the loops then winding it around eight times. I put it around my neck and wore it under my coat. I didn't have it hanging out or anything, but a woman asked me about the rope and I showed her. 'She said give that to me. Don't be so stupid.' So I gave it to her. I guess suicide is a sin isn't it? It may even be one of the commandments… I'm not sure.

"I got to quit drinking. I tell myself that I can, but I don't do anything. I talk the talk, but don't walk the walk. I also have to get back on my meds. My worker is going to help me with that. I did go to church yesterday."

I asked, "Did you go with Marcia?"

"That drunken whore? No, I went with a woman who attends university. She's a nice girl. She invited me to church, but was surprised that I actually showed up. It was nice, singing songs, that sort of thing. It got me thinking.

"At the end of term she's leaving for Paris. She'll be staying with a Parisienne family; they'll provide her meals. She has to pay for her flight and other expenses. She hopes to find work teaching English.

"Paris isn't the safest place in the world right now with the bombings, shootings, other terrorist attacks. I hope she'll be okay."

Rehab Clinic

"Good morning, Ted, I have some questions for you. If you don't mind."

"Go ahead, shoot."

"There is a group that is planning to open an addiction clinic in the downtown area. Do you have any thoughts on that?"

"Is this going to be a safe injection site?"

"No, not specifically. It'll be housed in an existing building. The facility will have twelve beds. There will be doctors, nurses, psychologists, pharmacists and counsellors. What do you think of the idea?"

"Yeah, it sounds like a good idea."

"Do rehabilitation centres work?"

"Yes and no. I've been in rehab five times. I'm still an alcoholic, but they kept me clean for a while. The longest period was five years. That's when I was living five miles in the bush out west. The outreach workers were great. Each Friday they'd walk the five miles into my camp to see if I was okay. They'd bring soup and other food supplies. I felt guilty so I said to them, 'Instead of you walking here, I'll be on the highway at eight o'clock every Friday evening.' So, that's the way we worked it out."

"What was the best facility that you stayed in?"

"That would be in Vermont. It's closed now. My dad arranged an intervention. He came to my apartment with two goons, they kicked the door in, threw me in a van and took me to this rehab centre. It was really expensive. I stayed a month and said I was ready to come home. He phoned the administrators and told them, 'He's not ready to come home. Keep him for another month.' I was clean for about two years after that. It boils down to people, places and things. I was told not to associate with other alcoholics or drug users; to stay away from places that serve alcohol and to avoid anything else that I associated with drug or alcohol use. I have some brochures at home. I'll bring them to you."

"Thanks Ted, I'd appreciated that."

"What about priority."

"Well, old farts like me are a waste of time. It's the youth that need guidance and treatment. You saw the Paramedic van in front of the youth shelter yesterday? There were two kids that had overdosed. Later a woman came over to me and asked for a smoke. I asked her if she knew anything about the two people who were brought out on stretchers. She said, 'Yeah, that was me and my boyfriend. We'd overdosed on Xanax. They couldn't wake us up in the morning, so they called 911.'

"I know so much about those places I could be a counsellor. In group sessions when you first arrive you have to give a statement. It would start with, 'I am an addict and I can't control my addiction.' Sometimes, when young girls were asked to describe their situation they'd start crying and say they couldn't talk about it, the counsellor would say, 'Go over and talk to Ted. He knows what's going on.' So, they'd come over and I'd say. 'You have to be open and honest. You say you can't talk about what happened, but the truth is that you're not willing to talk about it. The only way this program is going to help is if you put your heart in it.'

"The counsellors would question me and I could tell them just what they wanted to hear. They'd say, 'Ted you have such good retention of information.' It was like going for a school exam when I'd taken the same exam five times before. These places all asked the same things."

"So how are you doing now, Ted?"

"I drink, smoke a bit of pot, occasionally take meth. I don't drop two tabs like some of these kids; I cut a tab in half and take that. It helps with my sexual performance, if you know what I mean.

"I made a commitment this morning. I'm going to cut out the hard stuff. A couple of days ago I got really wasted. When I woke up this morning I had the shakes, my legs were twitching. I had two beer, 4.9 per cent, and it leveled me off. From now on I'm going to stick to beer."

Later, I was talking with Little Chester, "A group is proposing a drug and alcohol addiction facility in the downtown area. Is that something that would interest you?"

"No, but it would be good for the youth."

"Have you ever been in a rehab program?"

"Yes, three times. Each time I told them the same story and each time they said, "We don't want you here."

"What was the story that you told them?"

"I said, "Each morning I wake up, get drunk, fall down and have fun."

Debbie R.I.P.

19 May 2017

Bearded Bruce was sitting on the sidewalk with his back against the polished granite of an office building. An empty coffee cup was held in his outstretched hand. When he saw me approach he said, "Hey, Dennis, have you got a few minutes to talk. I'll pull out a piece of cardboard for you to sit on. So, how are you doing, man. It's great to see you. Loretta and I were just talking about all our friends. Did you hear that Debbie passed away? Loretta took that pretty hard. Nick and Trudy are back. They both have cancer. Nancy's is incurable. Nick is doing everything he can to make her life comfortable. Raven passed away and I guess you heard that Shark and Irene are both gone. Loretta stayed home because she was feeling depressed. When she feels depressed she wants a drink. She's been sober for two years. She's decided that what she wants to do is study to become a drug and rehab counsellor to Inuit people. She's had a lot of experience with that."

I said, "A group I know of: doctors, nurses, psychologists, pharmacists and philanthropists are interested in providing accessible, mental and substance abuse/addiction care for the homeless in the downtown area. We have in mind an existing building with twelve beds. Is this something that you'd be interested in? Is twelve beds enough?"

"A thousand beds wouldn't be enough, but twelve would be a dozen more than we have right now. Follow up and job placement would be mandatory. These people would need to trust that there was someone to turn to if they had a relapse or things went bad. AA has a helpline that alcoholics can use if the need for a drink is too great. They can also go to meetings whenever they want, some go once a day, some go five times a day.

"You're asking me about this in what capacity? I'm not interested in rehabilitation for myself. I'm different than a lot of people who we both know who need drugs and alcohol. If they don't get their fix or a drink for a couple of days they get symptoms of nausea, headaches, sweats, diarrhea, insomnia, and anxiety, among others. In extreme cases, alcohol detox can cause death. Sometimes, drugs are used to lessen the effects of alcohol detox.

"I'm not one of those people. For me it's a lifestyle choice. I want alcohol, but I don't need it. Deciding to give up sex doesn't mean that a man doesn't get a hard on. The want is always there. I used heroin for a while, but didn't get addicted because I don't have an addictive personality. Also, I wasn't trying to escape from anything. There was nothing that I wanted to forget. I came to Canada with five friends, we called ourselves a gang. Can you guess how many of them are still alive? One, and that's because he's serving twelve years in prison for murder, or manslaughter. Have you seen the movie Trainspotting? If you haven't you should. It was filmed near where I used to live. Do you remember the urinal scene. I was there. My friends were just like the characters in the movie.

"If you're thinking of a model rehab situation you should look at Holland. Prohibition never works. See what happened in the States, it put all the money in the hands of organized crime. In Holland, what they did first was to eliminate the money. A drug or alcohol addict could get a government licence and he would be provided a limited amount of the alcohol or drugs of his choice. He didn't have to buy from underground sources, so they dried up.

"The overall vision puts addiction clients in charge of their own addiction treatment, by shifting the care towards empowerment, reintegration and self-regulation of the clients. Since the start of 2014, addiction care has been provided in a three-stepped approach: with frontline support from a general practitioner or a general practice mental health worker, followed by the primary mental healthcare and secondary mental healthcare. http://buff.ly/2rDPSiz

In case after case, those who have completed the drug rehabilitation program in Zutphen state that this treatment center saved their lives. One woman told a terrifying tale of years of crime perpetrated to maintain her drug habit. When she woke vomiting blood one day, she realized that she would die within a week if she did not get help. She had heard that the Narconon drug recovery program in Zutphen could help and she went to them. It took several months for her to finally rebuild the life that was destroyed by substance abuse, but she did it. She got completely clean and became a productive employee again, also restoring her relationship with her family. http://buff.ly/2qCvWPz

Bruce continued, "You must be willing to accept people who are drunk and/or on drugs. At present these people are turned away from AA and the Salvation Army. They demand that an addict be clean for twenty-four hours before entering their premises. There is a small window where addicts have hit rock bottom and may decide that they desperately want recovery. If an addict or an alcoholic can resist for twenty-four hours they don't need a program. In Scotland and Holland, addicts commit to seventy-two hours where they are locked in and sometimes tied down. After that it's their decision to stay or go.

"There would need to be a pharmacist to administer the drugs of choice. Methadone is not a substitute for heroin, it replaces the craving and is administered to a user who has given up the drug, much like a nicotine patch is used by someone quitting smoking. You can't just slap a patch on a smoker and expect any results. They have to have a deep desire to quit. Being told by a doctor that you either quit or die is often enough motivation.

"It's essential that there be representatives on the board who were down and out drug users or alcoholics and are now in recovery. Nobody else would know the hell that recovering addicts go through. As an example a man wouldn't be effective as a counsellor at a rape crisis center, unless the man had himself been raped. A healthy youth wouldn't be effective counselling to elderly arthritis sufferers about how to deal with their pain. As a parent you wouldn't be effective counselling pedophiles, you'd look down at them with disgust. Am I getting my point across?

"Another thing you would need is security. If addicts can't get money for drugs they'll resort to violence and stealing. This causes bad feelings. If both the thief and the person stolen from are in the same room, or if one is outside and the other is inside, they'll break down the door to get revenge.

If you'd like I'd be willing to speak to this group, and could refer other people who may be of value in the program."

Home Brew

26 May 2017

"Hi Dennis, I'll be getting my new place on Monday. They've moved it up a few days. I've got roaches where I am now so there's a lot of stuff I can't take to my new place. I've heard that roaches are the oldest living insect. They originated over two hundred and eighty million years ago. So, they're pretty tough. I don't mind them so much, but they spread disease.

"My new place is bigger so I'll be able to make wine again. That'll save a lot of money and I can sell some on the side. It's easy to make and it's not illegal. I've made my own beer. My wife didn't like that because I'd have guys ringing the doorbell at two thirty in the morning. They'd be yelling, 'Ted, we've got some bitches in the car and we want to party. Bring us down a couple of two fours.'

"Another time I was making my own vodka. I had all the distilling equipment hidden in the attic. I'd send out bottle pickers to get me sparkling water bottles. I'd give them thirty cents a piece. They were happy. I was happy. My room was on the main floor so I'd have people banging on my window at all times of the night. These guys, alcoholics, would be drunk and noisy. They'd shout, 'Ted, get out of bed you lazy asshole. We need a couple of bottles.' It cost me a little over a dollar to make and I sold it for ten, so I was making big money. If someone bought more than ten bottles I'd throw in a free one. Other guys would want me to front them because they had no money. I'd tell them, 'I'll give you this bottle for free, but don't ever come by again without money.'

"My landlady didn't like the noise and had the police come by. They knocked on my door and asked if they could come in. I said, 'Do you have a warrant?' The cop said, 'No.' I said, I'll let you come in, but I'll stay with your buddies in the hallway.' He went in, saw all the bottles and asked, 'Ted, are you making alcoholic beverages here?' I said, 'Just a bit of wine. There's no law against that is there? When vodka is fermenting it's a dark color. It looks just like wine. The cop asked, "Do you mind if we look through your drawers and closets?' I said, 'Go ahead.' They came around a couple of times. After the second inspection where they didn't find anything they said, 'We won't be coming back again.' If they'd come a third time I could have charged them with harassment.

"My landlady was still ticked off so she invited me for lunch. She paid. She said, 'Ted, this isn't working you'll have to move out.' I said, 'No problem. Give me two months to organize my stuff and I'll be gone.' "

Going Fishing

"Hi Dennis, I'm in my new place now. It's huge, about four times the size of my old one. I found one roach, that's not bad. They have the baseboards and all the cracks caulked. The building has steam heating, you know, with radiators. The problem with that is they have open cold air registers. Bugs can travel from apartment to apartment.

I asked, "Do you have a bed yet?"

"Yeah, but they sent a single bed. I told them I can't use a single. I haven't slept in one of those since I was a kid. When you're used to sleeping outdoors you get used to rolling around from side to side. Maybe it's to get the circulation going. I've already fallen out on the floor a couple of times. And if I have some bitches over… You know what I mean.

"The place is quiet though. The landlord asked me if I minded being on a floor that is mostly elderly people. I said, 'I just turned sixty. I'm no spring chicken.'

"I read in the newspaper that this weekend people are encouraged to put at the curb any old furniture, even clothes they don't want. They attach a sign saying 'Free' and anybody can take them. I really need a sofa and a table. I had to leave most of my stuff behind and now I have so much room to fill.

"I got my fishing licence. I hope to go down to where the canal empties into the river. I've caught big muskies there. Last year I went with a couple of women and they kept telling me that I didn't know how to fish. I brought some frozen fish, slit them from asshole to gills, then cut them into six inch chunks. I buried three hooks deep inside and let the bait rest on the bottom of the river. Muskies are scavengers, they feed off the bottom. I waited a while and pulled in a thirty pounder. I think the record weight is sixty-nine pounds. You watch, I'm going to catch a record breaker and you'll see my picture in the paper. They've set size limits for each of the twenty provincial zones so you need to read the regulations before you fish. At some of the northern lakes you're not allowed to catch a muskie smaller than fifty-four inches or a northern pike smaller than twenty-seven inches; that's because the larger ones may be spawning. For walleye you're not allowed to keep anything smaller than eighteen inches.

June 2017

I got rid of my worker

13 June 2017

"Good morning Dennis, I got rid of my worker, a real porker. I saw her Friday and asked if she'd contacted my landlord about the three months rent he owes me, since everyone was evicted due to construction. She said, 'No, I didn't call him. He's your landlord, you call him.' I said, 'Alright, give me his phone number, I'll call him.' 'No,' she said, 'I'm not going to do that.' She thinks that because I'm passive, a nice guy, a pacifist that she can yell at me and treat me like shit. I don't care that she's a lesbian, but I want her to be professional. I've been really nice to her… I gave her a silver bracelet that I found. She said she wasn't allowed to accept gifts, but I said, 'If you don't tell; I won't tell.'

"And that stupid single bed she got me. I told her beforehand that I didn't want it. I said I'd chuck it in the garbage. Well, I've tried it, fallen off a couple times. It has a thin mattress; it's like a toy bed. Three of the screw in legs are smashed, so the mattress is on the floor now. I'm two hundred and sixty pounds. How did she expect that I'd be able to sleep on something that flimsy. Now they want to meet with me to find out why I want to change workers. It isn't too often that they get requests like that. I won't say anything bad about her, but I wonder what she told them about me. I guess I'll just have to wait to find out. Now I have my old worker back.

"I heard a party going on in the park near my building. It was a bunch of native guys, they were all drunk. We shared a few drinks, so I made a few friends. Every ten minutes they wanted to shake hands with me. I guess they'd forgotten who I was. I found a hundred and sixty-two cans in that park. I'm not a bagger, but I bagged those and hid them where nobody would find them. They were hidden so well I had trouble finding them myself, even when I was standing right next to them.

The weather's getting nice for fishing now. I can't wait to get out.

Raccoons

21 June 2017

Ted was sitting in the rain. A blue tarp covered his lower half, an umbrella hat deflected the water from his face. The look on his face was one of resigned discouragement.

"Good morning, Ted. Are you managing to keep dry?"

"Hi, Dennis. The water is running under my tarp. I'm soaked, but I'm keeping warm. I haven't been around for the past few days. My brother and I were helping my mother to get rid of some raccoons — real nasty fuckers. They were tearing a hole under the eves trying to get into the attic. Two of them were snarling and hissing, the third one was easy going. He'd probably been fed regularly by some of the neighbors. We put him in the truck and released him. Did you know that the law states that you aren't allowed to move them more than a kilometre from where they're caught. I think that they're afraid that it may cause a spread of rabies. Also, they may have cubs nearby and you don't want to separate families.

"I have my trapping licence so we baited the trap with cooked bacon and caught the two vicious ones. I must have skinned a hundred raccoons over the years. I made coonskin caps for my sons when they were young."

I asked, "Have you ever eaten a raccoon?"

"No, they're scavengers, like rats. They eat road kill. When you cut them open there's a horrible smell. I have to cover my nose with something when I'm skinning them. It's different with bears. Most people don't realize it but bears are mostly vegetarian. Eighty-five per cent of what they eat are berries, roots, insects, larvae, grass and other plants. The West Coast bears are so much larger because they have access to the salmon spawning in the rivers."

"So," I asked, "have you been able to get a larger bed?"

"No, not yet. My mother, who is eighty, promised me a bed but then she said, 'Maybe I should keep it in case that German girl comes back to visit.' That German girl visited twenty-seven years ago and hasn't kept in contact. I said, 'Okay Mom, whatever you say.'

"I've been approved for O.D.S.P. (Ontario Disability Support Program). I'm also receiving Social Assistance so I won't get the full amount. I don't know how much I'll get; my worker will let me know.

"Did I tell you I got my fishing licence? I had to pay thirty bucks and the season is half over. They discounted me two bucks. Don't you think they should have charged half price?"

I said, "In winter you could also go ice fishing. Have you ever done that."

"Yeah, I used to go out with my sons to fishing derbies. They had an area fenced off and holes augered in the ice. It would be about two to three feet thick. We got three holes fairly close to the shore. If you looked into the hole you could see the bottom of the river. You weren't allowed to bring coolers because they didn't want any foreign bait introduced to the lake. Also, in a cooler you could hide an award winning fish. We caught the largest northern pike at twenty-nine pounds and the largest walleye at eleven pounds. We also could have won largest yellow perch but we told the judge to give it to somebody else.

"Do you want to hear something sad? Between my new place and the river is a baseball diamond. In the gravel bed behind home plate, a turtle decided to lay her eggs then left. When I walked past this morning, shit hawks were pecking away at the eggs. I yelled, waved my arms and chased them away. A lot of good that did. They came back as soon as I left. In some areas they create turtle nesting places along rivers and build underpasses out of drainage pipe so they don't get run over on streets and highways."

July 2017

People Dying All Around Me

After stepping off the bus I saw a familiar face. It belonged to a man I once referred to as St. Nick since he prepared sandwiches and delivered them to homeless people sleeping under bridges, in parks and other places that were not publicly known. This he did from his own money collected from panning on the street. I said, "Hi, Nick, I haven't seen you for ages."

"Yeah, I was out of town for a while then came home for Anne's funeral. Trudy is also sick. I've been on the streets since winter. I'm on my way to see my worker. I've got liver disease and colon cancer. I need an operation, but they won't arrange that until I have a place to stay. I'm going to tell her to get off her fuckin' ass and find me a place. I'm really pissed off that she's taken this long to do anything."

"Take care, Nick. I hope that everything works out for you."

...

Later I saw Ted.

"Hi Dennis. I'm kind of pissed off this morning. Reah stood me up last night. I talked to her this morning. She said that a friend came into town with four hundred dollars and they partied. I guess I would have done the same thing. Instead, I polished off a bottle of vodka.

"Did I tell you that when I was fishing the other day I caught a beaver. I was dangling my feet in the water and saw this little thing swimming towards me. I thought it was an otter, you know how friendly they are. I quickly reached down and grabbed it by the neck. I was surprised to see that it was a baby beaver. They really have sharp teeth. I held it a while, rubbed its belly, felt its tail then let it go. I was thinking of taking it home and putting it in my bathtub. I could have put in some poplar branches and kept it for a pet. I thought better of it and let it go. It would have been illegal anyway."

...

After work I was waiting for my bus when I heard someone holler, "Dennis, over here!" Seated on a piece of cardboard was Bearded Bruce. He asked, "Do you have time to sit for a few minutes? Here, I'll move the cardboard so you can rest your back against the brick wall. So, What have you been up to?"

"Same old, same old," I said. "How about you?"

"I've been thinking of moving on. I've got bed bugs in my place again. They've sprayed once and will be coming back to do it again next week. That's a real pain. I have to cover everything. When they've finished I'll have to wash dishes and anything that's been exposed. I washed all my clothes and dried them on high heat. That whole mess has got me down."

"Where do you plan to move to?"

"I'm not sure. I might just travel and work for a couple of weeks. If I'm away for more than a month I'll lose my apartment. It's crazy, if I went to prison they'd hold it for me, or guarantee a place when I got out. I've got a one person tent that weighs three pounds. I need a big eight or twelve gallon back pack. I may go to the Niagara region to pick grapes and tend vines. I may go to Leamington to pick tomatoes. I'll just have to find out what's ripe for picking and where. It could be apples, peaches, strawberries or other berries.

"I'm pissed off with this Brexit situation. I was born in Scotland, but if Britain separates from Europe I'll need a passport to travel out of the country. I have a friend in Ecuador, he says there are plenty of harvesting jobs there.

"I guess I told you that Debbie died. That hit me hard. It seems that everyone around me is dying. I want to go somewhere that people are living."

Baby Blues

11 August 2017

"Hi Dennis, I'm in recovery mode this morning. I've been hitting my homebrewed wine too hard. Fuck, that's potent stuff. I let it ferment eleven days longer than I was supposed to. Maybe that's what made it so strong. My vodka should be ready in three days. It's really frothing up in the metal container. I'm going to stay away from drinking that stuff. It's too hard on me."

"Do you plan to sell it?"

"Yeah, that's the idea, to make extra money. I've thought of offering it to the people in my building. There's a group that hangs around the back wall, drinking beer and smoking. I've had problems with landlords before. It probably wouldn't be a good idea to have a lineup of noisy drunks coming to my room at all hours."

I asked, "Do you have a bed yet?"

"No, I was supposed to go Tuesday, but I was too drunk. I was supposed to go yesterday, but I had a visitor. Marcia came over and stayed the night. I can't keep up with her. I don't know what mental problems she has but she gets an injection from her doctor once a month because she can't remember to take her pills. I can't even have a conversation with her. She'll be laughing, then ten minutes later she'll be screaming at me. She doesn't listen. I can see it in her eyes, maybe she's thinking about what to say next."

I said, "She's probably taking other drugs as well."

"You bet. She asked for some meth yesterday so I gave her half a tab. Fifteen minutes later she was screaming for more.

She was into my wine too. I gave her a bottle, but took a big swig out of it first. A full bottle will even put me out. She saw the big glass container in the fridge and wanted more. Just because I've got a lot doesn't mean we have to drink it all at once. I'm a drunk, but I've got a level where I'm still functional and I quit drinking there. Not her.

"Then she started getting upset about her kid. She had to go to court to sign a form releasing the baby for an additional six months. I told her, 'Sign it off permanently. You're in no shape to take care of a kid. Let it go to a family that can give it a good home, take care that it's fed right.' Marcie wasn't allowed to breast feed because of all the junk in her system. She looked at me kind of funny. I told you that there is a possibility that I'm the father. I can barely take care of myself."

I asked, "Is Marcie still staying at the women's shelter?"

"She does the rounds. One week she'll stay with her mother, the next week will be the Shep then the other place."

"If I knew for positive that it was my kid I'd find some way of taking care of it. I'd take the blood test, offer financial support. My mother, brother and sister would insist on helping. My sister would probably take it."

"I told you I've still got that tiny mattress. I've also got five sleeping bags piled on the other side of the room. I said, 'You sleep there.' She flipped out at that, called me a queer because I didn't want to sleep with her."

"I know a lot about mental illness but I don't know what her problem is. There's no way I can help her. Maybe I'd have to take courses. I can't stand to be with her for too long. She'll probably be by this morning with an apology."

"The good news is I've been out fishing. I caught some nice sized pickerel the other day."

Welfare Cut Off

4 August 2017

While waiting for the bus I saw Bruce approaching, "Hi Bruce, how is everything going?"

"Hi Mate, I'm going through a hard time. Someone photographed me panhandling and now my welfare has been cut off. I went to their office to see them and I nearly lost it. All I'm getting now is three ninety-five a month. I said to the guy, 'Where am I going to live on three ninety-five. The cheapest boarding house cost four fifty. ' He said, "Well, you could quit smoking.' I said, 'I don't smoke, at least I don't buy them. Every once in awhile I'll bum one. Could you live on three ninety-five a month?' He said, 'No.' I said, 'If I was a prostitute you'd accept that as working, but if I say I'm a panhandler you won't accept that!' He said, 'You're right panhandling is against the law, prostitution isn't, as long as there is no solicitation involved.' You see, if a high price call girl with her own apartment does tricks she can claim that as income. She even has to pay taxes on it. It's a crazy world we live in.

"They should decriminalize panhandling, street prostitution and drugs. And I mean all drugs, heroin included. Methadone doesn't cure heroin addiction it only lessens the craving, but an addict has to want to be cured. It's the same as if you slapped a nicotine patch on a smoker. If they didn't have a strong desire to quit it would have no effect.

"You see these new fancy bus shelters they're putting up. The 10 installed shelters cost two hundred and three thousand dollars. Habitat for Humanity, with volunteer labor, can build a house for forty-seven thousand. Now why can't the government build affordable housing?

"I've been able to pick up a few jobs landscaping. That will be going toward my rent payment. Now I'm heading downtown to the bar strip. I stay there from eight o'clock 'till two in the morning. I leave then because that's when the real rowdies come out.

New Batch

14 August 2017

"Hi Dennis," said Ted, "my vodka is still bubbling. I gave it a stir this morning. It's supposed to be between seventy to eighty degrees. I'm at the bottom end of that, maybe that's why it's taking so long. I could get a heating pad. I'll see how it goes. After that there's an additive to stop the fermentation and a filter to clear it. My new batch of wine is really good. I took a bottle to my friend up the street. She's always good to me. There were these other two guys there asking, 'Can I have one? Can I have one?' They were loaded to begin with. I said, 'I'll sell you a bottle for ten dollars.' They checked through their change and said, 'We've only got six.' I said, 'I'll let you have this one for six, but next time it's ten.' Do you think I did the right thing? I don't know.

"After that I panned in front of the hotel. There were a lot of guys holding hands and some gorgeous women, but, like a friend advised me, 'Look for the Adam's apple.' Sure enough this woman had an Adam's apple. I didn't care, they were handing me fives, twenties, I ended up with a hundred and sixty dollars. I guess that Pride Week starts next week so I got a schedule of the events and I'll make sure I'm there. Is that okay?"

"I think it's okay Ted. I don't see that you're doing any harm."

"After that I met a gorgeous woman. She's thirty-two years old. We went over to my place, had some wine. She asked if I had any drugs. I said, 'I have some meth.' That didn't appeal to her so I gave her sixty bucks and she went out and got what she wanted. I don't know what it was but she was really buzzed. She cleaned my whole apartment. It's never been so clean. She stayed the night and I'm going to see her again this afternoon. She's really nice. If I treat her right she might be a keeper. Who knows?"

"I see you have a guitar. Do you play?"

"No, a guy I know was short of cash so I loaned him forty bucks and he left his guitar as collateral. He's never come back so I'm going to give it to a friend who put me up for seven months. He wouldn't take a cent for rent."

"It's a semi hollow electric bass. I don't recognize the brand, but it's probably worth a couple of hundred dollars."

"I'm not going to sell it. I'll give it to my friend."

I don't want anything to do with you...

14 August 2017

"Hi Dennis," said Ted, "My vodka is finished. I tried a few bottles It's really potent, but it didn't kill me and I didn't go blind."

I said, "You can regulate the alcohol content, can't you?"

"Yeah, I did. I added more yeast."

"If you wanted it less potent you could add distilled water, couldn't you."

"Yeah, but why would I want to do that?"

"It does seem to be counter productive."

"That's a good way of putting it. I only had eight bottles, so I'll hang around the liquor store and wait for customers who are returning empties. I don't mind paying them the regular refund price.

"I came down today because my worker has arranged for me to get a new set of keys. I had a woman stay over about a month ago. She ran out of cigarettes and dope. I gave her forty bucks. My keys were on the kitchen table. She took them on her way out; she never came back. I don't mind about the forty dollars, but I'm lost without my keys. I told my worker that I lost them, so she talked my landlord into giving me a special deal. If she'd said they'd been stolen it would have cost two hundred dollars. There's the electronic outdoor key, the mailbox key and the swipe pass for my apartment, plus they'd have to replace all the locks. By telling him they were lost he's charging me fifty for the keys and twenty-five for the swipe pass. When I get that taken care of at noon I can go get my bed. I can't do that until I get the keys.

"I've been having fun with Julia. I met her a couple of weeks ago. She wanders around topless and has a lot of piercings. She has piercings everywhere. She has piercings in places I didn't know you could get piercings. She said to me, 'Ted, you should get a piercing through your cock.' I said, 'There's no way I'm going to do that.' Can you imagine?"

"There's no way I'd get that done either. I hurt myself enough by accident. I don't want to pay to have someone hurt me."

"Anyway, that first night I talked to her -- I'd seen her around before but we'd never been introduced -- she he sat down next to where I was panhandling. I said to her, 'I don't mind you sitting here, but you're going to have to put your top on. It makes me uncomfortable and I'm sure my regulars would feel the same way. We had some wine then she asked me if I had a place. I said, 'Yeah, I have a place.' We went there, smoked a few joints and she started taking her clothes off. She just doesn't like being dressed. When she took off her shoes there was a terrible smell. I'm not just talking about foot odor, this was rotten. Two of her toes were bandaged. I've taken first aid courses so I took the bandages off and it was a mess. She was supposed to go back to the hospital two days before to have her bandages changed, but didn't bother. I had her soak her foot in an epsom salt bath. The water was filthy. I had gauze so I rebandaged them and applied antibacterial cream, but I'm not a doctor. He told her that if she didn't take care of them they'd have to be amputated. I saw one of the outreach workers today and asked if he knew Julia with all the piercings. He said he knew her. I said, 'For Christ's sake, get her to a hospital to have her toes looked after.'

"Another thing, she was drug sick and so shaky that she couldn't use a needle. I was on that stuff, but not for the past ten years. I figured if she kept trying on her own she'd miss a vein and create an embolism. You can die from that. So, I shot her up, quite a few times. She lay down and I covered her up. She slept about five hours, woke up, we talked then she slept for another six hours.

"Before she left this morning she said, "We should do something regular." I said, 'I got some movie passes. Do you want to go to a movie on Friday?' So that's what we'll be doing.'

"I was really pissed off with Roger this weekend. We were going fishing then we figured on hanging around to see the fireworks across the river. Quebec doesn't want people from this side of the river to see the fireworks for free, so they put up a steel fence where the rivers join, that's where we usually fish. We walked across the bridge to the island. It's controlled by First Nations people. A guy stopped us and asked why we were on their property. I said, 'We'd like to watch the fireworks and do a little fishing while we wait.' 'Certainly,' he said, 'you're Canadians, you're welcome here.' So, we continued down a trail to the point where we had a good view and a place to fish. Roger set up about fifteen feet behind me. I caught some nice pickerel, watched the fireworks for about an hour and a half, then went back for Roger. His backpack was there, but there was no sign of him. Everybody else had left the island. I was worried. We'd both had a lot to drink. There were slippery rocks. I thought he may have fallen in the river. I spent about an hour looking for him. That's just the way I am. I've been trained you never leave someone behind, but I'd searched everywhere, so I went back to our regular panning spot near the hotel. There was Roger, sitting like there was nothing unusual. I said, To him, 'You stupid fuck, where'd you go?' He said, 'I got bored and decided to leave.' I asked, 'Did you not think of letting me know. I found your backpack and thought you may have fallen in the river.' He said, 'I never thought of that. I'm sorry.' I said, 'Stay away from me. Don't talk to me. Don't come around me.' The next night I was panning near the hotel and he came by. I held up my hand and said, 'No, stay away. I don't want anything to do with you.' He left, but I'm sure he'll be around tonight."

More Raccoons

1 September 2017

"Hi Dennis," said Ted, "I've been staying at my mom's place for the past five days. It had been three months since I last visited. I got rid of some more raccoons. My stupid brother doesn't kill them. He catches them, but the law states that you're not allowed to relocate them more than a kilometre from where they were caught. I can understand that, they're worried about spreading rabies. Killing them is illegal, but if you don't they just come back. I have my trapping equipment stored in my mom's garage. I set four Conibear traps and used meat as bait. These are called a body gripping traps that quickly and humanely kill the animal once the trap activates. Although most people can compress the 110 pound spring by hand, many people are unable to compress a 220 or 330 pound spring. These larger sized traps can be set using tongs that use leverage to easily compress the springs. I didn't have the tongs and broke a finger trying to set the traps. My mother was worried that rabbits would get caught but I told her that rabbits are vegetarian, they wouldn't come near a trap with meat in it.

"I got my new key. I'm not giving this to anyone. I saw the stupid bitch that took my last set, but I didn't do anything. What am I going to do, start a screaming match with her in public? I decided to just let it go. I haven't seen the other woman with the infected toes. I don't know if she had to have them amputated. I hope not.

"I went to see some live theatre last week. Blood on the Moon is about murder of Thomas D'Arcy McGee, and the accused James Patrick Whelan. The evidence against Whelan was purely circumstantial, yet led him to his death before thousands of jeering spectators in what would become Canada's last public hanging. Some 135 years later, Whelan's ghost still haunts the streets, determined to prove his innocence and rewrite the history books. It leaves the the audience with a decision to make, did he or didn't he?

"I'm looking forward to fishing this weekend. Richard wants to come with me. He hasn't fished before. Did I tell you that he left me behind on the island? I spent an hour looking for him. I found him back at his panning spot near the hotel. I was pissed off. He couldn't understand it. He kept asking, 'Why are you mad at me, Ted?' I couldn't talk to him.

"I've sold all my wine. My vodka is in the fridge. I have to add a clearing agent then it will be ready to drink. It scares me. I hear these voices in my head. One will say, 'Stay away from that stuff, Ted It'll kill you.' Another voice says, 'Just have one drink. You can handle it.' The problem is that once I've had a drink my resistance goes down and I'll keep drinking until I'm unconscious. I'll wake up and not remember anything."

Wolf R.I.P.

14 September 2017

I was about to step on the bus when I heard someone calling my name. "Dennis, mate, hold on!" I felt a large hand on my shoulder, turned and saw Bearded Bruce. I waved the bus on. "I have some important news. I came down here especially to see you. Our friend Uncle Wolf is dead. It happened yesterday. My girl, Loretta and I were having a cup of tea and it came to mind that you'd have no way of knowing about his passing. Funeral arrangements are still up in the air. You've still got my phone number don't you. Call me, we'll get together for tea.

"Let's cross the street where we can sit down. I'm not allowed to pan within so many feet of a bus stop. It's called captive audience solicitation. Here sit on my bag. It's not soft but there's nothing breakable in it."

I asked "What about Shaggy? Who's going to look after her?"

"His brother came down and is taking the dog. There was somebody else there. I can't remember. It's someone I don't like."

"Was it Chris, maybe?"

"No not him. I'm still pissed about what he said after Weasel's funeral. He knew we were friends and said, 'Good riddance to bad rubbish.' You don't say things like that about the dead, especially to family."

"Was it Outcast?"

"Yeah, that son of a bitch. He's stolen from a lot of my friends and I don't like the way he treated Little Jake. He's a bully. I can't stand bullies. In my book they're just like rapists and wife beaters."

I said, "Joy didn't like Weasel, but after his death she said, "they'd had their differences, but she had nothing against him.' Little Jake was in tears and she comforted him."

"Yeah, Joy spoke her mind, but she backed it up. When she was living with Big Jake there were so many times he'd beat her. I said I'd take care of him, but she pleaded with me not to hurt him. When I was in prison five years ago I got him alone. I showed no mercy, wiped the floor with him. He was hospitalized for two days.

"Another person who was beat up is Magdalene. She really had the shit kicked out of her. She'd probably mouthed off, or stolen from somebody. I don't hit women, but I've been tempted to tell her to shut up and then punch her in the face."

I said, "Her boyfriend Alphonse was such a nice guy, before he committed suicide."

"Yeah, I liked Alphonse. He was solid."

"So", I asked, "how have you been doing?"

"I've been able to pick up a few jobs landscaping. That will be going toward my rent payment. Now I'm heading downtown to the bar strip. I stay there from eight o'clock 'till two in the morning. I leave then because that's when the real rowdies come out."

Even More Racoons

22 September 2017

"Hi Dennis," said Ted, "I've been staying at my mom's place for the past five days. Caught three more racoons. One was a big bugger, about forty pounds. I didn't like it though. I gave up trapping years ago, swore I'd never do it again. The problem was I set a live trap and my brother was supposed to check on it, which, of course, he didn't. So, I had to take this animal out of the cage and kill it. It hurt me. What am I going to do?

"My mother is really going batty. She asks me the same question over and over again. What is that?"

I said, "My wife used to work with clients who had dementia or Alzheimer's. It could be one of those."

"I saw a program on tv, a scientist said that the brain doesn't deteriorate. That's why these rich guys have their head and spine removed to be frozen and brought back to life some time in the future. I guess you can't always believe what you see on tv. My mother watches the wrestling channel. That's the only channel she watches. I went out to the yard for a few minutes, when I came back in I asked her who won that last match. She said, 'I don't know.' She could watch the same match over and over again and never know the difference. My brother and sister are talking about putting her in a home. I was helping her clear her attic. I hauled down five boxes of boots and shoes. Some had hardly been worn. She has two extra bedrooms upstairs. I found bundles of dresses and blouses, still in their original shop bags, still with the labels on. What's that about? Is she just acting like a big shot, showing people how much she can buy?"

I said, "I can't explain women and shopping. If my wife and I have an invitation for dinner, she'll ask me what dress she should wear. I'll pick out something and she'll say, 'I can't wear that. I wore it last time we visited, a year ago.' I'll say, 'They probably won't remember and what's the harm if they do?' I can't figure it."

"Katrina visited me a few days ago. Al, the guy she'd been staying with had beaten her up something fierce. What is it like when a person has schizophrenia?"

"I've known a few people who've suffered from that. Seeing, hearing, or even feeling things that no one else can. Difficulty with memory or paying attention. Disorganized thinking, such as trouble organizing thoughts or connecting them logically."

"That's her alright. She's on powerful meds, but can't remember to take them, so she gets shots once a month. She's pregnant again. I asked her, 'What's this bulge?' She said, 'I'm having cramps.' I said, 'No you're not, you're pregnant?'

"I gave her half a tab of speed and she wouldn't shut up. It was driving me nuts. Did I tell you that she has these long scars on her legs and arms because her veins collapsed. That happened because of shooting drugs. It looks like

Frankenstein. She wanted to stay at my place, but when I told her I wasn't going to give her money or drugs she walked out.

"I went fishing again — caught three pickerel. They were too small so I used them for bait, but I didn't catch anything. Did I tell you about the muskie I nearly caught last week. I was sitting on a two foot wall beside the canal, dangling my toes in the water. I caught a decent sized pickerel, three or four pounds. It would have been good for eating, but I embedded three hooks in its belly and threw it back in, letting it sink to the bottom. After a while I got a giant tug on my line. I fought that fish for fifteen minutes. I was alone and drunk and had a hell of a time trying to get it out of the water. At one point I even had my fingers underneath tickling its belly. That calmed him a little, but I couldn't get a good hold and he snapped my line. The world record is fifty-eight pounds. I don't think this one was that big, but close. Do you know how much fishing line costs now? Seventeen bucks, and a large lure costs nine. That's ridiculous!"

No, I'm not going to split with you!

27 September 2017

Ted was reading a newspaper as I arrived at his sidewalk panning spot. I asked, "Are we involved in a nuclear war yet?"

"Hi, Dennis, no we aren't at war, but it's coming. That Kim Jong-un needs to be straightened out.

"I've been doing a lot of fishing lately, but haven't had much luck. I hooked a big muskie, about four feet long. The world record is sixty-nine pounds, eight ounces. That was back in 1949. The government has netted some twice that size. They weigh, measure then release. I was drunk and down on my belly trying to grab for him. They have a huge mouth with rows of razor sharp teeth. I was looking down his throat. I nearly had my fingers in his gills, but he jumped and snapped the line. I also caught a big pickerel. facepalm You know that I'm a commercial fisherman. I'm ashamed to even talk about this, but I made the most rookie mistake. I felt him strike, but didn't set the hook. You know, jerk the line to embed the hook deeper. I started reeling him in. There was a lot of weight. He came straight up from the bottom, opened his jaws and spit the lure at me. Did I ever feel foolish.

"My mother had another racoon. She got my brother to put out a live trap three days ago and he was supposed to check on it regularly. Mom phoned me to say that a raccoon had been caught. I asked her if my brother had taken care of it. She said he hadn't. I asked if it was still alive. She said that it wasn't moving. I phoned my brother. I said, 'You stupid asshole. You put out a live trap three days ago and you didn't bother to check it. We've been having a heat wave. Can you imagine how much pain that animal must have suffered with no shade and no water? That's the worst way to die and it's the most inhumane thing I've ever heard of. I phoned him and yelled, '**Get over there, dig a hole and bury it.**'

"My mom also wants me to move a tree for her. It's about twenty feet high. I remember when it was planted. A trench will have be dug all around and underneath. Roots will have to be cut, then I'll have to pull it down with a rope, move it twenty feet and replant it. That's a big job."

I asked, "Wouldn't it be better to just chop down the tree and buy a new one to replace it?"

"Yeah, that would be the easy way, but there's no reasoning with Mom when she gets an idea in her head. I'll see what I can do."

"I went to my doctor yesterday. He says I need to lose weight. I know that. I told him, 'I walk about fifteen miles a day.' He said, 'That's no good. You've got to elevate your heart rate, get breathing heavy and raise a sweat. Walking is hard on your joints. You should ride a bike.' I said, 'I can do that.' I rode yesterday afternoon. When I came home my tee shirt was soaking. I'll have to buy a lock. I had another bike that I left leaning against my building. By morning it was gone.

"The next few days should be good for me. Most of the panhandlers will have gotten their checks and won't be on the street. I was in front of the hotel last evening with Richard. He had an open bottle of beer in front of him and a bag from the liquor store. People don't want to see that. One woman handed me a takeout box of Chicken alfredo. It was really good. Another guy dropped me a five. Richard said, 'I'll take half of that.' I said, 'No you won't. I didn't ask you to sit and pan with me, so, no, I'm not going to split with you."

She said she was 27

29 September 2017

"Good morning Ted," I said, "you look comfortable sitting in the sun. It was a cold night."

"Morning, Dennis, I saw Bernard this morning. Said he'd been in jail, that's why he hadn't been able to pay me." I said to him, 'Your check should have arrived. Everybody else has theirs.' He said, 'I'll go to the office and check.' When he got back he said, 'Mine hasn't come in yet, but I'll give you half of the money I have.' He pulled out two twenties and gave me one. I said, 'I thought you didn't get your check. Where did you get that money?' He said, 'Panhandling last night.' Yeah, right, you don't get two twenties panhandling. He probably blew the rest on crack and weed. He has a real problem with that stuff."

I said, "The last time I saw Bernard was in December."

"I remember exactly the last time I saw Bernard. You know he was sleeping at my place. On Christmas day I was approached by a woman who said she was new in town, had no money, nothing to eat. I said, 'If you'd like, I'll walk you to the Mission, they have their big Christmas meal today.' She didn't want that. I said, 'I share a small place with another guy who sleeps on the floor. If you want you can spend the night, but I'll need to see some id first. She said, 'I'm twenty-seven.' I said, 'You don't look twenty-seven, you look under twenty-one.' She had no id. We went to my place, Bernard was there. At night I gave her some blankets. I crawled into my bed. I don't know where she slept. I heard strange noises in the night, but didn't pay it any mind. In the morning she was arguing with Bernard. I don't know what it was about. She was pissed. She went out, slammed the door then pulled the fire alarm. Of course that brought the police. By that time she and Bernard were long gone. I made a statement to the police and told them she said she was twenty-seven. The cop laughed and said, 'She isn't twenty-seven.' He asked where he could find Bernard I said, 'He could be anywhere.' They seemed to know Bernard, maybe he had some priors. I didn't ask.

"I hope to do some fishing tomorrow then I'll be going to my mothers to catch more raccoons."

"Enjoy your weekend, Ted."

"You too, Dennis."

October 2017

I know you, but I forget your name…

Standing at the bus stop, reading The Dain Curse by Dashiell Hammett on my Kindle, a man approached me. I didn't look up. He didn't say anything. I lifted my head to see who it was, I recognized Little Jake. I gave him a hug and said, "Jake, I haven't seen you for ages."

He said, "I know you, but I forget your name."

I said, "It's Dennis. How are you. I've spoken to Bearded Bruce lately."

"Yeah, he just threw me out. I'm walking around in a fog. I don't know where I'm going."

I said, "You're looking good."

"No, I'm not."

I reached into my wallet looking for a five to hand him."

"I don't want your money. I don't want anything."

I said, "I was sorry to hear about Wolf passing. He was a great guy."

"Yeah, it's going to be my turn next. I'm not interested in money. I'm not interested in anything." His blue eyes started to tear. He patted my shoulder then shuffled off down the sidewalk. I was at a loss for words. I didn't know what to do. I just watched him drift away.

Mom has Dementia

11 October 2017

"Good morning Ted," I said, "the weather is getting colder. There's a frost warning for tonight. How late in the season are you allowed to fish?"

"Trout spawn in October and November so the season is closed for them, but for all other game fish I'll be fishing right through the winter. I need to get some new equipment. For sinkers I've been using nuts and bolts and I broke my rod. I had it in my backpack and forgot to duck when coming through a door. I caught one fish my last time out. It was a good size for eating so I gave it to somebody I met by the river. I was so drunk I fell about a dozen times, in the water three times, I was soaked up to my chest. The rest of the times I fell on the rocks. One time I didn't think I'd be able to get up. I was sure I had broken a bone, but everything was moveable. I decided then to go home before I killed myself. Look at the scratches on my shin. My knee was swollen the size of a grapefruit. I'm still having trouble bending it.

"I spent the last week with my mother. She'd like me to move in, but I can only take so much of her. She's getting really bad, watches wrestling all day long. When we were watching together she asked me who won. I said, 'Ma, you were watching. You should know who won.' She said, 'I must have turned away for a minute or fell asleep.' Half the time she's watching vintage wrestling from twenty years ago. Who does that? We had a power failure, she sat in front of the television for five hours waiting for the wrestling to come back on.

"My brother and sister want to put her in a home, but she's against the idea. She has trouble getting up and down steps. When my dad was alive we had an elevator that went up the circular staircase. It cost about five thousand dollars. She sold it for twelve hundred. I can't imagine what they cost now. On the main floor we have a bathroom and an extra room that was used as an office. I said to her, 'Mom, I can move your bed, your dresser and all your bedroom furniture down here. You'll have access to everything you need.' She said, 'No.' Also, she can't keep herself clean. There's shit all over the floor. I can't deal with that."

I suggested, "You could hire a Personal Care Worker. They would help her wash, dress, go to the bathroom, even cook her meals."

"No, she wouldn't want that. She's very independent and bossy."

I asked, "Have you caught any more raccoons, lately?"

"No, I didn't see any. Her neighbour told her to stop feeding the birds because it was attracting the coons. So she stopped feeding the birds. We have six big bags of bird seed in the garage, she's been doing this for years. I don't know if raccoons were eating the seeds, but they're garbage eaters. You never know."

Bernard is Back

13 October 2017

I saw Ted's green upturned hat. When I approached he appeared to be asleep. I was about to walk past when I saw his eyes open. "Good morning Ted."

"Good morning, Dennis, I drank four tall boys already this morning, so I'm a bit wasted. I've had a fever for the past two days. Yesterday I stayed in my sleeping bag. I pulled it over my head and that's the way I spent the day. My face is frying. I must have some sort of infection, maybe in my teeth. I need an Advil or something."

"Did you buy a new bed?"

"No, I used the money to exploit women. That's the way I am."

I said, "Maybe you should go to a walk-in clinic, or do you have your own doctor."

"Doctors! What do they know.

"I read that in Australia they've had their worst 'flu season in ten years — a hundred and seventy thousand cases so far this year. Two and a half times more than last year. They've already had seventy-two deaths from the 'flu. From the flu! I'd go get a shot, but I can't while I have this fever. Make sure you get yours.

"Have you seen Bernard? I told you he gave me a twenty towards the money he stole from me. I was really drunk last night, but I briefly awoke to see him going through my wallet. I just rolled over at the time, but I remember. He's a slimy bastard. I told you that when Rhea pulled the fire alarm he said he had to leave because the police were coming. I think he's a pedophile. I've never asked him about it. He'd lie anyway, but he did go to prison shortly after he was with Rhea. I wouldn't put it past him."

I asked, "Will you be here on the weekend?"

"No, I don't do well on weekends. I don't see any of my regulars. I'll go fishing instead. I'm going to leave now. I'm going to the pharmacy to buy some Advil and a new pair of glasses so I can read the newspaper."

I asked, "Did you lose your glasses?"

"Well, yes and no. I know exactly where they are — at my fishing place. I put them a few feet from where I usually sit, so I could reach them when needed."

Ted's Mother

25 October 2017

I saw Ted's green upturned hat, then saw his boots sticking out from behind a column of the church. When he came into view I said, "Good morning, Ted how was it staying with your mother?"

"It was okay, I got her in to see the doctor. He fixed her up with a puffer and a pump to get the fluid out of her lungs. She's still as cranky as ever. Did I tell you she smokes from five to eight packs of cigarettes a day. I've been trying to get her to cut down to three. It's hard for her since I smoke too. I should give it up."

"Did you catch any racoons?"

"No, I didn't see any around. I've got a trap set. I'll leave it there until the snow falls, then I'll be able to see if there are any tracks."

"How long does it take to go to your mother's place."

"About forty-five minutes. I take a bus to the outskirts of town then take a taxi from there.

"Today my worker is going to take me to the Salvation Army warehouse to pick out my furniture. They have free delivery. It'll be good to have a real bed for a change. I get sore sleeping on the floor.

"I was panning in front of the hotel last night and this East Indian guy stopped and gave me a bag of food from a restaurant. It was delicious. I love Indian food. This morning a guy dropped me a twenty. I went to the pizza place and ordered a breakfast sandwich with egg and sausage, home fries and a coffee. I'm still full.

"I met a woman the other day. She's slept at my place for the last three nights. She's really nice, tidied my apartment, cooked a nice meal and did the dishes afterwards. It felt homey. I've missed that. She's not like most of the women I've been involved with lately."

"She sounds like a keeper." I said.

"Maybe, we'll see how it works out."

"You didn't give her a set of keys, did you?"

"No, I've learned my lesson there. Richard stayed over one night. I had to kick his ass to wake him in the morning. He said, 'Just let me sleep a little while longer. Can you leave me a key?' I said, 'No way! I'm going to work and you should as well. Don't bother coming back because I won't let you in.'

"I'm not going to stay here too long. I've got a bitch of a headache. I'll buy some Advil on my way home."

Sidewalk Conference

26 October 2017

Lost in thought, listening to music on my iPod, I heard, "Dennis! Mate!" It wasn't anybody I work with since they were coming from the wrong direction. Without my glasses I could barely make out the figures of a big man walking beside a small man. As they approached I recognized Bearded Bruce and Little Jake. I hadn't seen either of them for about a month.

I reached out to shake Bruce's hand, but he said, "I don't want to shake your hand, come here give me a hug, brother. Don't hug Jake, he's contagious. Jake and I were just saying, 'We haven't seen Dennis for a while. We should go visit him. Have you got a minute to sit and talk?

"Sure, I said, "I'd like to catch up on news from the street."

Bruce continued, "I've got cardboard for you to sit on so you don't get your pants dirty." We sat and Bruce put his empty paper coffee cup out for donations.

"How have you been? I asked.

Jake spoke first, "Not so good. I have a blood infection. I'm taking medication for it.

"The last time I saw you was on the bus, wasn't it?"

"No, I was waiting for the bus and you came up to me. You weren't feeling too well. You said, 'I'm walking around in a fog. I don't know where I'm going.' "

"Yeah, I remember that."

I asked, "Have you seen anybody around that I would know. Does the gang still meet at the park?"

Bruce answered, "No, since Wolf died, Jacques doesn't come around. Everybody else is dead. That sounds harsh but it's true. Wolf mentioned to me he missed the conversations that he had with you. He didn't like most people. I see Little Chester near the mall. He's still annoying. It drives me crazy to be around him. The two gay guys have Wolf's dog Shaggy. You remember them. They used to bring Wolf a half dozen eggs and a loaf of bread. They showed me a picture of Shaggy. She looks like she's doing well."

I asked Jake, "Do you have your furniture yet?"

"Yeah, it took two years, but I'm set now. Have you been to your cabin lately? Duck season is opening soon. Do you hunt?"

"No, I don't hunt, but I get scared during duck season. I saw a couple of guys armed with shotguns in a boat. It looked like they were shooting at me.

"Do you hunt?"

"No, my brother does. Since my mom died he's living in her house. He bought my share. I don't go there any more."

Bruce said, "Jake and I were heading to my spot near the restaurants and bars. Here doesn't seem to be working for us. Maybe you're too well dressed."

I replied, "Ted says I'm good luck for him. He always gets a few drops when I'm sitting with him."

Bruce said, "Luck is luck. I'm superstitions. I always have my lucky penny, and bear token in my cup."

Several colleagues from work walked past. One smiled, one frowned and the others ignored me. Bruce yelled at them, **"He's just visiting. It's just me and Jake that are panning."**

It's been seven years that I've known Bruce and Jake. I always look forward to our conversations. When I first met them they were both living in a cardboard box near the dumpsters in back of Starbucks. Now they are both housed and their alcoholism seems to be under control. Bruce limits his drinking to two beers a day. He got up and reached out his hand to help me to my feet.

I said, "I've got something for you." I reached into my wallet and saw that I had two twenties. I handed one to Jake and the other to Bruce.

Bruce said, "Are you sure you can afford this? I always ask that of people. We saw Jenny last night. She had been drinking and was laughing. She reached into her pocket and pulled out some bills. She handed me a fifty. I don't want you to think that I'd take advantage of somebody who was under the influence. I asked her, 'Are you sure you can afford this?' She replied, 'Yes.' I saw that she also had a twenty and a ten in her hand. I asked, 'Are you sure you don't want to give me the ten?' 'No, I'm sure.' she said. So, I'm asking you again, Are you sure you can afford this?"

It's been quite a while since I've given money to any street people. They simply haven't been around. I thought about what other things I would use that money for. Nothing of any consequence came to mind, however with it Bruce and Jake would be able to go to Bruce's place for supper. They would have made their price for the night. Their alternative would have been to sit on the cold sidewalk for six hours until the bars closed and the streets emptied. It gave me great pleasure to be able to have a positive effect on their lives. I consider them my closest friends and looking at Jake I didn't know if I would see him again. I said to both of them, "I'm sure I can afford this." We hugged and went our separate ways.

November 2017

Used, Abused and Stolen from ...

7 November 2017

Ted had an upturned fur hat on the sidewalk. He'd retired his green plastic St. Patrick's Day top hat. "Good morning, Dennis, I've been really sick this past week. I really thought I was going to die. I had one foot in the grave the other on a banana peel. I'd been on a drunk for three days and I was having trouble peeing. I'd go to the bathroom and only a few drops would dribble out. My back was really sore. Finally, I went to the hospital. They told me that I was dehydrated. Not enough fluid in the body can lead to kidney failure. That's what I had. Anyway, since October 20th I've been drink free. I still have a bottle of vodka in my freezer. I'm going to return to A.A. meetings. They're going to tell me to get rid of the vodka. One of their principles is to disassociate yourself with people, places, and things that you identify with drinking.

"I still don't have my bed. There was a worker who came by to evaluate where I was living. He made a list of the things I needed: a bed, dresser, curtains, plates. He said to contact one of their stores within a month. The request would only be valid for thirty days. They have free delivery. I phoned the store to make an appointment, they said they had a five month waiting list. So, that was a waste of time.

"Eight thirty Sunday morning I heard a banging on my door. By the time I got up and looked out in the hall the guy was banging on someone else's door. He was taping a flyer from management saying that they'd be doing inspections. I said to the guy, 'What's the idea of banging on people's doors at eight thirty, Sunday morning. People are trying to sleep.' I said, 'You can just as easily slide the flyer under the door.' So, that's what he started doing. When they do the inspection they'll see the cockroach problem, maybe then they'll decide to spray. It's because of the hot water heating. There are pipes leading from the furnace to every apartment. I'm really clean. I don't cook. I don't leave food out. I scrub the floors. When I moved the fridge to clean underneath I saw about a hundred cockroaches. I sprayed them with pesticide, waited until they were dead then swept them up. When I moved the stove, same situation. I keep my knives and forks in a sealed plastic container in the fridge. That's the only place I'm sure they'll stay clean. They're better than bed bugs, but roaches carry a lot of diseases."

I said, "The last time we spoke you mentioned that you were seeing a woman. How's that going?"

"I don't see her anymore. She stole my weed pipe, sleeping pills from my medicine cabinet and borrowed forty bucks. I know where she is. I could see her at the Mission any time, but she says she doesn't have the money. What am I going to do? I wouldn't hit a woman. I could get a woman to hit her, but I still wouldn't get my stuff back. The people who stay at the Mission are all the same. I'll just add her to the long list of people who have used me, abused me and stolen from me.

I'm going to put down that I'm a hooker...

14 November 2017

Work was over for the day. I was standing at the bus stop, my bus pass in one hand, my Kindle in the other. I was reading Dragonfly in Amber (Outlander series Book 2). I've been watching it on Netflix, but I'm understanding more by reading the book. I heard someone holler, "Hey, old man," I looked up and it was Bearded Bruce. He said, 'That was funny, I called 'Hey, old man' and immediately you looked up. I hope you know I didn't mean any offence. So, are you back from your vacation?"

"No," I said, "we'll be leaving Sunday and will be gone to San Diego for a week."

"Oh, I thought it was last week. So where were you last week? I stopped by to see you a couple of times. Where were you?"

"I was in my usual places," I said. "Maybe I left work early a few times. That may be why you missed me."

Bruce continued, "I wanted to let you know that everything is in order now. I saw my worker and he offered me and my girl a place in their housing program. Only one hundred and ninety-one people have been chosen. He told me that I could claim my earnings as tips because panhandling is illegal. Now, I have to figure out what job I'm earning these tips from."

"Have you decided on an occupation?"

He replied, "I going to put down that I'm a hooker, or a stripper, working part time. They'll accept that but not panhandling. I had to tell them about my situation. People tell me that 'It's a problem being an alcoholic,' or 'It's a problem being addicted to drugs,' I say, 'It's not a problem for me. It's you people who see it as a problem.' The guy asked me, 'Are you depressed,' 'Depressed?' I said, 'The only thing that depresses me is you guys cutting off my money.' He asked, 'How does that make you feel?' I said, 'It makes me want to blow people up.' No, I was just kidding. My girl says that I've been cranky lately.' I said to her, 'If you don't like it then get out.' She went to stay with her cousin for a week. She's back now. She told the guy some things about her past, but not everything. It's looking good. We'll know by next week if we're approved. We're feeling positive."

"That sounds great, Bruce. I see my bus coming, so I'm going to have to leave. give my best to Loretta."

She said to me, 'So, you're going to talk to Dennis, your bitching post.' She didn't mean that in a bad way, it's just that I wanted to tell you our good news. It feels better when I talk to you. You really listen."

"Take care, Bruce," I said. When I found a seat at the front of the bus -- I always sit at the front in case the bus lurches and I fall down. Sitting across from me was Chris with his cane and a pack of beer, eight tall boys."Hi, Dennis, my backpack was stolen this afternoon. I was panning and walked across the street to the hotel to take a piss. When I returned, my backpack was gone. I was really upset. It had my bus pass, my bank card. In the summer when I used to wear shorts and a tee shirt I'd attach my keys to the backpack. Lucky for me I have lots of pockets now and had my keys with me. I would have been in deep shit if I came home without my keys. I guess I could have phoned my landlord. He could have come down and let me in, but he wouldn't have been happy about it. I have an extra key in my apartment. My birth certificate and my health card were at home. I got a new bus pass. It won't be valid until three thirty tomorrow afternoon. The guy didn't even charge me a fee for the new card and he gave me two bus tickets so I could get home. I cancelled my bank card. They'll send a replacement in the mail. I always request that they send me a card without a chip. If it's got a chip and it gets stolen it would be too easy for someone to drain my account. I've only got a hundred bucks in there, but it's the only money I have.

"I hope there's someone in my building who can lend me a backpack. It's too hard carrying beer otherwise. I feel naked without that weight on my back.

"Anyway, my stop is coming up. Take care, Dennis."

People, Places and Things to Avoid

15 November 2017

I'd been looking for Ted's upturned cap. From a block away I could tell if he was panning or not. As usual he was sitting on the concrete with his back against the stone wall of the church. He was reading the newspaper. "Hi Dennis, I was just reading that Justin Trudeau was slammed by the Philippine leader for asking about human rights. Trump congratulated Duarte, they're best friends now."

"How are you feeling, Ted."

"Today I'm sore. I went to the dentist yesterday and he pulled four teeth. I've got two others with cavities. On the twenty-eighth I go again to have those filled, then I'll have a partial plate made. I might as well since the government is paying for it. I thought the dentist was going to recommend that I have all my teeth pulled. I haven't had them checked for about fifteen years, but no, he said I could keep most of them. One was really hard to pull. He worked on it for about half an hour. He clamped it with some kind of rod and would tap it with a hammer then wiggle it back and forth. He stopped for a while and I said to him, 'If pulling that one tooth is so difficult why don't you tie a piece of string around it with the other end secured around a door knob. Then you'd just have to give the door a good yank and the tooth would be out.' He laughed at that.

"I've picked out some furniture: a dresser, kitchen table, some bedding. It will be delivered on Friday."

"Will you be getting a bed?"

"No, I haven't been able to find one. A new one would cost three hundred. There's no way I could afford that. I was at Canadian Tire and was looking at an inflatable bed for eighty-nine dollars. What do you think of that?"

"I've had bad luck with air mattresses. They always get punctured and I end up on the floor."

"I don't think I told you, but I haven't had a beer for thirty days now. At first I got really sick. It was like the 'flu. I'd have sweats one minute then I'd be shivering my ass off. My kidneys shut down. I didn't pee for three days. After four days I went to the doctor. I told him my problems. He said I was suffering from alcohol withdrawal. He said I could have died. I didn't know that. He said I should have cut down to three beer a day for the first week, then two a day the next week, and one a day for the following week. Then it would be okay to quit altogether. I've had diabetes for the past ten years, so cutting out the beer will be good for that as well. I bought three bags of milk the other day, put two in the freezer. I was reading the ingredients. There is a lot of sugar in milk. I didn't know that, but one cup of milk has a teaspoon and a half of sugar.

"I've stopped panning in front of the hotel. I've left that place for Richard. He'd always be offering me a beer or a slug of whiskey. In AA they emphasize people, places and things. I should stay away from Richard, stay out of places that serve drinks and avoid things that remind me of alcohol. I used to belong to AA but I haven't attended a meeting for ten years. My worker wants me to start attending again. Ninety meetings in ninety days. I used to go for an hour each day at noon. I'm also trying to cut down on smoking. I now smoke six or eight a day. My worker said I should take it slow, baby steps at first. I guess he's right.

"I do feel better now that I'm not drinking. I've been here too many times. It's a cycle: panhandling, booze, drugs, homeless... I have to get off that wheel. Starting January I'm going to be looking for a job."

Porky Hunting

30 November 2017

From a block away I could see Ted's upturned Christmas hat in its usual place. He was reading the newspaper. "Hi Dennis, I've got a bitch of a toothache. I went to the dentist yesterday for two fillings, so that part is taken care of. I told him about how much pain I'd been having because of the extractions. I'd phoned his office twice telling the receptionist how much they hurt. She didn't suggest that I come in for an appointment. He asked me what I did for the pain. I said, 'I just went down to the market and got hopped up on drugs.' He was shocked, but then I said, 'I was just joking. I used Advil.' He said the cause of my pain was from dry sockets from the extractions. I'll be having a root canal next Tuesday, then he'll have me fitted for a partial plate."

I asked, "Do you have a bed yet?"

"Yeah, I bought a futon. I don't have a base for it yet so it sits on the floor. It's a bit difficult for me to get up and down -- old age. I hate it. I find I'm slower getting around. I have aches and pains. My memory is going. I'm getting a new pair of glasses. They'll be ready next week. I didn't get bifocals because I tend to trip over things. I got the ones for distance viewing. I'll still use the glasses I bought at the drugstore to read the newspaper.

"I knew it was going to happen -- my roommate skipped out on me last night. He was supposed to pay me eighty bucks a week to stay at my place, but was always borrowing from me. He borrowed twenty bucks, went downtown and spent it all on beer. He came back and wanted to borrow money for food. I said, 'Hey man, I gave you twenty bucks, you made a choice to spend it on beer instead of food. That's not my problem.' He was always asking, 'Can I have a cigarette, can I have a beer, can I have something to eat, can I have some money.' The guy is thirty-four years old. I'm not his dad. Last night I awoke at nine thirty. He was sitting in his sleeping bag in the middle of the floor. He said, 'Ted, I need ten bucks. The beer store closes at ten and I'm all out. I've only got a half hour to get there. My check will be in my bank at midnight so I'll pay you the hundred bucks I owe you.' So, I was half asleep and said, 'Okay, I'll give you the money.' At eleven o'clock he received a text from his mother in Montreal. He said she was in hospital. If she was well enough to text it couldn't have been that serious, but he was fidgeting and crying. I went back to sleep. At three this morning I heard the door slam. He'd moved all of his stuff out and didn't even leave the key. I'm stiffed for a hundred bucks. I told security what happened and to keep an eye on my place. This guy is not allowed access. I may have to have the lock changed. He could come in and steal my bicycle, my fishing gear and anything else I have.

"I didn't realize before how much I value my privacy. This roommate hung around my place all the time. He'd go out and pan for a few hours, then he'll come back to the apartment. He sleeps about eighteen hours a day. I'd like to hang out with myself for a change. I'm glad that he left. From now on it's no roommates. The only people coming through my door will have tits and a pussy.

"Did you see the football game yesterday. I nearly put fifty bucks on Toronto to win against Calgary, they were such a long shot. I looked at the Pro-Line application. The print was so small and I couldn't figure out what I was supposed to, so I left. Wouldn't you know it, Toronto won. That could have been a pile of cash in my pocket If I'd bet.

"I was reading in the newspaper that women are going to be losing their grip on men. They're making these robotic dolls in China. Their skin is warm and soft. They have three holes that can do everything you'd want, if you know what I mean. No nagging, no spending your money, no rules.

"I could have had three women last night, but I've gotten to know them. I didn't want the hassle. One stayed over the other night. She lives at the women's shelter. She's on heavy meds. Her conversation would jump over the place. As far as listening skills, she had none. Every so often I'd get half a sentence in, then she'd interrupt.

"I'm going to be fishing this weekend. I broke the end of my rod, so I have to buy a tip for it. They come in a plastic bag with assorted sizes. They're easy to put on. Sometimes you have to sand your rod a bit, then slide the tip on with a bit of glue. I have a twenty-four shot disposable camera with about seventeen pictures taken so far. When I've finished I'll bring you some photos of some of the big fish I've caught.

"After the first snowfall I'll be snaring cottontail rabbits as long as I can keep clear of the game warden. I'll check the snares at about four in the morning. Have you ever eaten rabbit? It's really good. What I do is cut the legs and arms off, then split the carcass in two. I put the six pieces in a big pot with water, a teaspoon of salt and two teaspoons of baking soda. I leave it in the fridge overnight, then cook it slowly the next day. Throw a few vegetables in and it makes a great stew. The meat just about falls apart it's so tender.

"I used to host wild game dinners for the Knights of Columbus. I'd serve duck, moose, bear, even porcupine. A friend and I were driving along the highway when I saw a porcupine up a tree. Of course I was drunk. I told my friend to pull over, got the chainsaw out, took the tree down and with my heavy gloves, grabbed the porky. It even made the newspaper the day. 'Tree cut down and left for no apparent reason.' Of course, they didn't know about the porky. Another way we used to catch them was in hollow trees. We'd make a ball of barbed wire. I'd hold onto one strand, climb the tree and drop the ball through the highest opening. My friend would be waiting for them to come out and he'd hit them with a hammer. Those were good days. I miss them.

"You won't see me here in the new year. I'm sorting myself out then getting a job.

December 2017

A Guy Pulled a Knife on Me

7 December 2017

When I approached Ted he was reading the newspaper. I said, Hi, Ted, what's happening in the world?"

"Oh, not much. I got a box here for you to sit on. I've got a bitch of a toothache. I went to the dentist yesterday to have a root canal. He said 'I've already done five root canals, I don't want to do any more. I'll finish your fillings instead.' I thought that was odd, but he's the dentist. He even repaired my worn down teeth. It feels strange, but chewing is a lot easier and I don't have those gaps where food used to get stuck.

"I fucked up my drinking. I'd gone twenty-nine days sober then got blasted, so I've started again; I'm on day six now. It was all that stress of getting rid of my last roommate. He stayed seventeen days, ate my food, drank my beer, borrowed money then skipped out on the rent. I've had it with roommates. Don wants to move in, but I said no way. He asked if he could just come over for a beer and I told him three times on the way to my place, 'I'll let you stay for a couple of hours then you go.' He didn't have any bus fare so we walked. It was embarrassing, he'd go from one side of the sidewalk to the other looking down for things that people may have dropped. I asked him, 'Why don't you get a worker like I have. They'll show you places, fill in your forms, help you get furniture.' He didn't want that. He's barred from all the shelters for fighting."

I said, "That's the kind of roommate you want to stay away from."

"Yeah, I've thought of getting a woman. They'll still eat my food, drink my beer and borrow money, but at least there'll be benefits.

"Did I tell you that aa guy pulled a knife on me. It was on the same corner where another guy got stabbed. This guy is a booster; he steals stuff. I wanted some fishing equipment. I'd written a list and this guy said he'd get it for me. I saw him the next day, he was with his girlfriend, he didn't have my stuff. He said, 'I got a twenty dollar serloin tip steak. I'll sell it to you for ten dollars.' Now, the normal break for stolen goods is one third, but the guy said he needed diapers for his baby. 'Well, I said, since you need diapers I'll give you the ten. I'm waiting to go fishing so I want the other stuff by tomorrow.' He agreed. The next day I saw him he said, 'I don't have your fishing gear, but I got some gift cards, one for a hundred and one for one twenty.' I was pissed off, I said, 'I wasn't born yesterday, there could be any amount on those cards or none at all. Keep them and get me my stuff or I'll get someone who can.' That was when he pulled out his knife. It wasn't opened. I pulled out my can of mace and said, 'Go ahead, try to stab me and I'll blind you.' He settled down after that."

I asked, "Where do you buy mace?"

He said, "At any hunting supply store. It isn't the kind the cops use. What I have is coyote and dog spray. You can also get bear spray. That would be stronger." He showed me the can. It had a safety switch and the plunger was designed so that there was no danger of spraying yourself in the face.

"I've caught a lot of fish, they've really been biting. First thing when I wake up in the morning I think of fishing. My freezer is full. I think I'm over my limit, but I'll have to check the regulations. This weekend I'm going to invite a bunch of my friends over for a fish fry."

Swollen to the Size of a Tennis Ball

7 December 2017

When I approached Ted he was sitting in the snow with an agonized look on his face. "How are you Ted?"

"Horrible! I just got out of the hospital. I'm in pain"

I asked, "What was the problem?"

"My left testicle was swollen to the size of a tennis ball. Something similar happened to a friend of mine. He told me it happens when the spermatic cord rotates and becomes twisted, cutting off the blood supply. His doctor said he should lie on his back for three days and the swelling would go away naturally. Stupid ass me, figured I had the same thing. By the end of the third day I was in so much pain I checked myself into hospital. They told me that the swelling was caused by an infection, similar to the yeast infections that women get. I had a massive injection of antibiotics before I left the hospital and I have a prescription that I'll have filled at the pharmacy."

I said, "I've had a vasectomy. I remember spending a weekend on the couch with my feet elevated and a bag of frozen peas wedged securely between my thighs. I have some idea of the pain you're going through. I'm sure the antibiotics will give you relief. Sitting in the snow is also a good idea."

Ted continued, "Another problem I've had is the heat in my apartment. I have a thermometer hanging in the middle of the room. It's been reading eight degrees Celsius for the past four days. That's forty-six degrees Farenheit. It should be around seventy. I remember sweating in a tee shirt a couple of weeks ago."

"Have you spoken to your landlord?"

"He hasn't been around very much. When I finally got hold of him he came over and said that the radiator just needed dusting? Have you ever heard anything so ridiculous. I said to him, 'I usually hear popping and banging in the water lines, but now there is no sound at all. I think it's frozen.' He didn't seem to think so. I wouldn't be surprised if he had the water turned off. I eventually called my worker to complain since she got me the apartment. I told her that if it doesn't get fixed soon I want a different place to live. My landlord doesn't like me. He has sharks in the building checking on me to report if I'm selling drugs or using. Of course I'm not, but he doesn't believe me."

"Ted, what he's doing is illegal. You could take your case to the Landlord Tenant Association."

Ted raised his eyebrows and said, "I know I could and you can bet that I'll bring a big jar of cockroaches with me."

We Lost Another One

15 December 2017

Standing at the bus stop, headphones over my ears, I was listening to *Sessions for Robert J* by Eric Clapton. These are covers of the few songs recorded by Robert Johnson, an American blues singer-songwriter and musician who died in 1938 at the age of twenty-seven. Clapton has called Johnson "the most important blues singer that ever lived." The volume was turned to loud and I was oblivious to anything around me. I felt a tap on my shoulder and turned to see the chest of Bearded Bruce. He said, "Hey, Mate, I've got some good news to tell you."

I asked, "Is it about your housing application?"

"Yes, we've been approved. Everything is lined up. Loretta and I are really excited. Towards the end of the month we'll start looking for an apartment without cockroaches. This weekend they'll be treating the cockroaches in the place we're in now. Because of my girl's lung sensitivity they can't spray. They have to use some kind of gel. It's really expensive, but we don't have to pay for it. I'm not exactly sure how it works, but I still have to clean all the cupboards, cover and wrap all food and small appliances. We have to move the stove and fridge to mop underneath. They asked us to vacuum up any visible roaches and eggs just before the service visit then take the vacuum cleaner outside, remove the bag, seal it and discard in the trash. Then we have to take a damp cloth and wipe down the entire vacuum cleaner. If any cockroaches or eggs are seen after this is completed, re-vacuum or otherwise kill them. After they complete the treatment we can't wash the floors for two weeks. I'm going to start cleaning tonight.

"Loretta has been sick. She had a high temperature, her skin was burning hot. I filled the bathtub with cold water, had her soak in it for a while. She didn't like that. Then I wrapped her in heated blankets. I can remember my grandma doing that for me when I was a wee one. She's starting to feel better now. She's also in a better mood.

"I've also got some bad news. We lost another one. Chris, you remember Bicycle Chris. I was pissed off with him because after Weasel's death he said, 'Good riddance to bad rubbish.' Weasel wasn't easy to get along with, not many crackheads are, but it's just wrong to disrespect the dead. Chris knew that we were friends.

"Little Jake really took it hard. He doesn't deal well with death. He kept saying, 'It should have been me.' Considering the many times that Weasel beat Jake and trashed their apartment, I don't understand why Jake is so upset. He should be relieved that the beatings are at an end."

After allowing this to sink in I said, "I often used to ride the bus with Chris. He was using a cane because his hip had deteriorated to the point where an operation wouldn't save it.

Either that or he was denied surgery because of being an alcoholic. Usually when I saw him he was returning from the beer store. He'd often say, 'I can't wait to get home and put these in the freezer. I love cold beer.' That's the way I'll always remember him.

Requiem

15 December 2017

Our street family no longer exists. There are no more congregations at the park or elsewhere. The original crew who had been together for at least ten years included Jacques, the patriarch, who no longer visits since the death of Wolf. Their playful French-German rivalry, especially surrounding the FIFA World Cup soccer championship was particularly entertaining. Joy, the matriarch passed away in April of 2015. Shakes died in June of 2017, Shark and Irene within the past few months. There was nothing left to hold the group together.

I continue to talk to street people when I encounter them panhandling on the sidewalk. I keep five dollar meal cards and bus tickets in my pocket for such occasions. They are always appreciated. Most appreciated, however, is the acknowledgement and respect I offer them and the chance I give them to tell me about their lives. Most people show them no interest. They walk by them as if they were ghosts.

Joy and Me

Love is amazing —
when we give it freely
it doesn't diminish,
it enriches our souls.

Joy, is a panhandler
(incapable of anything else),
she is also my friend.
Each morning
(on my way to work)
I eagerly anticipate
her greeting and warm smile.

I sit with her
on the sidewalk,
as witness
to her blackened eyes.
I listen to her stories
of beatings and abuse,
give comfort
when she cries.
"Tears are a sign of weakness"
her father used to say.

I bring her tea
(cream and three sugars),
a bagel with cream cheese,
on mornings when frost
is on the ground,
and on the hearts,
of most passers by.

She gives to me
her hand to hold,
an attentive ear
to my daily problems,
and a hug
(when a hug is needed).

With her love,
Joy has enriched my soul
and filled my heart with tenderness.
She has given me so much
that I didn't know existed —
I am deeply in her debt.

In the Realm of Hungry Ghosts

26 April 2013

I've sometimes wondered why I'm drawn to homeless people. I've found some answers in the book, In the Realm of Hungry Ghosts: Close Encounters with Addiction by Gabor Mate, M.D.

Dr. Mate works with drug addicts in the former Portland Hotel, on Hastings Street, in Vancouver's Downtown Eastside, considered Canada's drug capital.

"What keeps me here?" muses Kersten Steuerzbech. "In the beginning I wanted to help. And now … I still want to help, but it's changed. Now I know my limits. I know what I can and cannot do. What I can do is to be here and advocate for people at various stages of their lives, and allow them to be who they are. We have an obligation as a society to … support people for who they are, and to give them respect. That's what keeps me here."

"Liz Evans began working in the area at the age of twenty-six. 'I was overwhelmed,' she recalls. 'As a nurse, I thought I had some expertise to share. While that was true, I soon discovered that, in fact, I had very little to give — I could not rescue people from their pain and sadness. All I could offer was to walk beside them as a fellow human being, a kindred spirit.'"

Conclusion

I hope that you've enjoyed reading about my friends. Every person has a story, these are just a few. This is the end of Book 4 and it seems to be the end of an era. I have enjoyed my relationship with these wonderful people. Visit my blog, Gotta Find a Home at: http://gottafindahome.com to read about recent adventures, promotions and links to my new books a soon as soon as they have been released.

To conclude, in the eight years I have been conversing with street people I have no ultimate solution. From my position as a controlled alcoholic with mental issues for which I take medication I have some suggestions: more affordable housing; pro choice concerning drug use similar to laws concerning the consummation of alcohol; alcoholism and drug addiction are diseases and should be treated as such; there need to be more accessible rehabilitation clinics; convicts whose only crime has been the use of illegal substances on their own bodies should be released from jail; ex convicts regardless of the crime they have committed should be given the opportunity of training and subsequent employment; there should be more funding for homeless outreach services so they won't be understaffed and overworked; there should me easier access to mental health facilities to handle the one in four people who have mental issues.

The next time you see a person begging for money on the street consider that not all disabilities are visible: they may have a physical or mental illness that prevents them from working. They may suffer from some form of Post Traumatic Stress Syndrome. The majority are victims of physical, emotional and sexual abuse beginning as early as childhood. They may be a war veteran; they may have a university degree. They may previously have been the head of a major corporation. Without exception they are just like us, seeking happiness and and end to suffering.

Thank you for your support in buying and reading my books. If you enjoyed them, I would be very pleased if you posted a review (no matter how short) on Amazon, Goodreads and any of your social networks. All author royalties go directly to people forced onto the streets and to Ottawa Innercity Missions, Street Outreach Program. As of March, 2017, $1745.00 has been contributed to the OIM. The dollar amount donated directly to my friends on the street is incalculable, as is the love they have shown to me.

Ottawa Innercity Missions

I can't do much for these people except to show them love, compassion, an ear to listen, perhaps a breakfast sandwich and a coffee. I want to do more. To know them is to love them. What has been seen cannot be unseen.

All profits from the sale of these books will be used to support those forced onto the streets or to the *Ottawa Innercity Missions, Street Outreach* program.

OIM's *Street Outreach* teams come to walk alongside the poor and homeless in the downtown core. Volunteer teams provide relief provisions, pastoral care, crisis intervention and referrals.

Street Outreach is the main component of OIM's work. Through *Street Outreach* our trained volunteers meet men and women living on the street, create trusting relationships, and can work to filling both physical and personal needs. Last year (2012) OIM connected with 7,672 individuals on the street in downtown Ottawa, 2,735 of whom were youth.

The Red Vests

If you see two or more people walking down the street wearing a bright red vest with the OIM logo on it then you have run into one of our mobile outreach teams!

OIM's *Street Outreach* volunteers are out meeting with people and handing out snacks and toiletries six days a week.

We have teams on the street Monday to Thursday nights (7pm – 9pm), including late Wednesday (9pm-Midnight). Additional teams are out during the day on Wednesdays & Saturdays (10am-1pm) and Thursdays & Fridays (1-3pm).

You may donate directly to *Ottawa Innercity Ministries* by contacting Canada Helps.org at: http://buff.ly/1pHYBPy

More books by the author

Continue reading similar stories in

Gotta Find a Home: Conversations with Street People
Gotta Find a Home 2 : More Conversations with Street People
Gotta Find a Home 3: Conversations on the Streets

Read about these characters in real time on Dennis' blog
http://gottafindahome.com/

A generous portion of the proceeds from the sale of these books goes towards helping the homeless.

You can help in this goal by leaving a review on Amazon.com, Goodreads, wherever you purchased this book, or on any of your social media networks.

Thank you so much!
Dennis Cardiff, author

Connect with the author:

Follow Dennis Cardiff on Twitter:
https://twitter.com/DennisCardiff

Like Gotta Find a Home on Facebook:
https://www.facebook.com/gottafindahome/

Subscribe to Gotta Find a Home blog:
http://gottafindahome.com/

Email Dennis Cardiff at:
AuthorDennisCardiff@gmail.com

www.ingramcontent.com/pod-product-compliance
Lightning Source LLC
Chambersburg PA
CBHW071235290326
41931CB00038B/2971